Reaching and Teaching the Child with Autism Spectrum Disorder

of related interest

Planning to Learn
Creating and Using a Personal Planner with Young People on the Autism Spectrum
Keely Harper-Hill and Stephanie Lord
ISBN 978 1 84310 561 9

Asperger Syndrome in the Inclusive Classroom
Advice and Strategies for Teachers
Stacey W. Betts, Dion E. Betts and Lisa N. Gerber-Eckard
Foreword by Peter Riffle
ISBN 978 1 84310 840 5

Everyday Education
Visual Support for Children with Autism
Pernille Dyrbjerg and Maria Vedel
Foreword by Lennart Pedersen
ISBN 978 1 84310 457 5

Practical Sensory Programmes for Students with Autism Spectrum Disorder and Other Special Needs
Sue Larkey
ISBN 978 1 84310 479 7

Tales from the Table
Lovaas/ABA Intervention with Children on the Autistic Spectrum
Margaret Anderson
ISBN 978 1 84310 306 6

The Verbal Behavior Approach
How to Teach Children with Autism and Related Disorders
Mary Lynch Barbera with Tracy Rasmussen
Foreword by Mark L. Sundberg, Ph.D., BCBA
ISBN 978 1 84310 852 8

Assessing and Developing Communication and Thinking Skills in People with Autism and Communication Difficulties
A Toolkit for Parents and Professionals
Kate Silver with Autism Initiatives
ISBN 978 1 84310 352 3

Understanding How Asperger Children and Adolescents Think and Learn
Creating Manageable Environments for AS Students
Paula Jacobsen
ISBN 978 1 84310 804 7

Teaching Children with Autism and Related Spectrum Disorders
An Art and a Science
Christy L. Magnusen
Foreword by Tony Attwood
ISBN 978 1 84310 747 7

Teaching at Home
A New Approach to Tutoring Children with Autism and Asperger Syndrome
Olga Holland
ISBN 978 1 84310 787 3

Reaching and Teaching the Child with Autism Spectrum Disorder

Using Learning Preferences and Strengths

Heather MacKenzie

Jessica Kingsley Publishers
London and Philadelphia

First published in 2008
by Jessica Kingsley Publishers
116 Pentonville Road
London N1 9JB, UK
and
400 Market Street, Suite 400
Philadelphia, PA 19106, USA

www.jkp.com

Library of Congress Cataloging in Publication Data
A CIP catalog record for this book is available from the Library of Congress

British Library Cataloguing in Publication Data
A CIP catalogue record for this book is available from the British Library

ISBN 978 1 84310 623 4

Printed and bound in the United States by
Thomson-Shore, 7300 Joy Road, Dexter, MI 48130

*To Lorne and MacKenzie
who taught me so much
about autism, the world
and about myself.*

Acknowledgements

My husband, Bill, needs the greatest expression of gratitude. He supported me on this writing journey and allowed me to remain submerged in my thoughts and ideas for weeks on end.

I am deeply grateful to my colleagues who so graciously reviewed an earlier version of this manuscript and provided valuable feedback. These people include Karen Duff and Carmen Hengeveld, both expert speech-language pathologists and valued colleagues, Johanna Brown, an exemplary teacher and treasured friend, Susan Deike, a skilled writer and mom of twins, Janice Rigg, a very knowing mother of three, Teeya Scholten, an important source of motivation, Allison Waks, a psychologist par excellence, Bev Appel, and Linda Whitney, an indomitable spirit especially when it comes to her sons.

I extend a special thank you to MacKenzie Whitney who so generously provided his thoughts on what helped him as a child and young man growing up with autism and what he would find helpful.

Contents

Preface

A NEW CLINICAL PERSPECTIVE

Over the past 15 years, I have searched and researched current thinking and approaches to helping children with autism. I believed that I needed to understand autism from the 'inside-out' – that is, what the person with autism was experiencing and why he did what he did.

When I began my career over 30 years ago, I used traditional therapeutic approaches which, at that time, had little emphasis on teaching and learning in the 'real-world'. I became increasingly disenchanted with the 'approaches of the day' because I was not seeing my clients learn at the rate I thought they should.

I recall reading a 'break through' article outlining the functional basis to echoing behavior in children with autism. This struck a chord with me because I believed that behavior in children with autism was neither random nor totally egocentric. I saw and was told by parents about the 'connectedness' they sometimes experienced with their child. I was determined to develop a clearer understanding of people with autism and how to reach them. I was surrounded by people and approaches which were being embraced by therapists and families. The approaches were usually based on what was 'wrong' with the child with autism and not what was positive and strong about him. Very often, the content of these programs was outlined and 'dictated' by strict developmental principles and/or external behavior. Little attention seemed to be focused on what drove and motivated the child.

My desire was and is to shift the attitudes and beliefs of others who care about children with autism. My determination and drive were given a lift from an article about five common characteristics of leaders in the field of education. I related strongly to these commonalities. The five features of educational leaders were strong core beliefs, courage of conviction, a sense of social responsibility, seriousness of purpose, and situational mastery.

1. Core beliefs

I have always believed that every child with autism wants to learn and wants to feel competent.

My idealistic side knew that children with autism were trying to make sense of their world and cope in whatever ways they could. I knew I needed a new understanding of how children with autism think and perceive the world. I believed that the pursuit of improved approaches for children with autism was important and eminently worthwhile, although at times I wavered when others shrugged off my ideas.

To my core, I knew that children with autism can achieve at a higher rate if the program of instruction is well-suited to them. I observed children with autism in special education and regular classrooms and saw that, for the most part, they were underachieving. Other professionals seemed to see the children as being disabled, 'mentally retarded' and unable to learn much more than lifeskills. I believed that my work could change how others view children with autism and that programs for these children could have more authentic 'real-world' potency.

I observed that a great deal of focus is placed on behavior and dealing with behavior of children with autism. This is often done to the exclusion of program content. For example, I have been told on many occasions by teachers, parents and therapists, "I'm still working on behavior. As soon as I can get some compliance, I can start teaching him."

2. Courage of conviction

While the government and other agencies were funding and touting behavioral approaches to autism, I continued to develop an approach which emphasized the child and what he cared about and what things made a difference for him. I persevered and continued to develop my concepts and constructs.

In 2003, I presented the *Learning Strengths and Preferences* (*LPS*) model, which is the core of this book, at the American Speech-Language-Hearing Association annual convention in Atlanta, Georgia. The reception was overwhelmingly positive. A crush of people came to speak to me at the end of my presentation and then people stopped my husband and me on the street, in elevators and in the halls of the convention for days after to indicate how excited they were. I knew then that I had something special and that others could sense my passion and understand how I was approaching children with autism.

My 'de-pathologized' model of autism caused quite a stir at the 2004 International Conference on Psychological Type in Toronto, Canada. An understanding and appreciation of psychological type in children with autism is a core concept in the *LPS* model. I have continued dialogue with others interested in the area of psychological type and autism since that time.

3. Social responsibility

I have been deeply affected by the children I worked with. It seemed an injustice to leave educational and developmental approaches as they were and are. There are some reasonable approaches that are being used but they typically do not focus on strategies that ensure generalization into everyday life and increasingly independent lifelong learning in the children.

I am committed to making sure children with autism get the best education possible and are allowed to contribute meaningfully to our world.

4. Seriousness of purpose

I have read extensively and been involved in development and implementation of a variety of programs. The majority of these have been strongly behavioral in orientation, broadly developmental and clearly cognitive in their approaches.

My years on this journey have prompted me to examine very carefully how I and others approach teaching and learning in general but, especially, in relation to children with autism. I knew I had to develop a framework that could encompass at least three main features for each child:

1. learning preferences, including how the child relates to the world and gathers information

2. learning strengths, including what modalities (visual, verbal, physical and so on) are more efficiently processed and meaningful to the person, and

3. the 'inner world' of the person, his interests and affinities.

I have searched diligently for theories, models and approaches to development and education for both typical children and those with a variety of special needs that would 'fit' with the three features above.

Having said this, I am not ignoring the fact that children with autism also face many learning challenges. I know, however, that they want to learn. It has become my goal, as an educator, to find and 'harness' each child's *Learning Preferences and Strengths* to enhance his learning and development.

5. Situational mastery

Over the last 20 years, I have developed and tested my approach and techniques with children I worked with in private practice. I have seen the developments and 'blossoming' that are possible. Feedback from the parents of those children has been extremely positive and encouraging.

Seven years ago, I took a large 'leap of faith' and established a preschool program for children with autism using the *LPS* model. I was fortunate to find key staff and families who believed in improving the future for children with autism. The program confirmed my beliefs about children with autism and provided the 'proving-ground' for many of the techniques presented in this book.

DEVELOPMENT OF THE *LPS* MODEL

In the area of learning strengths, I searched for a cognitive model that did not simply define 'intelligence' as a singular factor, set of factors or a score on a test. Given the typically uneven developmental profile of children with autism, I was drawn to Howard Gardner's (1983) model of *Multiple Intelligences*. Gardner believes that each person possesses a number of different 'intelligences', each of which can be nurtured to enhance learning.

In addition to addressing learning strengths, each person's learning preferences need to receive attention. I not only had to address the intellectual side of each child but also other characteristics that influence the person's thinking, motivation and behavior. The 'preference' construct had to include what each person cared about, what made sense to him and how he wished to deal with the world. People try to adapt to the world around them with the internal resources they have available. The concept of learning preferences drew me to personality theories.

The search for a model that deals with personal preferences within people brought me to the work of Carl Jung, Swiss psychiatrist. Jung addressed questions such as how people gain energy, take in information, make decisions and relate to the world. He worked to clarify the differences observed in human behavior within his theories of psychological type. Jung's constructs have been applied to career planning, team building, marriage counseling, and to the field of learning.

Starting with these theories as a foundation, I defined and refined my *LPS* model. The approach focuses on reaching both brain power and heart for learning in children with autism.

I have been able to observe and measure the impact of the *LPS* model on the learning of children with autism in the preschool I established. By honoring both their *Learning Preferences* and *Strengths*, we have made a significant impact on these learners. The intervention program based on the *LPS* model has proven to be positive, effective and much more fun for parents, teachers, therapists, caregivers and children. In addition, parents are now looking at their children as learners rather than as people with an array of disabilities.

ADVANTAGES TO THE *LPS* MODEL

There are many advantages to the *LPS* model. The model:

- *Looks at each child as unique* with a specific set of learning strengths and preferences. It emphasizes that all brains are wired to learn.

- *Does not focus on pathology and deficits.* Although learning and developmental difficulties are addressed, the model does not work from a pathological base. The diagnostic label is not the focus. Each child's unique profile of strengths, preferences and needs provides the basis for the program. This helps everyone look for and find the things the child is doing well and why. The child is helped to view learning positively which acts to boost his motivation.

- *Looks at learning from the learner's point of view.* This feature helps everyone involved with the child understand him from a more positive and productive point of view. Each person learns how the child perceives objects, events and people around him and prefers to deal with them. The child himself also learns about how his brain works more easily and what things are a little more difficult.

- *Allows principled predictions* by the parents, teachers, therapists and other caregivers about how the child will respond to different events, settings and tasks.

- *Helps understand the child more quickly.* For many children with autism, a great deal of time is spent trying to understand their learning. The *LPS* model helps you get there more quickly. The warm-up and start-up time can be reduced significantly.

- *Is easily blended with other assessment information.* The information from the *LPS* can be used as an overlay for other data and measures.

- *Can be used in any setting.* The strategies and approaches outlined in this book can be used in any setting, including home, day care, segregated treatment programs, or inclusive classrooms. The knowledge gained about the child can be used by all people involved in his life. The same principles can be used with other learners, such as those with Fetal Alcohol Spectrum Disorder and Fragile X.

- *Encourages involvement of all people important in the child's life.* The knowledge gained about each child encourages participation of the child and his family in the learning process. The model also engages teachers, therapists, support workers, and other caregivers. It can also help extended family members (e.g. grandparents, aunts, uncles, cousins) understand the child's behavior in a more positive manner and encourage more rewarding interactions.

WHAT THIS BOOK CAN HELP YOU DO

This book is intended for parents, teachers, therapists, and support workers involved in the lives of children with autism. The approaches described will also help children with autism better understand themselves. The strategies presented in this book are intended for use with children from 2 to 12 years of age.

It is my hope that the *LPS* model will stimulate different ways of thinking about people with autism. It will also encourage different approaches for treatment and education of children with autism. The model should prompt new perspectives into research in the area of autism intervention.

My website is an opportunity for all of us to share questions, successes, data, and anecdotes about our children and the *LPS* model. It also includes information about presentations, conferences, and special events.

This book will help the reader view autism from a broader perspective. Autism is part of the human spectrum and strategies focus on skills important to lifelong learning. The model provides a comprehensive framework for understanding and dealing more effectively with children with autism. The reader will gain greater insight into the person with autism as well as the ability to predict responses and project future learning needs.

In Chapter 1, I will review the traditional defining characteristics and symptoms of autism. I will then provide a 'reframing' of autism which emphasizes more positive aspects. The major categories and characteristics of *Learning Preferences and Strengths* will be presented in Chapter 2. My research into the *Learning Preferences and Strengths* of people with autism will be reviewed in

Chapter 3. Chapter 4 will provide a brief overview of the major components of the *LPS* program and key features. Suggestions are given for the order of program implementation and ways to motivate and get the most from children with autism. Each program component will be explained in subsequent chapters along with practical applications and examples. Anecdotes will be presented to illustrate approaches and what I have learned from the children. Chapter 8 examines *Learning Preferences and Strengths* of children with autism and research on type dynamics to better understand their behavior. We will learn about 'triggers' for behavior problems. Understanding of *Learning Preferences and Strengths* will also enable us to use appropriate resources and strategies to restore more normalized behavior. In Chapter 9, I will provide thoughts and suggestions of further directions for children with autism.

Chapter 1

Reframing the Traditional Definition of Autism

TRADITIONAL DEFINITION OF AUTISM

The typical clinical description of Autism Spectrum Disorder (autism) includes the following trio of characteristics:

1. impairment of social interaction with others, including

   ○ lack of spontaneous seeking to share enjoyment, interests or achievements

   ○ lack of social or emotional reciprocity

2. impairment of verbal and nonverbal communication, including

   ○ using stereotyped, repetitive, and idiosyncratic language

   ○ difficulty initiating or sustaining conversation with others

3. impairment of make-believe or social play and imaginative activities and restricted, repetitive, and stereotyped patterns of behavior, including

   ○ preoccupation with one or more stereotyped and restricted patterns of interest

   ○ inflexible adherence to specific, non-functional routines or rituals

   ○ stereotyped and repetitive mannerisms

   ○ persistent preoccupation with objects or parts of objects.

This triad of social, communicative and behavioral features makes up the hallmarks of autism. These behaviors pervade all aspects of the child's life. Autism is found in all economic, racial, educational, religious and social groups around the world.

NO TWO PEOPLE WITH AUTISM ARE THE SAME

Autism is referred to as a 'spectrum' because the amount or severity of each of the major characteristics varies considerably from individual to individual. Some children may be talkative and seem to have quite good communication skills. On digging a little deeper, it may be found that the child is using a lot of 'scripted' language learned from videos and/or other people. The child may also show strong verbal fluency only when talking about favorite topics, like trains or dinosaurs, but conversation is not truly interactive – more like a very interesting monologue. This same child may exhibit a great deal of rigidity about how things need to be done in day-to-day life. For example, the same route must be driven to familiar places or the same routine for getting dressed must be followed.

Oliver Sacks (1995), a neurologist who has eloquently written about a variety of neurological conditions, stated, "No two people with autism are the same; its precise form or expression is different in every case" (p.250). Given this, it is little wonder that making a diagnosis can be complex, requiring input from a number of individuals who know the child and have extensive experience with autism.

STRENGTHS IN AUTISM

The most striking thing about the traditional diagnostic criteria for autism is that they are all stated in the negative. Criteria include terms such as 'impairment of...', 'lack of...', 'failure to...' Durig (2005) indicated that "autism and normalcy have been defined as mutually exclusive" (p.18).

Savant abilities, or exceptional skills or knowledge in a particular area, such as mathematics and geography, occur in less than one per cent of the general population. Yet one in every ten people with autism have savant abilities. Other strengths often observed in people with autism are interest and memory for word strings, such as movie scripts, for visual-spatial information, such as maps, and for music and rhythm. Affinities, or spontaneous strong interests, are frequently seen in people with autism. They may include interests in flags, clocks, maps, calendars, electrical cords, cars, and trains.

LOOKING BEYOND BEHAVIOR

Another striking feature of the criteria for diagnosis for autism is that they are based primarily on behavior observed and little on the inner workings and personality of the individual. The behavioral criteria are important for making a diagnosis but they are less helpful for developing a comprehensive intervention and educational program for the child. Peter Szatmari (2004) stated, "greater understanding of disruptions and perplexing behaviors (in children with autism) is possible once we can see the world through the child's eyes" (p.ix). He went on, "the most important ingredient associated with successful outcome… (is) having a family or a teacher understand what it's like to be inside the mind of a child with autism spectrum disorder" (p.x).

LEARNING FROM THOSE WITH AUTISM

We have learned a great deal about autism from people with autism themselves. Temple Grandin is perhaps one of the most famous people with autism today. She has autism but also has earned a Ph.D. in animal sciences and is an expert in both areas. Dr. Grandin has revolutionized the design of animal holding facilities because of her knowledge and her personal perceptions of the world. It was not until Dr. Grandin began writing and speaking about her life that people in the field of autism began thinking about the inner life of people with autism. She described, with Margaret Scariano (1986), her experiences as a child with autism. She spoke of her hypersensitivity to different sensations. For example, she could hear and feel everything at full intensity, both relevant and irrelevant information. Everything seemed disorganized and she could not figure out what were regularities and rules.

Oliver Sacks (1995) pointed out that, "in autism, it is not affect in general that is faulty but affect in relation to complex human experiences, social ones predominantly" (p.288). In the social realm, Temple Grandin found that, as she matured, she was able to learn simple universal emotions, often in the form of mathematical equations. She referred to her social learning as "strictly a logical process". Grandin had to learn how to put pieces of information together in order to understand social regularities, rules and motivations. For example, she was able to work out that there were three main categories for social rules. The first are those that are 'really bad', such as stealing, destruction or injuring others. The second are those that are 'sins of the system', such as smoking and sex. In the third category are 'illegal but not bad acts', such as speeding or illegal parking. Grandin continues to experience difficulty with social games and social subtleties.

AUTISM REFRAMED

Oliver Sacks (1995) reported that Temple Grandin

> thinks that there has been too much emphasis on the negative aspects of
> autism and insufficient attention, or respect, paid to the positive ones. She
> thinks that (people with autism) unquestionably have great problems in
> some areas (but) may have extraordinary and socially valuable power in
> others – provided that they are allowed to be themselves. (p.290)

Without question, people with autism have areas of difficulty or 'impairments'
but they also have many positive characteristics. Among them are:

- they are very frank, forthright and honest

- they tend to be fiercely loyal, intensely moral and have a passionate
  sense of right and wrong

- they are usually perseverant and single-minded about things that are
  important to them. They have a great intensity of thought and strong
  passion for their affinities

- typically, people with autism are strongly visual

- they often have precise and powerful memories for music and
  rhythm.

The characteristics outlined above are not typically considered to be 'impairments' or 'disabilities'. The features of frankness, honesty, loyalty, strong sense
of right and wrong, perseverance, etc. are honorable qualities. Within the
context of a disability, like autism, these same attributes are sometimes viewed
as problems.

Consciously or unconsciously, when we view someone as 'disabled', 'im-
paired', or 'disordered', we perceive that person differently. We approach him
differently and we are very likely to miss his assets. If we think of the person as
having a disability, we are much more prone to interpret his behavior as pathological. In addition, our expectations of that person tend to be somewhat lower
than for others without the diagnostic label. The following example should
speak for itself.

Example: During snack at preschool, one of the children started flapping his hands. We had not seen that behavior in the month he had been with us. His teacher looked and thought "Well, I guess the honeymoon is over. He is self-stimming." She then turned to him and asked, "Are you okay?" The child looked toward her and said, "I'm just drying my hands!" and rolled his eyes.

We could have left the handflapping as a behavior consistent with the child's diagnosis of autism or we could try to understand what the child was experiencing. By responding neutrally to this child, we learned an important lesson: do not view behavior as disordered until you have pursued all angles.

AUTISM AS A COGNITIVE STYLE

There has been increasing discussion of autism as being less a disability than a 'cognitive style' or 'learning difference'. Simon Baron-Cohen (2000) cited 12 differences in children with autism to support his argument that "behaviour in Asperger Syndrome and High Functioning Autism is not better or worse than that seen in typical development" (p.490); it is simply different. The list includes:

- the child spends more time involved with objects and physical systems than with people

- the child communicates less than other children do

- the child tends to follow his own desires and beliefs rather than paying attention to or being easily influenced by others' desires and beliefs

- the child shows relatively little interest in what the social group is doing or in being a part of it

- the child has strong, persistent interests

- the child is very accurate at perceiving the details of information

- the child notices and recalls things other people may not

- the child's view of what is relevant and important in a situation may not coincide with others

- the child may be fascinated by patterned material, be it visual (shapes), numeric (dates, timetables), alphanumeric (license plates) or lists (of cars, songs, etc.)

- the child may be fascinated by systems whether simple (light switches, spigots), a little more complex (weather fronts), or abstract (mathematics)

- the child may have a strong desire to collect categories of objects (bottle tops, train maps) or categories of information (types of lizard, types of rock, types of fabric, etc.), and

- the child has a strong preference for experiences that are controllable rather than unpredictable.

QUALITATIVE DIFFERENCES BETWEEN BRAINS

If we begin to consider autism a cognitive difference, Baron-Cohen (2000) points out that the notion of a spectrum in autism is much easier to understand. He believes that the neurological differences in people with autism cannot be taken as evidence that one brain is better or worse than another. Baron-Cohen stated, "if environmental expectations change, or in a different environment, they (people with autism) may not necessarily be seen as disabled" (p.497). Szatmari (2004) added, "in some individuals, the distinction between a disability and a gift or talent is hard to establish" (p.61). Baron-Cohen (2000) mused that, if we shift to the notion of autism as a cognitive difference, the diagnosis would become akin to being told your child is left- or right-handed.

SYSTEMATIC AND SOCIAL BRAINS

Baron-Cohen and Hammer (1997) and Baron-Cohen (1999, 2002) described the autistic cognitive style as being more object-oriented and more focused on detail. Baron-Cohen suggested that the male brain is "more spatial (mathematical, geometric, relational) and less social (empathetic, sensitive to mental states of others)" (Baron-Cohen and Hammer 1997, p.196). The male brain 'systematizes', analyzing inanimate things and constructing systems, focusing on details and forming 'if-then' rules. Baron-Cohen cites research on male toy choice, occupational choices and superior constructional abilities as supporting this notion of the male systematizing brain. He indicated that the female brain is more empathizing and socially-oriented. Baron-Cohen suggested that autism is an example of the extreme male systematizing brain.

Baron-Cohen, *et al.* (2003, 2005) conducted research to examine empathizing and systematizing in autistic and non-autistic males and females. They found significant differences between the male and female subjects in systematizing and empathizing, as predicted. In addition, they discovered that males with Asperger Syndrome and High Functioning Autism received significantly higher systematizing scores and significantly lower empathizing scores than the non-autistic males.

Interestingly, Baron-Cohen and Wheelwright (1999) discovered that obsessions of people with autism also had a largely systematizing focus. The obsessions were most likely to relate to physics, building, categorizing and sorting. Sensory experiences, like touching and smelling, plus films/movies, videos, cartoons and food were also common obsessions.

Lending further support to the notion of the systematizing brain, Baron-Cohen *et al.* (1997, 1998, 1999) found that fathers and grandfathers of children with autism were twice as likely to work in the field of engineering, a systematizing profession, as compared to families without relatives with autism. In the families of children with autism, 28.4 per cent had at least one relative who was an engineer.

COHERENT AND PIECE-MEAL BRAINS

Francesca Happé (1999) supported the notion that "deficit accounts of autism cannot explain…the assets seen in this disorder" (p.216). She went on: "progress in understanding this disorder…will arise chiefly through exploration of what people with autism are good at" (p.216).

Frith (1989, 2003) proposed the theory of Weak Central Coherence to explain the uneven profile of abilities typically seen in autism. Frith (1989, 2003) and Happé (1997, 1999) hypothesized that, on tasks that required relatively piece-meal processing with little emphasis on central coherence or bringing the pieces into a whole, people with autism would have an advantage. If a task required recognition of global meaning or 'the big picture' such that there was stronger emphasis on central coherence, people with autism would perform more poorly.

Happé (1997) found that people with autism exhibit superior performance on visual-perceptual problems, like block design tasks, and visual illusions, like Ebbinghaus circles, as compared to non-autistic and learning disabled subjects. Because people with autism tend to see the pieces and not the whole, they are not 'seduced' by the desire to integrate information into a gestalt, or whole.

Frith, Happé, and Baron-Cohen clearly show that people with autism can have superior abilities in specific areas.

LEARNING PREFERENCES AND STRENGTHS

The *Learning Preferences and Strengths* (*LPS*) model presented in this book arises from my desire to account for the 'person' with autism. I believe we have a responsibility to respect and honor each child's interests and affinities as well as his *Learning Preferences and Strengths*. Temple Grandin (1995, p.100) stated, "I think there is too much emphasis on deficits and not enough on developing abilities." We cannot and do not ignore areas of difficulty but we can increase our effectiveness in addressing those areas of need by adopting the *LPS* model.

Any model of teaching or therapy should have at least five key features, including:

1. a *comprehensive model of thinking and learning* that focuses on the learner through to adulthood

2. a *clear philosophy* of learning and education

3. *goals that follow logically from the model and philosophy*

4. *strategies that are consistent with the model, philosophy, and goals*

5. *goals and strategies that are applicable to all settings* in the life of a person with autism and all aspects of his learning and development, including behavior and motivation.

Each of these key features is included within the *LPS* model. The five features will unfold as you proceed to the chapters describing program components.

The *LPS* model gives an entry point for planning intervention, not an end-point. It provides a positive approach to teaching and learning. *LPS* is both practical and effective in matching intervention goals and strategies to individual children. The *LPS* model provides principles and frames for action to optimize learning in people with autism. The 'match' between learner preferences and strengths and teaching structure, content, and processes creates a remarkable synergy among learner, teacher, task, and environment. The model does not, however, set out a script for the adult to use. The focus, instead, is on forming a productive, dynamic relationship with the child which centers around specific goals and principles.

Overall, the *LPS* model differs from other programs for children with autism in terms of:

- how to teach
- what to teach
- the child's participation
- goals of teaching/intervention
- role of the teacher/parent.

The impact of the *LPS* model on learning in children with autism at the pre-school I established has been powerful. The changes it has induced in teachers, therapists, parents, and support workers and their feedback have also been extremely compelling. Typically, we have seen one-and-a-half months' gain in development for every month of enrolment in the *LPS* program, based on results of the *Psychoeducational Profile – Revised* (1990). Greater gain tends to be seen in children who showed evidence of autism from an early age, versus children who exhibited typical early development with later regression.

The *LPS* model is not prescriptive. It permits us to make educated assumptions and projections about children with autism while keeping in mind that each child is a unique individual.

There is something that is much more scarce, something rarer than ability. It is the ability to recognize ability.

– Robert Half (undated)

Chapter 2

Learning Preferences and Strengths Model

LEARNERS AS "CRYSTALS"

A few years ago, a colleague, who views people through feelings and images, referred to children as "crystals". I was initially skeptical about the rather esoteric nature of her comment. After a great deal of thought about this metaphor, I began to realize how this notion fits with my own beliefs.

I believe that each learner should be valued and approached as an individual who has many strengths and abilities. Learners, from this viewpoint, are like crystals. Each learner:

- is multi-faceted and complex

- gives different reflections and refractions dependent upon the situation, setting or activity

- has physical and optical properties that vary dependent upon how you view them

- is unique yet shares universal characteristics and tendencies.

Hold a crystal up to the light. Examine these features and properties. It becomes apparent that a learner, with the right focus and direction, can take on the same glistening quality. By viewing him in certain ways, you can see the potential he has and his unique qualities – or you can focus on his flaws.

Commonalities in *Learning Preferences and Strengths* of children with autism permit us to make educated projections about how to approach each child more effectively and efficiently. It must always be kept in mind that each child has his own unique features and facets. The *Learning Preferences and Strengths (LPS)* model is intended to give us a head start and clearer conceptual framework for planning and implementing teaching and learning programs.

LEARNING PREFERENCES

The learning preferences presented in this book are based on the work of Carl Jung, Swiss psychiatrist, and the interpretation and extension of his work by Isabel Briggs Myers and Katharine Briggs.

Katharine Briggs and her daughter, Isabel Briggs Myers, studied and elaborated the work of Carl Jung. Myers began developing the *Myers-Briggs Type Indicator* (MBTI®) after seeing "waste of human potential in World War II" (1998, p.5). Briggs noted that some people were more comfortable and suited to certain types of work than others. Briggs and Myers then set out to examine work and careers relative to personality type. They took on the challenge of meeting the demands of tests and measurement while honoring Jung's theory. The MBTI® is a self-report questionnaire for adults designed to make Jung's theory of psychological type understandable and useful in everyday life. The MBTI® is the most widely-used instrument for understanding normal personality differences. It is used to examine career choices, work satisfaction, group dynamics, marital satisfaction and education.

Learning preferences are derived from the MBTI® model. The four pairs of preferences include how the learner prefers to maintain or re-establish his energy for learning, gather information, make decisions and relate to the world. The preferences combine to make up 16 possible 'personality types'. Before reviewing the four pairs of preferences, it is critical to keep a few things in mind. These include:

- *All people have one preferred set of type pairs.*

- *Type is inborn.* The way we gain energy and relate to the world are enduring throughout our lives. The manner in which we gather information and make decisions tends to change over time and with life circumstances, cultural values, family influences and educational practices.

- *Preferences are not abilities.* They are preferred ways to use your abilities.

- *One's true type is natural, automatic, effortless and easy to use.* Living your 'true' type is like using your preferred hand: you can use your other hand but generally not as easily and effortlessly.

- *One type is not better than another.* Briggs and Myers refer to the types as "gifts differing". Different type preferences have slightly different ways of viewing and interacting with the world but each type uniquely contributes to and blends with other types. In addition, having a type preference does not mean you cannot use other preferences. The 16 type combinations are like a 16-room house: you can enter and exist in all 16 of the rooms but there is one room where you are most comfortable.

- *All 16 types are found in every culture.* The distribution of type preferences varies in different populations and population subgroups, however.

Most people teach or intervene in a manner that is consistent with their own preferred type. As you read through each description below, try to determine your preferences for each pair. You may want to locate a qualified MBTI® practitioner to obtain more valid and extensive results. There are a number of quick on-line type questionnaires you might try. Keep in mind, however, that their validity and reliability in relation to the MBTI® are not established.

Four learning preference pairs

1. ENERGY SOURCE

The first preference refers to how and where a person recharges his personal battery. This type pair describes how we prefer to interact with the world and receive stimulation and energy.

Introversion

The term 'Introversion' is used to indicate that the person prefers to gain personal energy from internal ('intro-') sources. The person with Introversion preferences needs some 'down' time to refresh himself. He needs a little more time to take in information and to reflect on it before being asked to respond. He may have to reflect on and rehearse what he wants to say before expressing it. The Introvert also prefers to watch an expert or view an example before attempting a task. He needs time to warm up to new situations or activities before he decides whether or not to join in. He can appear somewhat extroverted and more talkative when in comfortable familiar situations with people he knows and/or when talking about favorite topics. The Introvert prefers to work in quiet with few interruptions. He looks inward for energy and satisfaction and may resent having someone watch over his shoulder. He typically can work without a great deal of encouragement or praise; in fact, he may become suspicious if a person is too complimentary.

Introverts can be mis-perceived as aloof, inhibited, insensitive, unfriendly, or withdrawn.

Extraversion

The term 'Extraversion' is used to indicate not that the person is outgoing but rather that he seeks personal energy from the outside ('extra-') world. The person with a preference for Extraversion gains energy from being around other people and tends to be attuned to the external world. His personal battery will deplete if he is required to spend extended time alone. He becomes restless when alone because he lacks the group which helps him form his own identity. He is usually energetic and vocal but may seem to 'open his mouth before he engages his brain'. Thinking out loud is very important to helping him clarify his ideas. Often, he will have difficulty knowing what he thinks unless he is given a chance to express it. Sometimes it is easier for an Extravert to talk than listen. Extraverts tend to be responsive and enthusiastic and plunge readily into new and untried experiences.

The Extravert can be mis-perceived as being boastful, intrusive, a social butterfly, flippant or loud.

2. INFORMATION GATHERING

The next set of preferences deals with how the learner prefers to gather or take in information about the world.

Sensing

The person with a Sensing preference needs to learn about things by using his five senses. He may need to touch, see, taste, hear, smell something before he can truly understand it. This means he prefers to watch tasks and touch materials before trying them out himself. He typically prefers tasks and activities that have tangible results or end-products without surprises. He notices details others may not; that includes details that may or may not be relevant, like whether the picture on the wall is straight. He tends to be a 'bottom-up' processor preferring step-by-step, detail-by-detail approaches to tasks and activities. He may become stressed if a task is too open-ended. He may not notice the 'big picture' (the forest) and just recognize the next step (the trees).

The Sensing person can be mis-perceived as being fussy, concrete, picky about details or obsessive.

Intuiting

The person with an Intuiting preference tends to enjoy new ideas and is very good at seeing the big picture or overall concept (the forest) before the individual details (the trees). He is not particularly interested in small details but enjoys looking for new possibilities. He prefers to scan situations and information in order to see relationships among thoughts or ideas. The Intuiter is more likely to trust and act on hunches and may become irritable when pushed for details. He likes to think about future possibilities and may seem uninvolved and inattentive to the present.

The Intuiting person can be mis-perceived as being a dreamer, imprecise, impractical or unrealistic.

3. DECISION-MAKING

This set of preferences deals with how people make decisions about information they gather from the world.

Thinking

The learner with a Thinking preference values logic, fairness and truthfulness for making decisions. He is naturally quite brief, businesslike and to the point. The Thinker makes decisions based on what is fair and truthful. He places great value on being right and is only secondarily concerned about how others may feel about what he does or says. He does not readily pick up on the feelings of others and may be unaware of the emotional climate around him. Thinkers do not easily express emotions and may be unaware of how they feel.

The Thinker can be mis-perceived as being blunt, argumentative, cold, tough-minded or unfeeling.

Feeling

The learner with a Feeling preference values harmony and good feelings among others. It is important to remember that the term 'feeling' does not mean 'emotional' and having a feeling preference does not preclude his ability to use logic. The Feeler places value on meeting others' needs and on being liked; being right is usually secondary. He takes others' feelings into account when making a decision and will sometimes overextend himself in order to meet others' needs. He usually performs small services for others and is heartened by appreciation and recognition.

The Feeling person can be mis-perceived as being hypersensitive, wishy-washy or evasive.

4. RELATING TO THE WORLD

The final set of preferences deals with how the person prefers to respond to the world and events around him.

Judging

The learner with a Judging preference likes to be decisive and to finish tasks. The term 'judging' does not mean judgemental; it refers to the person's acting like a judge in wanting things to be decided and finished. The Judger likes to have things settled and finished and takes pleasure in completing a task or activity. He will often forego play until he finishes what he started. The Judger prefers organized and predictable environments and may balk at surprises and changes. He prefers clear rules and may try to ensure that others also follow them.

The Judging person can be mis-perceived as being impatient, rigid or compulsive.

Perceiving

The learner with Perceiving preferences likes to keep his options open and may balk at too much structure. He prefers to live in the moment and can readily adjust to the unexpected, being flexible, adaptable and tolerant. He may feel he does not have enough information in order to make a decision and may find it stressful to come to closure. The Perceiver is energized by starting things but enthusiasm and attention may dwindle as the task or project proceeds. He may leave work until later if new and more exciting options present themselves.

The Perceiving person can be mis-perceived as being unreliable, scattered or a procrastinator.

LEARNING STRENGTHS

Learning strengths derive from the work of Howard Gardner. Gardner (1983) developed the theory of Multiple Intelligences as an explanation of how different minds work. He originally proposed seven distinct forms of intelligence. He arrived at this conclusion after examining patterns of strength in people with brain injury, idiot savant and giftedness. The different intelligences are distinct, neurologically verifiable, have discernible stages of development and a core set of information-processing operations or modalities.

Learning strengths or intelligences are neither good nor bad. One is not better than another but our educational programs and curricula do show a clear bias for Verbal-Linguistic and Logical-Mathematical strengths. Gardner believes that most people have highly developed skills in some intelligences, moderately developed skills in others and they have some areas that are relatively undeveloped. Given appropriate encouragement, enrichment and instruction, most people can develop all intelligences to at least a moderate degree. The same intelligence may, however, be expressed in different ways by different people.

The seven different types of learning strengths Gardner originally proposed include: Verbal-Linguistic, Visual-Spatial, Bodily-Kinesthetic, Musical-Rhythmic, Logical-Mathematical, Interpersonal and Intrapersonal. These strengths and their implications for learning and teaching are presented below.

Seven learning strengths

1. VERBAL-LINGUISTIC

Verbal-Linguistic learning strengths are seen in the learner's ability to think in words, to use words to express what is on his mind and to understand language. He may use his abilities in reading, writing and/or speaking. He enjoys playing with language, manipulating the sounds, words and structure with relative ease. Listening tends to be a strength and he can easily understand, interpret and remember what has been said or read. His ability to communicate clearly and precisely with others is strong both verbally and in writing. The person with Verbal-Linguistic strengths likely learns other languages with relative ease. He is interested in language and strives to refine and enrich his language skills.

Poets, writers, journalists, newscasters, orators, speakers and lawyers tend to have strong Verbal-Linguistic intelligence, for example: Shakespeare (author), Maya Angelou (author), Mark Twain (author), Martin Luther King (orator), Winston Churchill (orator and author).

2. VISUAL-SPATIAL

Visual-Spatial learning strengths are seen in the learner's ability to envision, create, manipulate and remember things he sees or imagines in his mind. He can create and recreate visual experiences in his mind. He can perceive and/or produce designs and crafts, showing sensitivity to color, line, shape, form, space and the relationship among them. He tends to remember visual details readily and use visual images to aid his recall. A learner with Visual-Spatial strengths enjoys learning and using visual representations like graphs, maps, diagrams and charts. He may like to doodle or draw pictures about his thoughts and feelings.

Engineers, architects, pilots, chess players, dentists and sculptors tend to have strong Visual-Spatial intelligence, for example: Pablo Picasso (artist), Frank Lloyd Wright (architect), Coco Chanel (designer), Garry Kasparov (chess master).

3. BODILY-KINESTHETIC

Bodily-Kinesthetic learning strengths are seen in the learner's ability to use his body or parts of his body to express ideas and feelings and to produce things. He exhibits strong fine or gross motor coordination and dexterity. He can think in terms of movements and use his body in skilled and complicated ways. He may be very skilled at acting, dancing, sewing, sculpting, track and field, bike-riding, skateboarding or keyboarding. The person with Bodily-Kinesthetic strengths prefers to explore the world around him through touching and moving.

Athletes, gymnasts, surgeons, sculptors and dancers have strong Bodily-Kinesthetic intelligence, for example: Alvin Ailey (dancer, choreographer), Marcel Marceau (mime), Laurence Olivier (actor), Hank Aaron (athlete), Tiger Woods (golfer), Wayne Gretzky (hockey player).

4. MUSICAL-RHYTHMIC

Musical-Rhythmic learning strengths are seen in the learner's ability to appreciate and understand music, rhythm, and rhythmic movement. He may be able to compose, play or conduct music. The person with Musical-Rhythmic strengths will seek out music and listen with great interest. He may enjoy listening to a variety of sounds, including music and environmental sounds. The learner may develop the ability to play an instrument on his own and/or remember songs, rhythms and melodies after only one or two exposures. The person may be sensitive to pitch, rhythm, melody and tone. He can hear patterns and recognize, remember and manipulate them. He can more readily express his thoughts, perceptions and feelings through music, rhythmic movement or dance.

Composers, orchestra conductors, instrument makers, singers, musicians, and audiophiles have strong Musical-Rhythmic intelligence, for example: Leonard Bernstein (conductor, composer), Andrew Lloyd-Webber (composer), Itzhak Perlman (violinist), Luciano Pavarotti (opera singer), Eric Clapton (singer, composer), Oscar Peterson (pianist).

5. LOGICAL-MATHEMATICAL

Logical-Mathematical learning strengths are seen in the learner's ability to use and reason with numbers and mathematical operations. He may see logical relationships and patterns among objects and events around him. He can use reasoning to solve problems and discern rules and regularities. The learner with Logical-Mathematical strengths likely enjoys gathering information, forming hypotheses, developing paradigms and building arguments. He can understand numerical and quantitative abstractions quite readily and is keen to engage in activities involving them.

Engineers, computer programmers, mathematicians, accountants, and scientists have strong Logical-Mathematical intelligence, for example: Albert Einstein (scientist), Stephen Hawking (scientist), Carl Sagan (astronomer), Bill Gates (founder of Microsoft).

6. INTERPERSONAL

Interpersonal learning strengths are seen in the learner's ability to think about and understand people and to empathize. He may have a great capacity to understand the moods of others, their intentions, motivations and feelings. He interacts, cooperates and communicates effectively with others. He readily forms and maintains friendships and social relationships and builds rapport. He may be able to influence others' actions and opinions. He adapts well in different situations, easily determining the expectations and rules. He also understands different perspectives on social or political issues.

Skilled therapists, religious leaders, teachers, actors, skilled salespeople and politicians tend to have strong Interpersonal intelligence, for example: Mahatma Gandhi (peacemaker), Helen Keller (educator, humanitarian), Oprah Winfrey (talk show host), Tony Robbins (life coach and motivational speaker).

7. INTRAPERSONAL

Intrapersonal learning strengths are seen in the learner's awareness of himself. He has a deep understanding of himself, his strengths, limitations, intentions, motivations, emotions and desires. He exhibits the ability to control and develop his feelings and thoughts. The Intrapersonal intelligence encompasses many of the features of executive functions. Among these are impulse control, persistence, judgement, decision-making, goal-setting and self-regulation. The learner with Intrapersonal strengths tends to be motivated to identify goals and pursue self-actualization. He develops a strong ethical value system and ponders issues such as meaning, purpose and relevance of life events.

Philosophers, theologists, psychiatrists, mediators and psychologists tend to have strong Intrapersonal intelligence, for example: Carl Jung (psychiatrist), Mother Teresa (humanitarian, spiritual leader).

Chapter 3

Learning Preferences and Strengths in Children with Autism Spectrum Disorder

LEARNING PREFERENCES

When examining each learning preference, I was struck by the parallels between the features of **Introversion-Sensing-Thinking-Judging (ISTJ)** type and the key characteristics of autism. Examination of each preference is presented below and examples within the realm of autism will be highlighted.

Introversion

A person with an **Introversion** preference, as an energy source:

- is slow to warm up to new settings, people, information, and activities
- feels more comfortable receiving input than initiating contact and is generally selective about sharing thoughts
- focuses in depth on specific, selective interests
- is not easily influenced by others' desires or beliefs
- takes initiative if an issue is very important to him
- likes to work alone or with others he knows well
- dislikes being singled out.

Example: Time to warm up to new situations can be protracted for children with autism. One child I worked with walked the perimeter of my office exactly two times before he was able to focus on people and activities. If I quietly stood back and let him do his two laps, he was then able to settle into work. If I disrupted the perimeter walk, he became upset and was not ready to work for a considerably longer period of time.

The characteristics listed above for Introversion are all frequently observed in children with autism. They also capture many of the features considered to be 'social impairments' in children with autism. The children are slow to warm up and tend to need prompting to initiate contact with others, preferring to play alone. They often have intense interests in specific areas which they are willing to share with others.

Hans Asperger himself stated, "The literature on personality types certainly includes those who show similarities to the autistic personality…above all, the introverted personality described by C.G. Jung. Introversion…may well be autism in essence" (translated by Frith, 1991, p.90).

Sensing

A person with a **Sensing** preference, as a means of gathering information:

- focuses more on objects, facts and concrete information than people; is grounded in the tangible world

- prefers familiar and practiced methods

- is observant, noticing and remembering specific details others may not but does not easily see relationships among details

- understands ideas and theories through practical applications and experience with them

- trusts information gained through the senses; as young children, they have clear likes and dislikes in relation to food

- distrusts others who are not careful about facts.

Example: Concreteness and living in the 'here and now' are frequently observed in children with autism. One day, a teacher noted that one child had removed his shoes and socks rather than put on his indoor shoes. She said, "Oh look, Bobby, you have bare feet." The child looked at his feet and grew angry, snapping back with: "I don't got no bear's feet!" This clearly exemplified his concrete interpretation of language.

The focus on objects rather than people is reminiscent of Baron-Cohen's description of the 'male systematizing brain' in autism. The ability to understand ideas and theories through practical applications also captures central features of his theory.

The preference for using familiar and practiced methods could readily be equated with the 'stereotyped patterns of behavior' noted in people with autism. The distinct food preferences are frequently a source of great frustration to parents with a child with autism.

The tendency of Sensing people to notice and remember details provides support to the theory of Weak Central Coherence. People with a Sensing preference tend to notice the 'trees' (details) and may miss the 'forest' (overall concept or configuration). The detail orientation is frequently reported in children with autism where they notice even minute changes in the arrangement of their environment. Temple Grandin reported having difficulty sorting out relevant and important information from the onslaught of details coming at her.

Thinking

A person with a preference for **Thinking**, as a process for decision-making:

- identifies what is wrong or different in a person, event or situation

- is 'tough-minded' and less concerned about what his social group is doing and may seem detached

- is analytical and interested in routines and rules

- prefers logic-focused rather than people-focused activities, valuing fairness and consistency.

Example: Frequently we find children with autism are 'enforcers' of rules because they value fairness and consistency. One child in class was remarkably tall and muscular for his age. He was prone to outbursts that included hitting, biting and scratching others. The outbursts were often difficult for a full-sized adult to deal with. At the 'welcome' circle time, he took a calendar card from the teacher. A child beside him, who was slight and decidedly small for his age, blurted out, "You're not s'posed to grab!"

We all held our breath, ready to intercede as needed because we expected the smaller boy to receive a thrashing. Fortunately, the larger child simply gave the card back.

The decreased concern for social matters of the Thinking person parallels the lack of empathizing Baron-Cohen found in autism. In addition, the analytical, logical mind and interest in systems capture important features of his 'male systematizing brain' theory.

Judging

A person with preference for **Judging**, as a way to relate to the world:

- likes to live in a planned and orderly way, with orderly details, orderly categories and functions better with schedules, routines and rules

- prefers to finish what he starts, persisting in his pursuit of what he desires

- is dependable and perseverant in relation to things that are important to him

- likes to have things decided, finding it hard to switch gears with short notice and to concentrate if time-pressured.

Example: We have found that categorizing can be some children's attempt to make sense of and control their world. One boy spontaneously began to organize people into either "circle-face people" or not. We found that "circle-face people" had round face shapes. He decided he did not like "circle-face people" so would have nothing to do with his nanny and his baby brother plus a few other people who had round faces. He made a sign for his bedroom door to make sure no "circle-face people" entered.

Temple Grandin speaks about the need for planfulness and orderly categories in her life. Her persistence with things of importance to her are apparent in her autobiographies. She uses schedules, routines and rules to help herself cope with and learn more about the world around her. When you see Dr. Grandin speak, she follows a script quite carefully and does not seem to switch topics or trains of thought easily.

To this point in my thinking, I was projecting from what I knew about personality type, or learning preferences, and what I knew about autism to arrive at my belief that autism may be an extreme form of Introversion-Sensing-Thinking-Judging (ISTJ) preferences.

To investigate the ISTJ hypothesis, I developed a parent survey to obtain learning preference and strength profiles of preschool and elementary school-aged children with autism. The *Learning Preferences and Strengths Profile* can be found in Appendix II. It was necessary to develop the survey because there are no standardized measures for examining learning preferences in children whose reading comprehension is below the grade two to three level. However, type preferences are identifiable by as early as two years of age.

The parents were asked to complete the *Learning Preferences and Strengths Profile* in relation to how their child responds most of the time. As indicated earlier, we can all use different preferences at different times, dependent upon the demands and expectations. I was looking for the typical and most natural responses for each child.

The data from 71 parent surveys are shown in Figure 3.1. The trends support the ISTJ–autism connection:

- Over half of the children were reported to have a preference for Introversion. The relatively high per cent with a preference for Extraversion was a rather curious result. Then I recalled that Lorna Wing (1997) found children with autism to fall into three main categories: socially aloof, passive or odd. The latter category may capture some of the children reported to have an Extraversion preference: these are verbal children who use a lot of highly scripted language and/or who speak at length on their favorite topic.

- Eighty per cent of the children had a Sensing preference.

- Over 60 per cent had preferences for Thinking.

- Over 60 per cent had preferences for Judging.

These data support the view that children with autism have a preference for Introverted-Sensing-Thinking-Judging (ISTJ) type. It must, however, be kept in mind that having preferences for ISTJ does not mean someone is 'autistic'!

I then examined this information in comparison with existing data for incidence of the ISTJ type in the general population, using the extensive research database on *Myers-Briggs Type Indicator*® (Macdaid, McCalley and Kainz 1995). This was compared to the rates in men in general and different types of engineers and computer professionals to see if a relationship existed with Baron-Cohen *et al.*'s (1997, 1998, 1999) studies. The results are shown in Figure 3.2.

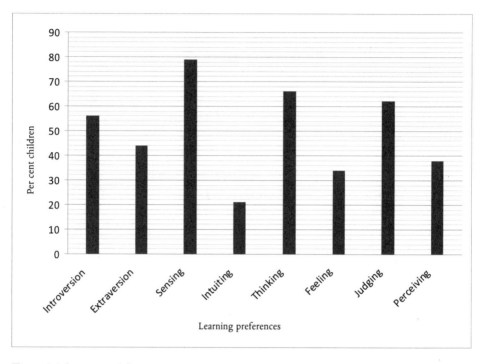

Figure 3.1 Summary of learning preference data obtained from parent responses on the Learning Preferences and Strengths Profile *(N=71)*

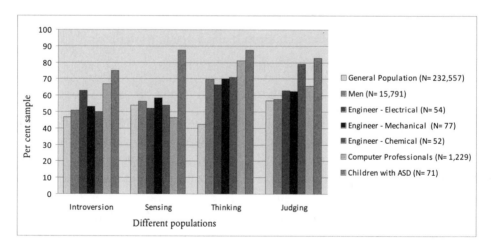

Figure 3.2 Per cent preference for ISTJ in different populations

The strongest trend was increased Thinking preference for all comparison groups relative to the general population. Electrical engineers and computer professionals also showed increased preference for Introversion.

Within the general population, 16.4 per cent of men have a preference for ISTJ but only 6.9 per cent of women have that preference. This lent support to Baron-Cohen's notion of the 'male systematizing brain'.

Further analysis was completed in my study looking at the relationship between learning preference and autistic characteristics in the normal adult population. Baron-Cohen *et al.* (2001) developed *Autism-Spectrum Quotient* (AQ) and used it to examine the normal adult population in England. The AQ is a brief, self-administered instrument for measuring the degree to which an adult with normal intelligence has the traits associated with the autistic spectrum. It is comprised of 50 items with ten questions in each of five areas: communication skills, social skills, attention to details, attention switching, and imagination. Each item scores one point if the respondent 'agrees' or 'disagrees' on the autistic-like side. Half of the items are worded to produce 'disagree' responses and half to produce 'agree' responses.

In my study, 89 Canadian adults of normal intelligence completed the AQ in addition to a learning preference screener. The overall results showed a close relationship between my data and those obtained by Baron-Cohen. In both studies, 2.3 per cent of the total adult group reported characteristics of the autism spectrum without any significant distress in daily life. I found a significant relationship between some learning preferences and total AQ scores. Significantly more people with preferences for Introversion and for Thinking had elevated scores on the AQ. Even though the number of subjects was somewhat small (N=89), these results suggested that at least these two preferences, Introversion and Thinking, are associated with autistic characteristics. When the five areas examined in the AQ were analyzed, a significant relationship emerged between Introversion preference and weak social skills and between Thinking preference and weak social skills as well as weak imagination (see Figure 3.3).

In summary, there appears to be consistent empirical support for people with autism to have preferences for Introversion and Thinking. Children with autism also exhibit a strong preference for Sensing which may not be apparent among adults. Anecdotal information from adults with autism lends support to the Judging preference.

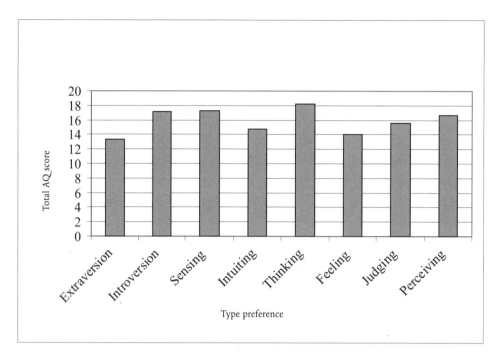

Figure 3.3 Summary of total scores on the Autism Spectrum Quotient *(AQ) survey and learning preferences (N=89) (*Significant at p<0.01)*

LEARNING STRENGTHS

When examining each learning strength, I hypothesized that children with autism would exhibit strengths in the areas of **Visual-Spatial**, **Musical-Rhythmic** and perhaps **Bodily-Kinesthetic** modalities. This view was based on years of work with children with autism.

Each of these learning strengths will be reviewed and their relationship to autism will be discussed below.

Visual-Spatial

A person with **Visual-Spatial** strength, as a means of learning and making sense of the world:

- readily understands, retains and remembers information he can see
- is able to create visual experiences
- shows sensitivity to color, line, shape, form, space, and relationships among them, often noticing minute details
- prefers orderly, tidy environments.

To a child with autism, seeing is believing. If visual schedules, plans, rules and Social Stories™ are employed with children with autism, they seem to understand and remember better. Some children can re-run entire videos in their heads. Attention to details and orderliness are two common features in autism.

Example: Strong Visual-Spatial reasoning can sometimes confound well-meaning adults. One day I was working with a child on a worksheet where the child was to place the number of small stones beside the corresponding printed numeral. The child kept placing one stone beside each numeral from top to bottom. I watched him complete the task several times when it finally dawned on me that we had constructed the task incorrectly for what we intended. The child was using quite flawless visual logic: going vertically the numerals matched the number of stones: one stone beside 1, add one more stone below and it adds up to two. If you looked at the worksheet logically, the sum of the stones matched the numerals only when you worked left to right. I put the numeral strip on the right-hand side and the child quickly completed the sheet in the manner we had intended.

Musical-Rhythmic

A person with **Musical-Rhythmic** strength, as a means of learning:

- seeks out music and rhythm and listening with interest

- enjoys and responds to a variety of musical and rhythmic sounds

- attends to, recognizes and remembers music, musical patterns and/or rhythm readily

- is sensitive to pitch, rhythm and melody, perhaps showing distress when music is off-pitch.

Example: Very frequent evidence of Musical-Rhythmic strengths are seen in children's response to their names. More often than not, if you sing the name of a child with autism, he will respond. If you just speak his name, he is considerably less likely to display attention.

Temple Grandin (1995) indicated that, "in some people, the brain circuits used for singing may be more normal than the circuits used for speech. Possibly the song rhythm helps to stabilize auditory processing and block out intruding sounds" (p.72). It is not unusual to find children with autism who can recall entire songs after one or two exposures. A number of parents have warned me that their children with autism will fuss, yell, cover your mouth if you sing off-key. This indicates a sensitivity to pitch and melody.

Bodily-Kinesthetic

A person with **Bodily-Kinesthetic** strength, as a means of learning:

- learns more readily when he can move his body or parts of his body, finding it stifling to sit still for periods of time

- retains information more readily when he can associate it with movement

- prefers to touch, smell or taste objects before using them

- is calmed and soothed or stimulated and enlivened by movement.

This strength overlaps considerably with the Sensing preference so I was not entirely certain that Bodily-Kinesthetic would be a distinct strength for children with autism. Sensory hypo- or hyper-sensitivity seen in many children with autism may be the source of some of the movement and sensory patterns observed.

To investigate the hypothesized learning strengths, I asked parents to complete the *Learning Preferences and Strengths Profile* and to indicate which statements in the learning strengths section best described their child. Each parent's checkmarks were added up and the category with the most checks was deemed the 'first rank' strength for that child. Only the top strength was identified for each child to simplify profiling. The data from 40 parent surveys are shown in Figure 3.4.

Trends found for the learning strength–autism connection were:

- Forty per cent of parents indicated that Musical-Rhythmic strengths were top-ranked for their children.

- Almost 40 per cent of the parents reported Visual-Spatial strengths as being top-ranked for their children.

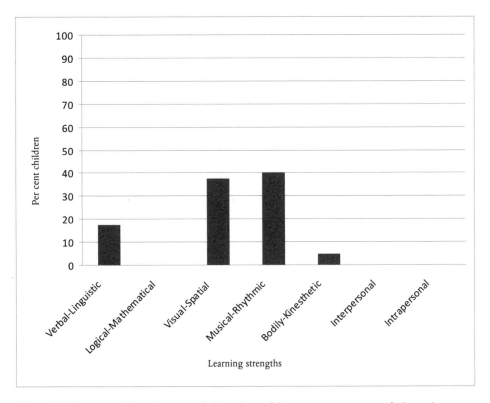

Figure 3.4 Summary of learning strength data obtained from parent response on the Learning Preferences and Strengths *Profile (N=40)*

- Interestingly, 17.5 per cent of the children were indicated to have Verbal-Linguistic strengths. This was not anticipated but likely was a reflection of the high levels of 'scripted' language used by some of the children.

- Only 5 per cent of the children were rated to have primary Bodily-Kinesthetic strengths.

With clear strengths in two main areas, Musical-Rhythmic and Visual-Spatial, children with autism have what is referred to as a 'laser' profile of intelligences or strengths. That is, they have a small number of clearly-developed peak intelligences. These results did not support all of my predictions but provided interesting and useable data for program planning.

DETERMINING THE *LEARNING PREFERENCES AND STRENGTHS* PROFILE OF A CHILD WITH AUTISM

Observing the child

The most important way to begin to understand a child with autism is to observe him. This should always be your first step. Watching him in everyday life helps you see how he tries to understand and make sense of the world, events and people around him.

Before you start, set aside all information you may have heard or read about the child. Do not think about him in terms of impairments or delays. Think about him in terms of how he may be trying to make sense of his world and make it more tolerable.

OBSERVING THE CHILD ON HIS OWN

Observe the child on his own at home where he is most likely to be at ease. Just sit back and watch to see what he does.

Ask yourself questions like:

- Does he approach as soon as I enter his space?

- Does he try to share an object or event with me?

- Does he spend more time with objects than people?

- Does he become upset if I try to re-arrange a toy or object he is playing with or I try to do something in a different order?

- Does he respond if I laugh or pretend to cry?

- Does he become upset or resistant if I suggest doing something different or if I suggest we go somewhere else?

- Does he resist putting away a toy or object he is playing with when I suggest it?

An example framework for observing the child alone is in Appendix III.

OBSERVING THE CHILD WITH PEERS

Observe the child with other children in his age group. Arrange the situation so that there is one main toy for them to play with and contribute to, such as Lego®, Duplo®, Meccano® or Marbleworks®. Using this kind of toy increases the likelihood of the children building a joint project.

Ask yourself questions like:

- Does he approach the other children as soon as he enters the space?
- Does he try to share an object or event with them?
- Does he spend more time with objects than the other children?
- Does he become upset if another child tries to re-arrange a toy he is playing with or try to do something he is doing in a different order?
- Does he respond to the emotions of the other children?
- Does he become upset or resistant if another child suggests doing something different?
- Does he resist putting away a toy or object he is playing with?

An example framework for observing the child with peers is included in Appendix III.

Gathering information about likes and dislikes

By obtaining information about the child's likes and dislikes, you can learn a great deal about his preferences and strengths. Also, if you include some of his strong interests in activities and tasks, you are more likely to 'hook' him and gain his attention and cooperation.

Ask his parents and other people who know him well:

- what are his favorite:
    - videos
    - games
    - TV shows
    - computer programs
    - books
    - toys
    - characters from videos, TV, computer games and/or books?
- what things does he dislike in relation to:
    - videos
    - games
    - TV shows

- ° computer programs
- ° books
- ° toys
- ° characters from videos, TV, computer games and/or books?

An example form is included in Appendix III.

Most commonly children with autism exhibit very strong likes and dislikes. Favorite things tend to be trains, dinosaurs, cars, computers, fans, flags, pipes, cartoon characters of the moment, letters, alphabet and numbers.

Completing the *Learning Preferences and Strengths* Profile

The *Learning Preferences and Strengths (LPS)* Profile in Appendix II is designed to provide information on the child's preferences and strengths in day-to-day life. The *LPS* Profile is intended to capture a picture of the child when he is relaxed and well-rested.

To ensure that you obtain a balanced picture of the child's *Learning Preferences and Strengths*, the profile should be completed by:

- parents, particularly the parent who spends the most time with the child

- teachers who have known and worked with the child for at least a few months

- support workers and other caregivers who have known and worked or lived with the child for at least a few months.

Information from therapists may be helpful but their exposure to children tends to be structured around specific therapeutic tasks. Often, therapists have only 'snap shots' of children because their time is typically briefer and more time-constrained.

Prompt everyone to complete the profile with the target child in mind. They must think about how he responds most of the time and look for trends. They should try not to become too focused on specific situations, responses or behaviors.

Once everyone has completed the profiles on a child, look at the consistencies and inconsistencies. If there is a marked difference in any area, discuss it with the person who completed the form in order to understand what they see in the child that others do not. Once you reach consensus or are able to achieve a reasonable profile for that child, you are ready to start planning his program.

Chapter 4

Program Planning with *Learning Preferences and Strengths*

KEY PROGRAM COMPONENTS

The *Learning Preferences and Strengths* (*LPS*) model is comprised of three key components: structure, content and process (see Figure 4.1). Excellent teaching is the fine art of connecting and integrating these key components for each child.

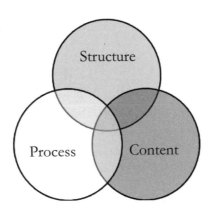

Figure 4.1 Learning Preferences and Strengths *model key components*

The individual child's preferences and strengths are at the heart of this model, guiding the structure, content and processes of his program. When there is a match between *Learning Preferences and Strengths* and program structure, process and content, a synergy is created that is greater than the sum of the parts. When the child's *Learning Preferences and Strengths* are engaged, his learning can be optimized and used in tandem to enhance other areas of preference and strength.

Emphasis on metacognition

Throughout the book, metacognition is a central focus. Metacognition refers to the child's being able to think about his own thinking. Metacognitive awareness helps the child become conscious of his thought processes and more engaged and in control of his own learning. By emphasizing metacognition, the child develops conscious understanding of:

- focusing and shifting attention
- identifying and defining important elements in a task, activity or event
- organizing, prioritizing and sequencing tasks and activities
- remembering and retrieving information from memory
- monitoring, checking, evaluating and revising his approach to tasks

in addition to regulating his alertness and sustaining his efforts and managing frustration, which are described under "Focus on self-regulation" below.

The initial goal is to help the child become conscious of his thinking and effective learning strategies he has learned to use. He then must progress to independent use of appropriate strategies. Ultimately, we want to help the child begin to reflect on his thinking and problem solving so that he can improve on his own.

Metacognitive learners become intentional learners who take control over their own learning and monitor their own progress. With metacognitive approaches, thinking is made explicit, visible and public. Bransford, Brown and Cocking (2000) have found three important developments in children who use a metacognitive approach:

1. learning is more efficient
2. learning outcomes are improved
3. transfer of learning, or generalization, to new situations is increased.

Focus on self-regulation

An important overall goal within the *LPS* model is to help the child become a self-directed learner. He must learn how to assume control of his body, his thinking and his emotions. The child must learn to shape his attitudes and efforts in order to achieve goals without adult reminders or cues.

Self-regulation means that the child learns to inhibit, subdue, maintain or enhance his own physical, emotional and cognitive awareness and arousal. He needs to learn how to reduce or increase the intensity of his actions, thoughts and feelings as well as slow them down or speed them up.

Self-regulated learning can be fostered through providing the child with choices, giving him responsibilities in the learning process and ensuring that the atmosphere around him is one that accepts errors as part of learning. He must learn that it is safe to take risks. The adults around him model these behaviors as well as teach the child self-regulation strategies directly.

Self-regulation is a critical skill in becoming a more reflective and thoughtful metacognitive learner. It allows the child to tolerate, adapt or react to everyday demands. Self-regulation also helps the child maintain his motivation and interest in learning.

Use of compartmentalization

I have found that there is a subtle but critically important way to refer to the child during learning. 'Compartmentalization' of a body part involved in an activity from the child himself can make the difference between his continuing to try and his resisting. This notion plays into the increased awareness of self we emphasize within the *LPS* program. Children with autism seem to accept more positively the healthy detachment of their body parts from their central selves. Compartmentalization seems to help us take personal judgement out of the learning process. It sets a boundary between the child and his behavior. Over time, the compartmentalization is reduced as the child gains greater control over his body and mind. The early effectiveness of this approach may be part of the concreteness children with autism prefer in their Sensing self in addition to their discomfort with being singled out.

I strongly recommend talking about the brain rather than just 'you'. For example, the child is prompted: "Tell your brains: don't get distracted, brain!" In the case of self-regulation, the body part is referred to as requiring help in controlling itself, not the child. He is prompted with statements like, "Tell your hands: 'you need to be gentle, hands!'."

Use of self-talk

As part of the development of metacognition and self-regulation, children are prompted to talk to their 'brains'. This self-talk is intended to help the children monitor and guide their own learning and use of strategies. When used effectively, it will assist the child in correcting himself, coping and using metacognitive strategies.

In young children, spontaneous self-talk is usually irrelevant to the task, such as about something that happened in another setting. Over time and with prompting and modeling, self-talk becomes more focused on the task, although the early content may not help the child complete the task. With further persistence and consistency, the child's self-talk will become more metacognitive and helpful to his learning.

In typical development, self-talk becomes internalized, or not spoken out loud, by middle childhood. However, when tasks are more difficult, both children and adults are more likely to talk out loud to help themselves focus and complete the activity successfully.

Importance of interpersonal trust

An important cornerstone to the *LPS* model is interpersonal trust. Trust refers to the child's confidence in the adults around him. If he can trust people he lives and works with, the child will be able to relax and learn more optimally.

Research has shown that four major elements combine to create interpersonal trust (Perrin 2007). These four elements include:

1. *Acceptance* – this means that the child is accepted for who he is. He is not viewed as being inferior or less able. The child must at all times receive the message that he is important to you. In everything the child does, he should be given the benefit of the doubt and his behavior should be carefully examined to try to understand why he did what he did without prior judgement.

2. *Reliability* – this refers to your doing what you say you will do when you say you will do it. The child can rely on you to do what you say and show him you will do. You can be trusted to keep promises even when it is inconvenient or circumstances change somewhat. The other important aspect of reliability is taking responsibility for yourself. That means that you will not attempt to blame someone or something else for your own feelings and actions.

3. *Openness* – this refers to honesty and willingness to provide candid feedback to the child about him and about you. If you make an error when working with the child, you should let him know. If he makes a mistake, he should be helped to understand it.

4. *Congruence* – this means that what you say and do is in line with what you believe and feel. There is a genuine and sincere interest in the child and his well-being in everything you do with and for him.

As you read this book, you will see how these four elements are carefully incorporated into all aspects of the *LPS* model. Those involved in implementing the model must commit themselves emotionally and cognitively to developing and nurturing trust in their relationship with each child.

WHERE TO START THE *LPS* PROGRAM

It is assumed that the child has already had all of the standard diagnostic and developmental assessments before you start. These pieces of information are important for obtaining ideas about where to start from a content point of view. The most important thing that I have found over the years is not to let standardized assessment information lower your expectations or change the way you view the child. The child is still the same person he was before the diagnosis. Most importantly, we know that he is motivated to learn and is capable of a great deal of learning.

In terms of the *LPS* model, structure, content and process are critically intertwined to form a solid program. It may seem like a complex and daunting task but I recommend not trying to do everything at once. The following chapters will introduce you to each component and provide guidelines and examples. I will lead you through understanding and developing each component.

I recommend starting with Structure, which is discussed in Chapter 5. You will see in that chapter, when the home and school environments are well organized around the child's *Learning Preferences and Strengths*, his anxiety and stress are reduced considerably. Because of this, his learning potential is enhanced.

The next step should be to develop the Content, described in Chapter 6. Content presented in this book will focus on the three main areas of need in autism: Learning/Cognitive, Social/Communication and Self-Regulation skills. Other content in each child's individual plan should follow national, state or provincial educational and developmental standards.

Finally, the Process component, described in Chapter 7, should be integrated. Process will focus on mediating the child's learning rather than teaching him. This requires active interaction on the part of the teacher using the Seven Pillars of Mediated Learning. It is within this component that the child's

Learning Preferences and Strengths are challenged most, prompting him to draw on less-preferred areas and modalities.

Within each section on structure, content and process, ways of 'challenging' the child in order to engage non-dominant preferences and strengths will be presented. For children with autism these other preferences and strengths center around learning such things as:

- determining the 'big picture' or main idea and constructing meaning from information they hear or see

- 'going with the flow' and becoming more flexible and less rule-bound

- dealing with uncertainty and change and accepting risk

- listening to and continuing conversations on a wide range of topics

- accepting other people's differences of opinion, appearance and thinking

- filtering out unimportant or irrelevant information

- self-regulating behavior, cognitive processes and emotions.

WHAT MOTIVATES CHILDREN WITH AUTISM?

Earlier, it was stated that children with autism have a desire to learn. Some would likely dispute that statement if they have worked with 'difficult to motivate' children with autism. Research into ways to appeal to and interest people with Introversion-Sensing-Thinking-Judging (ISTJ) preferences, conducted by Quenk (1993, 2000), provides us with some insight into motivating children with autism.

Things that motivate and energize children with autism closely follow their *Learning Preferences and Strengths*. Think about Introverts and their need for warm-up time, Sensers and their preference for gathering detailed information through their senses, Thinkers and their valuing logic and analytical approaches to making decisions, and Judgers and their preference for predictable settings and finishing tasks. Visual-Spatial learners are energized by use of visual images that are clear and precise. Musical-Rhythmic learners are motivated by songs, melodies and rhythms.

Factors that typically motivate ISTJs with Visual-Spatial and Musical-Rhythmic strengths are presented in Table 4.1 below. Example activities are also included.

Table 4.1 Motivators for children with autism and examples

Motivators	Example Activities
permitting him to use his learning strengths	visual matching, visual schedules and plans
incorporating his affinities and areas of high interest	use dinosaurs, trains, computers
allowing him time to warm up to and become familiar with activities and tasks before participating	watch others perform a task, present a model or picture sequence of how a task is to be completed
permitting him to gather information by using his senses	smell playdough, touch or sniff a toy, watch before trying an action, swing, spin
valuing his ability to gather detailed information	providing opportunities to tell others or demonstrate to others areas of strong knowledge
providing an environment that is predictable, organized and well-structured	use consistent 'rhythm' for working, break, working, break and so on
clarifying responsibilities and roles	use models to show the process for completion of tasks and the desired end-products
clarifying and agreeing upon goals, expectations and deadlines before starting a task or activity	make plan with pictures or words
finishing one task before moving on to another	remove items done from plan before starting next item
permitting him to be in control of his schedule	child decides every second item on his schedule or child decides the order of tasks assigned
making sure tasks have concrete, tangible results	child needs to print ten words, cut two circles, eat three spoonfuls

These motivators will be incorporated into structure, content and processes within the *LPS* model. Further discussion and description will be detailed in each chapter.

CONSIDER THE CHILD'S BASIC NEEDS FIRST

Before starting work with any child with autism, basic physiological needs must be addressed. Ensure that the child:

- has had sufficient sleep
- has eaten and continues to eat every two to three hours
- is wearing comfortable, dry clothing
- is warm or cool enough
- is not thirsty
- is feeling well.

Keep in mind that children with autism are particularly sensitive to these needs. Failure to attend to these can significantly reduce the child's ability to learn.

CONSIDER YOURSELF

Before starting work with a child with autism, it is important to look after yourself. The child with autism requires the adults around him to have a great deal of patience, understanding and energy to work effectively. Ensure that you:

- have had sufficient sleep
- are not feeling frustrated or on edge.

At the least, it is critical that you can behave in a calm and relaxed manner. This does not mean that you cannot express your feelings and emotions. They must, however, be related to the child and task at hand and not something extraneous to the situation.

Also, from a sensory point of view, it is best not to wear highly scented perfumes, deodorant or cosmetics as these may distract or irritate the child. The issue of body odors is also important in that halitosis ('bad breath') can stop some children with autism in their tracks.

It is essential that all people involved with children with autism develop an understanding of their own *Learning Preferences and Strengths*. Most of us likely enjoyed teachers at school who most closely matched our own preferences and strengths. We also tend to teach others using our own preferences and strengths. Because of this, we have to be keenly aware of our own learning profile. In Table 4.2 are some suggestions for monitoring your behavior in relation to the learning preferences typically found in children with autism.

Table 4.2 Balancing child and adult learning preferences

The child has a preference for	You have a preference for	Things you will need to monitor in yourself
Introversion	Introversion	talk out loud about your thinking and feelings and what the child is experiencing
		make sure you allow yourself some 'down-time' either midday or at the end of the day to recharge your personal battery
	Extraversion	keep your talk relatively short, concise and clear
		remember that you have increased tolerance for noise and interruptions but they cause considerable stress for children with autism
		try to tone down your energy, enthusiasm and excitement about things to a level that is more tolerable to the child; make sure you find other outlets for your wonderful zest
		do not worry that the child is not interested in joining groups or organized activities – work on a compromise over time
Sensing	Sensing	focus on the overall goal with the child
		be sure to help the child see the 'big picture' and broader implications of learning
		help the child not become too 'locked into' old procedures, slowly introduce change and flexibility
	Intuiting	ensure you do not miss or downplay details important to the child
		ensure the child has time for hands-on experiences
		help the child establish what he already knows before presenting new concepts or ideas
		pay attention to the child's need for using established procedures and predictability; be cautious when introducing new approaches
Thinking	Thinking	do not become too task-oriented and forget the relationship (emotional) side of your role with the child
		do not impose your need for truth and fairness on the child, especially when he is stressed; restore equilibrium first

Table 4.2 continued

The child has a preference for	You have a preference for	Things you will need to monitor in yourself
	Feeling	be careful your feelings are not hurt when the child says something 'blunt' or is uncooperative
		maintain objectivity and calmness when explaining rules, roles and reasons
		do not feel unappreciated or rejected if the child does not behave warmly toward you
		try not to feel harsh when you enforce a rule with the child
Judging	Judging	take your time in completing tasks to ensure the child understands and that he experiences a sense of ' being finished'
		do not become stressed if things do not follow the procedure or time-line you had planned; flow with the child's energy – you may be surprised where it leads
		help the child learn about coping and dealing positively with change
	Perceiving	do not be too 'go with the flow'; the child needs predictability and consistency in expectations, rules, routines, schedules and plans; a casual approach to day-to-day life can make the child feel insecure and uncared for – he may wonder who is in charge
		carefully forewarn the child of where, when and why things may change
		finish one thing before moving on to the next

Chapter 5

Program Structure

IMPORTANCE OF STRUCTURE

The structure of the learning environment must provide opportunities for the child to experience independent discovery, thinking and problem solving. Our overall goal is for the child to become a more autonomous learner and to develop skills and strategies for lifelong learning.

The term 'structure' refers to setting the learning stage so that it is more inviting and easier for the child to understand. It does not refer to rigid boot camp-like regimentation with adults controlling every aspect of the child's behavior. For children with autism, well-structured settings provide a sense of safety, security and certainty. They can then relax and learn more optimally.

Note on structure: Without a well-organized learning environment, the child seems to feel like you or I would when walking alone down an unlit lane at midnight: our every sense is on hyper-alert in a 'fight-flight' mode. This is not a situation where learning can readily take place.

Of all thinkers and investigators in the field of autism, the Treatment and Education of Autistic and related Communication-handicapped CHildren (TEACCH) model is by far the most advanced in honoring the needs of people with autism for clear program structuring. Important concepts from TEACCH have been extended and incorporated into the *Learning Preferences and Strengths* (*LPS*) model.

To understand the notion of structure a little better, think about the *Learning Preferences and Strengths* that are anticipated for children with autism and what they may mean for desirable structural features. Here are some key examples:

- sensory-reduced environment where sounds, sights, smells and other sensations are controlled so as not to overwhelm or distract the child

- organized and orderly environment so the child is not drawn to extraneous, irrelevant information

- clear, visually-obvious structure and organization so the child can see what he is supposed to do, when and where

- logical and clearly-planned structuring of tasks and activities so the child knows what to do and when he will be finished

- opportunities for down-time and privacy so the child can recharge and refresh himself and be ready for more learning.

Program structure occurs on three main levels. They include:

A. learning environment

B. schedules, plans and routines

C. tasks and activities.

The key to developing program structure is that, just by looking, the child should be able to understand the expectations.

Please note, you will not be keeping all environmental structuring features in place forever. The idea is to start the child's program with as much structure as possible and then slowly and progressively, as the child relaxes and learns to trust you and himself as a learner, reduce the amount of structuring.

Our ultimate goal is to make it possible for the child to exist in the real world while optimizing his learning. Some children will require a fair amount of structuring over the longer term. Some children will require more structure only on 'not-so-good' days.

The main emphasis of this chapter is program structure that honors the *Learning Preferences and Strengths* of children with autism. At the end of the chapter is a section intended to help the child develop non-dominant preferences and strengths, such as dealing with uncertainty, new activities and events and change in general.

At the end of each section in this chapter will be a Checkpoint. These will be used to summarize the *Learning Preferences and Strengths* incorporated within the strategies and provide any needed explanations. In addition, other preferences and strengths not typical to children with autism will be noted and described as Challenges.

A. LEARNING ENVIRONMENT

To engage strong Visual-Spatial abilities of a child with autism, the physical setting should be organized so that the child will know just by looking where different activities take place and where to find the needed materials. It is similar to the situation you would face traveling to a country where you do not speak the language and do not know cultural and social expectations. How do you figure out what to do? You watch very carefully, seeking out understandable signs and signals. I believe the child with autism feels very much this way so we must reduce his anxiety and provide him with information that makes sense to him.

The typical *Learning Preferences and Strengths* of children with autism suggest that the learning environment should include sensory-reduction, order and organization, visual designation of areas, reduced verbal language load and attention to the organization of seating. Each of these is described below.

1. Sensory-reduction in the learning environment

At the beginning of the program or school year, the environment should display only relevant and important information and materials.

Noise levels should be reduced as much as possible. Try to ensure that the child with autism is not seated next to an air vent or other source of noise. Even the sound of forced air can disrupt his ability to concentrate and work optimally. Having part of the room carpeted helps to reduce reverberation of sounds. Carpeting that is a simple weave without a discernible pattern is best. A pattern can be a visual stimulator for some children which will distract them from learning. Carpeting is important but you will also need a hard surface area for wash-ability purposes where painting and other 'messy' activities can take place.

Paint color and paint type for walls are issues that should be considered. Some paints smell more than others and the aroma may be overwhelming to children with autism, making it difficult for them to learn. In relation to color, neutral and relatively calming hues are preferable.

I recall working in one agency where the architects thought a child area should have a full range of primary colors depicting nursery rhyme characters. This was on the walls of a program area for children with autism. I arranged to have the walls painted a warm white. Some people were shocked that I had the works of art covered but the impact on the children of the now-muted walls was really noticeable. They seemed to be calmer and less readily aroused.

Lighting should include as much natural light as possible. If you are blessed with a lot of windows, you have an advantage. Some people with autism find fluorescent bulbs sufficiently bothersome that they cannot concentrate. Newer fluorescent lights have electronic ballasts that eliminate the old 'buzz' and they emit a full light spectrum.

If you cannot control all of these factors, do your best to be creative. Simple inexpensive drop-cloths or old bed sheets can cover busy walls as well as reduce some sound reverberation.

Checkpoint for sensory reduction: What *Learning Preferences and Strengths* did we incorporate?						
	Introversion	Sensing	Thinking	Judging	Visual-Spatial	Musical-Rhythmic
	✓	✓			✓	
Challenge:						

2. Order and organization in the learning environment

One of the most important things to remember is: Put things away! Storage cupboards and shelves are critical to maintaining a well-organized environment. Use whatever you can afford to ensure that non-critical things are out of sight. Some of the flat-pack stores have simple and relatively inexpensive systems that, along with drop cloths, can be all you need.

The parent, teacher, therapist or caregiver should have all needed material close at hand but out of sight to the child. Simple drop cloths, stop signs and other symbols can be used to indicate to the child that an object or area is a 'no-go' zone. A stop sign can be placed on a door of the house or classroom to indicate the door stays closed. Drop cloths can be used to drape just about anything you do not want the child to touch. Simply state, "The cloth is on so that's not available right now," or, "The stop sign is on so it tells us we can't go there right now." Point to the object or sign as providing the direction to the child and not you. It is a subtle but important difference that appeals to the concreteness and objectivity of the child with autism's thinking preferences. It can also keep you out of a tug-of-war with the child: After all, there is nothing you can do, it is the cloth, stop sign or symbol that is telling us!

 A simple drop cloth or old sheet acts to signal to the children that this object is not avalable right now

 A curtain with a stop sign placed on a computer monitor signals that the computer is not available right now.

Figure 5.1 Examples of stategies for restricting child access

The child's individual belongings and materials must have an organizational system both at school and at home. He needs a well-marked place to put his outdoor clothing and other belongings. Do not respond, "Oh, he can use any hook/shelf/drawer he wants, there are lots!" The child with autism needs help with organization and this will be one less stressor for him. Be sure to have:

- well-spaced out hooks, shelves or cubby-holes

- the child's name in print and his photograph, if needed, placed above the hook or on the shelf or cubby, keeping in mind the child needs to be able to see his name and picture even when his belongings are in place

| Simple coat hook, labelled for the specific child, and a mat for shoes or boots | Individual cubby-hole for clothing, shoes or boots, and backpack, labeled for the child. | Shelf unit with one shelf for each school subject area. | Individual boxes for different materials the child needs to remember. |

Figure 5.2 Examples of different organizational systems

- shelving for older children, divided by school subjects so that they can remain organized; also, the child should be able to put a completed subject back on a shelf which will give him a sense of closure and completion while keeping him organized

- bins with printed labels and pictures; for younger children, the bins may be for snacks brought by the children and for communication books; for older children, the bins may be for homework and communication sheets to be taken home for their parents.

Checkpoint for order and organization: What *Learning Preferences and Strengths* did we incorporate?						
	Introversion	Sensing	Thinking	Judging	Visual-Spatial	Musical-Rhythmic
	✓	✓	✓	✓	✓	
Challenge:						

3. Visual designation of areas in the learning environment

Just as houses are divided into function-related spaces so should the learning environment for children with autism. Use signs, barriers and furniture placement as dividers. I prefer to use barriers high enough so the children are not distracted but short enough so I can stand up and look around the room and see where everyone is. You can also use tri-fold cardboard presentation boards or cut-out cardboard boxes to act as individual screens.

Each space should have its own large label, along with a picture associated with that area. These should be posted at each area and the child's individual schedule should have a smaller version. This allows the children to use their typically powerful desire to match objects and pictures to guide them to the area of the room shown on their schedules.

AT SCHOOL

Typical areas at school include:

- *Entrance* where belongings, such as shoes, coats, backpacks or rucksacks, are placed on hooks, shelves or in cubby holes.

- *Schedule and transition area* where each child can learn what is going to happen for part or all of the day. This is the place where each child returns repeatedly to determine what to do next. As an extra benefit, allowing the children to get up, walk to the schedule, check and then go to the appropriate area will give them a chance to move and energize themselves.

- *Circle or group gathering area* where the children can get together for instruction, sharing and other activities.
  - ° Children usually respond best if there is a spot designated for each child within the group gathering area rather than having them sit anywhere. Carpet squares, free from most carpet dealers, or chairs with the children's names on them tend to work well.
  - ° Keep the area clear of too many objects. Activities and props should be obscured from the children's sight in a box, bag or cupboard that is close at hand.

- *Group activity area.* Each child should have a clearly demarcated space in which to work. It can be chairs at a table or desks. His picture and/or name should be shown clearly at the spot where he is supposed to be.

- *One-to-one and independent work area.*
  - ° The child should have his picture and/or name shown on the table or desk where he is supposed to work.
  - ° Tape can be placed on the floor to demarcate the child's working space that cannot be intruded by others.

- *Snack or eating area.* Ensure that each child has a specific place designated by his picture and/or name. If he is expected to eat in a cafeteria or other large room with many other students, I would re-think that plan. Most children with autism experience sensory overload in those types of places and simply cannot eat. You might form a 'lunch club' where a few students, including the child with autism, get to eat in a smaller room. The other students can be rotated so that it is a special privilege to join the 'lunch club'. Through the year, as the child with autism adapts to eating in a group of friends, he can be introduced to the larger room.

- *Toileting area.* Ensure that the bathroom has appropriate signage or the directions to it that are visually obvious. If the toilet is outside the classroom, use 'bathroom buddies' for younger children. This will ensure that the child with autism has support and does not go astray or end up experimenting with bathroom acoustics, just how much can be flushed down a toilet or what fun it is to play with water.

- *Play or hands-on experiential learning area.* Ensure that only necessary toys and objects are available. Having just one or two main toys or objects out can encourage the children to play in closer proximity to each other, perhaps even cooperate.

- *Break area.* There should be a place where any child can go to 'chill out' and regroup if he is becoming stressed. It can be an inexpensive tent purchased from a flat-pack store, cardboard box or a cut-out barrel available from large fruit juice companies.

Figure 5.3 Examples of settings for break areas

The schedule and group gathering areas should be like the 'hub' of the class-room. This is where everyone meets and greets, planning is done, completed tasks are checked off or removed from the list and where learning is summarized. The day should start and finish in this location. It is the central spot for checking the 'pulse' of the group.

AT HOME

Typical areas at home include:

- *Entrance* where belongings, such as shoes, coats, backpacks/rucksacks, are placed on hooks, shelves or in 'cubby-holes'.

- *Bedroom* where all of his clothes should be organized by type and labeled. A well-organized and labelled dresser can help the child:

- ○ remain calmer because everything is in its place
- ○ get dressed with greater ease, and
- ○ become increasingly independent.

The child's bedroom should be his special 'private' space and is best not used for work. It should be designated only for dressing, sleeping and quiet time. The child can go to his room to take a break if he is stressed or tired.

- *Bathroom* where the child will wash, brush his teeth, toilet and bath. This is an important place to work on consistent hygiene routines from an early age because ways of doing things, both effective and less effective, become solidified and less amenable to change.

- *Laundry* where the child can be helped to sort his dirty clothes for washing. Having a number of different-colored laundry hampers bearing labels can simplify sorting in preparation for washing and can ultimately increase the child's independence and accuracy doing the laundry himself. For example, one mother used a white hamper for whites, beiges and greys, a grey hamper for blues, greens and blacks and a third hamper for towels and all other colors of clothing.

- *Work area* where the child will do one-to-one and independent learning. The child should have a designated area that is not used for anything else. If that is not possible, use special cues like setting up a carrel for him to work.

- *Play area* where play is distinguished from work and all visual cues indicate this to the child.

- *Kitchen* which may act as the central point for schedules and plans. This is where the child can come to find out what will happen next and to remove pictures or printed words of activities already completed.

Children with autism find safety and comfort in certainty and predictability. Because of this, the location of activities should be the same every day for at least the first few months. After that, determine if the child is feeling relaxed and comfortable with the arrangement and then begin to make small progressive changes. If the child displays increased anxiety or off-task behavior, you can back up and replace the visual supports if needed. By slowly removing them, we are helping him learn flexibility but certain children will continue to need some types of visual supports.

Checkpoint for visual designation of areas: What *Learning Preferences and Strengths* did we incorporate?						
	Introversion	Sensing	Thinking	Judging	Visual-Spatial	Musical-Rhythmic
	✓	✓	✓	✓	✓	
Challenge:						

4. Reduced verbal language load in the learning environment

Children with autism have difficulties dealing with language for a number of reasons. Among them are extended processing time and difficulty understanding nonverbal cues. The learning environment can be arranged to help the child in these areas.

Children with autism tend to process verbal language slowly, especially when new ideas or topics are presented. In normal everyday conversation, we expect each other to understand and respond within less than five seconds. I have seen children take 30 minutes or more to take in and understand things said to them. Very often it looks like the child with autism was not even paying attention. Minutes or sometimes days later, you will find that he did take in the information.

Children with autism also have difficulty understanding differences in tone of voice, body language and gestures. Even if you say something with an emphatic tone and gestures, the child may not understand it is important.

These characteristics mean that you must be sensitive and tuned into each child's characteristics. Observe the child carefully to see how quickly and accurately he processes information. Look at how consistently he takes in and understands what you say. Do not reduce and simplify your language level too much because you need to balance what and how you say things with the child's understanding. Be very cautious about speaking to a low verbal or nonverbal child in too 'baby-like' a manner; his comprehension may be quite good. Also, do not take for granted that a highly verbal child will understand everything you say. Test it out and consult with your speech-language pathologist.

Always use visuals to reinforce what you say, whether in printed words or in print and pictures. Visual support can be in the form of environmental signs and visual schedules, plans and routines. It also includes writing or displaying important points on the blackboard or overhead projector or SMART Board™ and providing the child with an outline of the schedule or lesson plan. I have found that teaching very young children, five to six years of age, how to take brief notes during presentations and discussion helps them maintain their focus and increases their construction of meaning. Chapter 6 on **Program Content** provides more information in this area.

Checkpoint for reduced verbal language load: What *Learning Preferences and Strengths* did we incorporate?						
	Introversion	Sensing	Thinking	Judging	Visual-Spatial	Musical-Rhythmic
	✓	✓			✓	
Challenge:						

5. Organization of seating in the learning environment

The organization of seating is one more factor to consider when teaching children with autism. The orientation of the adult in relation to the child changes the dynamic and either increases or decreases the number of variables presented to the child. Each major seating arrangement and its implications for learning are presented in Table 5.1.

> I was asked to assess an elementary school-aged child with autism. I had read over his file and then chatted with the boy and his mother. I asked about some assessment results from the past, in particular an intellectual assessment that depicted the child as being severely delayed. Those results did not seem to go along with other assessment information and certainly did not fit the young fellow I was talking to. I asked his mother and she stated that the results were what the psychologist found. I then asked the child about being assessed by the psychologist. After chatting with him for a while, he finally told me that the psychologist had really bad breath and he just wanted to get out of the face-to-face setting with her. He said that he just did as little as possible so the assessment session ended quickly!

If you are working on early imitation skills, the side-by-side position is likely easier for the child. If you are working on reciprocity and social responsiveness, the face-to-face position is more appropriate. In the early stages of face-to-face work, lessen the task demands or the amount of reciprocity expected. This will ease the load on the child. In early stages of group work, the main focus should

Table 5.1 Different seating arrangements and their implications

Seating arrangement (gray = adult)	Implications of the configuration
Face-to-face in group Often used for group instruction. 	In face-to-face arrangements, there is an expectation that your partner(s) will listen and respond consistently. That means each person must listen, watch and respond to the group leader. This is in addition to dealing with sensory issues related to the physical closeness of other people and sounds, noises and actions other children may make. A multitude of demands in relation to paying attention and responding to the group leader while ignoring other factors are placed on the child in this type of arrangement.
Face-to-face in 1:1 Often used for assessment, communication and social activities. 	In the face-to-face setting where an adult works individually with a child, each is expected to pay attention and respond to verbal and nonverbal behavior of the other person. The child also has to deal with sensory issues related to being physically close to another person. These are in addition to working on a task. Again, a multitude of demands are being placed on the child simultaneously. In the 1:1 situation, the demands are reduced somewhat from the group setting because the child has only one other person to be concerned about.
Side-by-side Often used in helping a child develop new skills. This is a good configuration to use when teaching imitation because the adult model is parallel to the child. He does not have to provide a mirror image of the model.	When we are side-by-side, the focus on the task and the materials on the table is increased. This configuration places considerably less focus on social interaction. It allows more specific attention to the directions, materials and task at hand. The adult and child are looking from the same vantage point. This helps the adult understand how the child is perceiving the situation and the task. The child's role is simplified by reducing expectations for social interaction.
Teacher behind, child at table 	Presence of the teacher is lessened but close monitoring of the child can continue. This configuration promotes independence in the child and attention to the task, reducing reliance on adult cues. The arrangement can allow the adult to prompt the child physically, such as by pointing, nudging his elbow to start an action or by providing hand-over-hand assistance.

be on increasing the child's comfort level in sitting close to a cluster of other people. Tasks presented in these early groups should be relatively simple and adult support and assistance should be readily available.

Checkpoint for organization of seating: What *Learning Preferences and Strengths* did we incorporate?						
	Introversion	Sensing	Thinking	Judging	Visual-Spatial	Musical-Rhythmic
	✓	✓			✓	
Challenge:					Interpersonal	

Notes: Organization of seating stretches the *Learning Preferences and Strengths* in the following ways:

- *Interpersonal* – the person with Interpersonal strengths maintains and forms cooperative relationships with others, adapting well to different situations. The different seating arrangements challenge the child to become more responsive to others during interactions.

B. SCHEDULES, PLANS AND ROUTINES

For children with autism, a predictable and consistent environment feels safe and secure. When key people support the predictability by using schedules, plans and routines, the children are better able to relax, learn and become independent.

Well-structured visual schedules, plans and routines provide:

- advance warning of tasks and activities
- support during tasks and activities
- support for verbal directions and instructions
- isolation of key information
- clear expectations.

In this section, examples of schedules, plans and routines will be presented.

Note on schedules, plans and routines: When I bring up the subject of visual and/or written schedules, plans, and routines, I get a variety of responses. A fair number of people have said to me, "Oh, he doesn't need it. He understands everything." I have three main comments to that: (1) are you truly gauging the child's stress level accurately since children with autism can internalize a lot of anxiety, (2) why not support the child in ways that make it easier for him to understand, remember and learn and (3) adults tend to make lists to help themselves remember so why not allow the child this opportunity? If you really want to give the child with autism an optimal learning environment, use visuals. It takes nothing away and provides a critically important element.

Schedules

Schedules are the master plan for part or all of a day. They should be organized such that the child knows what activity he is supposed to do and in what order. Well-organized schedules allow the child to gain greater independence, handle transitions more calmly and become more flexible.

After each component on a schedule is completed, the child should be brought back to his master schedule where the completed task is removed and he checks what is next. This sense of rhythm during the instruction period should be: check your schedule, do the task, remove the picture of the completed task from your schedule and then go on to the next task or activity. Such a cycle is shown in Figure 5.4.

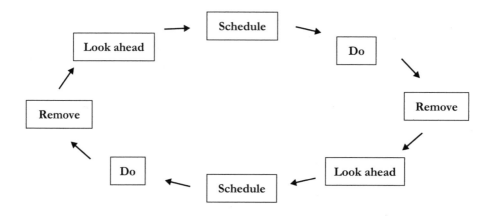

Figure 5.4 Rhythmic cycle of schedules

For younger children, it is best to start with schedules having fewer items. You may start with a simple 'first–then' card displaying just two activities. As the child progresses and is able to deal with and understand more information, the schedules can become more elaborate and lengthy. For older children who are comfortable with following schedules, the schedules can be more open-ended so the child is responsible for completing them. Examples and explanations of a variety of schedules are shown in Table 5.2.

Plans and routines

Plans and routines may involve activities that have a specific sequence or set of features, subroutines and/or more loosely-timed activities. Some examples are shown in Table 5.3.

The seemingly simple act of transitioning from one task to the next can be highly disruptive to children with autism. Music can help bridge this gap. Make up or adapt a simple song to signal the start of different activities or transitions from one activity to the next. Appendix I provides sites to stimulate your musical talents.

We have used a clean-up song to the tune of "Twinkle Twinkle" that went: "Twinkle twinkle little star, stop and clean up where you are, time to put our toys away, we can play another day, twinkle twinkle little star, stop and clean up where you are." Each child who helped clean up was given a star which he would use to replace his snack card on the 'Clean-up Star' chart. He would then take the snack card to the snack table. One parent wrote in the communication book that, over the weekend, her child was playing contentedly. On the television, "Twinkle Twinkle" was played. The child immediately put away all of his toys. He usually struggled with his mother when she asked him to clean up but did it spontaneously when he heard the 'clean-up' tune.

Children with autism do not automatically figure out rules in social situations. This includes things like looking at the person talking, listening when another person is talking and imitating the adult when she asks. We found during group work that, even when the teacher was tremendously animated and encouraging to the children, their responses were only intermittent at best. They loved the stories and songs but usually just sat there and sometimes even got up and went

Table 5.2 Examples and explanations of different schedules

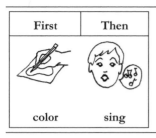

First	Then
color	sing

The first example is a simple 'first-then' schedule. In the early stages, start with one brief task followed by a highly desirable activity. As the child develops an understanding of 'first-then', extend task time and consider adding another step.

Pictures with printed words are attached by hook-and-loop circles. This makes it possible to use the base first-then card for different tasks and the child can remove the picture of a task once it is completed.

The second example is a partial schedule for a half-day preschool. Initially, each segment will last for only two to five minutes but some might extend to a maximum of 15 minutes. As the child becomes accustomed to using schedules, duration of each activity can increase.

Pictures with printed words are attached by hook-and-loop circles. This makes it possible to change tasks and order of tasks and permits the child to remove the picture of each task he completes.

Calendar	Thinking	Science center	Computer center	Snack

The third example is a partial schedule I made up for a junior high school student. We were working on helping him equate digital and analog time so he was expected to draw in the clock hands.

Because he had significant fine motor difficulties, I made up stickers for each school subject. He could then just peel and stick.

In the "work I need to do" column, the boy was expected to print basic directions or dictate them to a scribe. The teacher could then check if the boy understood the task.

The "check if done" column allowed the boy the satisfaction of checking off work completed.

The "what I need to do for homework" column was added so that (1) he would not fret about unfinished work (he had some place to put it) and (2) he took responsibility for completing his work.

Day_____ Date_____				
Start	Subject	Work I need to do	Check if done	What I need to do for homework

Table 5.3 Examples and explanations of different plans and routines

The first example is a set of task completion steps. It includes each major activity for completion of a craft as well as the model in the fourth square of what it should look like when finished. Each picture with printed word is secured with hook-and-loop circles so the child can remove the step as he completes it. Also, the numbered card can be used for other tasks. You can also fold over numbers for tasks with fewer steps.

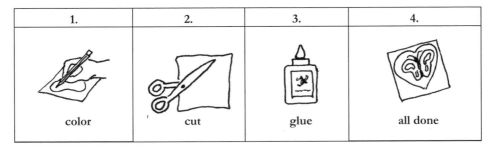

1.	2.	3.	4.
color	cut	glue	all done

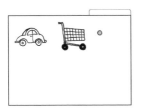

This example is a mobile planner that is made from a file folder. There is a storage envelope on the back for other activity options. These are ideal for situations where the child will be changing locations, such as home to school or around the home.

This example is a reminder for the special helper of the day. It reminds the child that he gets to help with the calendar and lead the line of children when they leave the classroom. Some children on their helper day try to wrest control from everyone else. This visual helps define roles more clearly.

Special helper	Calendar helper	Line leader

This example is a 'safe eating' routine I made up for a child who typically took an entire muffin in his palm and stuffed it whole into his mouth. Then he chomped on the muffin with his mouth open and crumbs fell everywhere. We were concerned he might choke. Also, other children were commenting on how messy he was. I incorporated a number of strategies into the rules. By prompting him to take a pinch of food, it was physically difficult to pick up an entire muffin. I also provided him with a size gauge which gave him a concrete, physical referent for bite size. Then he was cued to close his lips and chew three times before swallowing and starting the sequence again.

The child was initially frustrated with the new rules. Within 10 minutes, he was following the sequence with support from an adult. The other children spontaneously followed the rules and cheered each other on.

Rules for safe eating			
Take a pinch.	Same size as this.	Close my lips.	Chew 3 times.

This example is specific to hand-washing. It displays the most important steps in the process. By placing this sequence next to the sink in the bathroom, children can be more independent. The rules also help remind the children to control the amount of soap and number of paper towels they use.

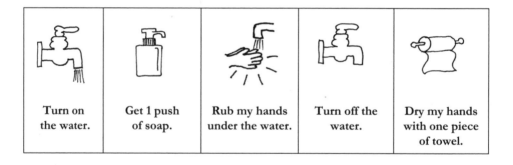

Turn on the water.	Get 1 push of soap.	Rub my hands under the water.	Turn off the water.	Dry my hands with one piece of towel.

This example is a specific routine I set up for a junior high school student whose teachers said that he spent an hour or more to get himself ready to work each morning. I suspected that the student was not entirely certain what he was supposed to do and then became distracted by more interesting things. It concerned both his mother and me that he was being allowed to miss almost one-quarter of his instructional day in wandering.

I made up this routine strip and, as soon as it was implemented, he completed the tasks each morning within about ten minutes. Also, he needed little reminding to complete the routine.

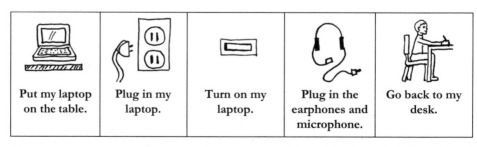

Put my laptop on the table.	Plug in my laptop.	Turn on my laptop.	Plug in the earphones and microphone.	Go back to my desk.

This example is a routine used at home to increase the child's independence in getting ready for school. It was made up into a four-page booklet that started in the bathroom, moved to the bedroom, then to the kitchen and to the back hall. Time limits can be set for each page so that the child starts learning a sense of time passage as well as time management.

Get up and go to the bathroom.	Wash my face and hands.	Brush my teeth.
Go back to my room and make my bed.	Get dressed.	
Go to the kitchen and eat my breakfast.	Take my vitamins.	
Pack my backpack with my lunch and everything I need for school.	Look outside to see if I need to wear a coat.	Hang up this book and go to school.

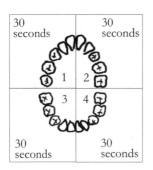

This example is a routine used by a parent to ensure that the child brushed all of his teeth. The mother took a tooth chart, obtained from the child's dentist, and visually sectioned it off into quadrants with time designated to each quadrant. You could be more specific by indicating that each tooth surface must be brushed for ten seconds: ten on each side and ten on top. Set up a timer, number each quadrant of the mouth and help the child learn to follow the routine.

What prompted setting up this routine was that the mother had found that her son was brushing only his front teeth because those were the teeth he saw most.

to another area of the classroom. I observed the children and it occurred to me: maybe the children did not understand the social rules and expectations. I made up the rule chart shown in Figure 5.5.

Before the next group session, the teacher explained the new rules: the teacher sits and the children sit, the teacher talks and the children look and listen, the teacher sings and the children sing, the teacher claps and the children clap. As the group proceeded, the teacher simply tapped her finger on a picture if children forgot. The children responded amazingly positively, almost like "Oh, so that's what you want!" Participation by all children increased exponentially.

It is critical to remember that rules and regularities may seem obvious to you but, to the child with autism, they need to be made explicit. Once a simple explanation is made, you will often see the child relax or show a response like "Oh, so that's how it goes!" We have occasionally found pictures from schedules, plans or routines missing, later to find them in the garbage or toilet. A child was simply making a comment that he did not want to do that, thanks very much! It was also an indication of how powerful visual cues are to children with autism.

This chapter has demonstrated how a well-structured program helps the child relax because he can see what is going to happen and when.

The mother of the student for whom I made the class schedule provided strong support for this concept. She sat down with her son each night and made up the schedule for the next day at school. She said that, after doing that, her son slept considerably better. He was no longer anxious about what the world held for him the next day.

Figure 5.5 Example of group participation rules

When developing visual schedules, plans and routines, there are some very practical things to do:

- Use pictures or photos and printed words or printed words alone for children who are readers.

- Set up the schedule, plan or routine in a left-to-right or right-to-left orientation so we can continually emphasize directions used in reading, printing and writing in the child's dominant language.

- Laminate all picture and print cards to ensure they last through everyday use; the cost of laminating will be out-weighed by the time and effort saved in making new cards.

The planning component should become an increasingly dynamic process. Children with autism learn by touching and doing so they need to be engaged physically and sensorally in schedules, plans and routines. The planning process should increasingly be shared with the children. They should help remove the picture of an activity completed and help make up schedules and plans. This will keep them involved and focused and feeling a sense of control.

Checkpoint for schedules, plans and routines: What *Learning Preferences and Strengths* did we incorporate?						
	Introversion	Sensing	Thinking	Judging	Visual-Spatial	Musical-Rhythmic
	✓	✓	✓	✓	✓	✓
Challenge:						

C. TASKS AND ACTIVITIES

One of our long-term goals with children with autism is for them to be able to work independently. That is, the child will be able to organize the task, systematically complete it, check for any errors and then put the activity away.

From the beginning of each child's program, we ensure he has opportunities for self-directed work in addition to one-to-one and group work. You can introduce more complex and challenging work in adult-assisted and group work situations. However, the tasks and activities for independent work have to be designed and set up so that the child experiences error-free learning. This means that independent work tasks and activities are initially very simple.

All tasks and activities, especially independent work, should have clear expectations and a clear beginning and end. They should be well-organized and only important and relevant information should be available.

1. Clear expectations for tasks and activities

At school and at home, the child must have clear expectations. Expectations center around a number of different features, including:

- *Time*, such as how long he is expected to spend with a task or activity until he must move on to the next item on his schedule. Use a timer so that the feedback to the child is concrete and objective.

  Different timers work better for some children than others. For children who love numbers, a digital timer is usually not the best choice: the child may simply watch the numbers on the timer rather than complete his work. A mechanical kitchen timer might be a reasonable substitute so long as the bell or buzzer is not too loud. For children with little internal sense of time, the use of time-passage clocks or sand/liquid timers is generally more helpful. With the time-passage clock, the overlay is moved back from the top zero point for whatever number of minutes you need. The overlay then moves toward the zero-point as time passes, closing the gap when time is up. With time-passage clocks and sand/liquid timers, time is seen as a concrete physical quantity.

- *Quantity*, such as how many activities he is expected to complete or how many items he must do before he is finished. Give him only the amount of work you want him to do and/or you believe he can reasonably accomplish. I recall the story of a young man with autism who started a job and was told his task was to sort a roomful of parts. He was not told that it should take him a week to complete everything. He refused to go home until he sorted all of the parts!

- *Quality*, or the precision and accuracy with which the task needs to be done. Providing a model of the completed task will allow the child to see what the end-product is supposed to look like. Some children try to complete tasks as quickly as possible, others work painstakingly for precision and finish very little. Each child's standard for quality must be individualized to reflect these differences. Placing quality reminders in front of the child can help. Examples are shown below.

Reminder for the speed demon	Reminder for the perfectionist
I need to tell my brain to slow down and do my best work 	It's okay to be a little bit jiggly. My hand and my brain are just learning  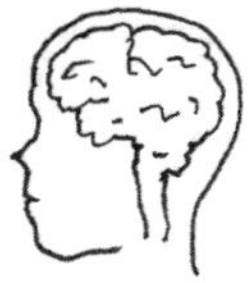

Figure 5.6 Examples of different quality reminders

Checkpoint for clear expectations: What *Learning Preferences and Strengths* did we incorporate?						
	Introversion	Sensing	Thinking	Judging	Visual-Spatial	Musical-Rhythmic
	✓	✓	✓	✓	✓	
Challenge:						

2. Orderly and organized tasks and activities

For all tasks and activities, only the materials needed to complete the task or activity should be visible in the work area. Use of a visual plan, as discussed earlier in this chapter, makes it easier for the child to follow the sequence in a multi-step task.

For independent tasks, the work area must be organized so that, just by looking, the child knows what to do, how much to do, when he is finished and what to do when he is done. Tasks should be organized physically so that:

- each task is separate and distinct: this can be accomplished by putting each task in a separate container such as a tub, binder, project case, file or box

- one task is completed at a time: the shelf holding the containers is numbered so that task 1 has "1" on the shelf below its container, task 2 has "2" on the shelf below its container and beside task 1 and so on, working left to right across the shelf or right to left if the child's dominant language in education follows that direction

Figure 5.7 Example of left-to-right task organization

- new activities are picked up on the left/right side of the work area and, once completed, placed on the right/left side. On the right/left side is either a shelf or box marked "done"

- each activity is independently understandable in terms of what the child needs to do: this can be accomplished by including printed instructions if the child reads, a plan card with the sequence of actions and/or a model of the finished product

- each individual task or activity should be designed so that the child works from left to right or right to left and from top to bottom or bottom to top, whichever is the direction used with his dominant language.

Some basic types of independent tasks are shown in Figure 5.8. Put-in tasks are generally the 'easiest' and most successful for the early stages in the child's program. Sorting tasks can become complex, such as by incorporating two- and three-dimension categorization.

The tasks shown in the pictures above appear very simple but you have to be cautious in their design. It is usually best to mock up a task and try it out with a child before you commit a lot of time and effort to it.

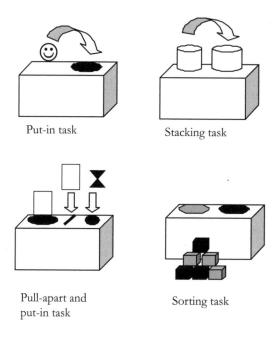

Put-in task   Stacking task

Pull-apart and   Sorting task
put-in task

Figure 5.8 Examples of different types of independent tasks

We had a sorting task using red and black dominoes. The set-up was similar to the sorting task shown above. A photo of a red domino was placed above the hole where the child was to place the red dominoes. A photo of a black domino was placed above the hole where the black dominoes were to go. An education assistant was working with a nonverbal child who appeared to have significant learning challenges. She tried the domino sorting task and the child either placed the wrong color in the hole or squawked. We both watched him for a while and then I ran to get some white correction fluid. I added white dots to some of the dominoes to match the photo models and the child successfully sorted by color. He was attempting to sort by color and number even though we had not intended him to do anything other than sort by color. We learned yet another good lesson about visual learners.

File folder games are well-suited to independent work tasks. If you are not familiar with them, you use a simple file folder and organize one activity per folder. Some printable file folder games and activities are included in Appendix I. File folder activities typically involve matching color to color, object to category, object to printed name, letters to letters and rhyming words.

Checkpoint for orderly and organized tasks and activities: What *Learning Preferences and Strengths* did we incorporate?						
	Introversion	Sensing	Thinking	Judging	Visual-Spatial	Musical-Rhythmic
	✓	✓	✓	✓	✓	
Challenge:						

This discussion of Program Structure has focused on honoring the *Learning Preferences and Strengths* in children with autism. The learning environment, schedules, plans and routines and tasks and activities incorporated many of the following:

- *Introversion* – people with Introversion preferences need extended time to process verbal information. The incorporation of visual information permits the child to use his strength in visual processing to support the slower, less certain auditory process. Visual information also allows the child opportunities to warm up to activities by looking ahead to see what is going to happen. People with an Introversion preference also need some solitary time to recharge and refresh. The use of one-to-one and independent tasks and activities affords them this opportunity. Incorporation of places for breaks and quiet time at school and at home help ensure the child re-energizes so his learning is more optimal and he remains calmer.

- *Sensing* – people with Sensing preferences focus on details and notice even small sensory details. By reducing sensory distractions, the child is more likely to be calm and focus on important information. By ensuring that the environment is orderly and organized, the child is less likely to be distracted by irrelevant information and cues. He is drawn to the tangible nature of the signs and pictures. Incorporating visual with verbal, the child is more likely to attend and understand more accurately and completely.

- *Thinking* – people with Thinking preferences value analysis and logic. The systems used in this chapter appeal to these features and make an enormous difference to the child's feelings of safety and security. The clarity provided by a well-structured environment, task and activity makes a significant difference to the child's willingness to attend and learn.

- *Judging* – people with Judging preferences like living and working in planned and orderly settings where things are decided and settled. The systems presented in this chapter are calming and assuring to Judgers.

- *Visual-Spatial* – people with Visual-Spatial strengths are sensitive to visual images and enjoy organized systems. The strategies provide a more naturally appealing situation because they emphasize what is important and reduce distracting elements. The use of visuals to reinforce and support verbal information acts to put the child more at ease because the visual modality is easier to use. The child is more likely to take in complete and accurate information. People with Visual-Spatial strengths are sensitive to color, form and space around them. By reducing or neutralizing sensory features, the child will more likely focus on learning-relevant information.

- *Musical-Rhythmic* – people with Musical-Rhythmic strengths are drawn to tunes and rhythms and seem to be able to process and retain melodic information more readily. Using simple songs can smooth the child's move from one task or area to another and reinforce the 'rules'.

STRUCTURE TO EXPAND *LEARNING PREFERENCES AND STRENGTHS*

We have focused thus far on engaging each child through his learning preferences for Introversion-Sensing-Thinking-Judging and his learning strengths for Visual-Spatial and Musical-Rhythmic information. We want to promote the child's developing some of the qualities of Extraversion, Intuiting, Feeling and Perceiving and some of the other learning strengths. This will help him become more 'balanced' and less firmly entrenched in his specific *Learning Preferences and Strengths*.

We do not, of course, attempt any of these 'challenges' to familiar and comfortable ways of thinking and doing things until the child has shown us that he feels safe with us. He must have complete and sincere confidence in people who work with him before any attempts are made to help him use non-dominant preferences and strengths. He will show that he is relaxed by flowing from task to task and activity to activity with relative ease and independently using strategies taught to him.

In terms of structure, we need to help the child learn how to deal calmly with uncertainty, with new activities and events and with change and unplanned events. Introduction of any of these can be highly unsettling for a child with autism so great care must be taken when planning for and trying any of these changes.

Dealing with uncertainty

Children with autism feel greatest sureness and comfort when they know what is going to happen. Introduction of uncertainty can be done only after the child has grown used to his regular schedule and follows it flawlessly. Then a bit of uncertainty can be brought in by adding a question mark to his regular schedule card. Referring to it as a 'surprise' gives the uncertainty a positive 'twist'. Following the surprise with a favored activity will also help him deal more positively with the uncertainty.

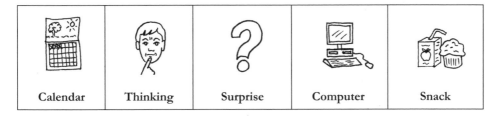

Figure 5.9 Example of visual schedule with introduction of a surprise activity

In the beginning, make the 'surprise' something fairly innocuous. For example, you may bring in a new book or toy or re-introduce something that has been put away for a while.

As the child begins to feel comfortable with 'surprises', you could help him prepare a surprise for someone else. You can also begin to make the 'surprises' more intense, such as by having a special visitor or going to a different location.

Dealing with new objects, activities and events

The child with autism likes to have his consistent routines and predictable ways of doing things. I have seen children with autism reject things I know they would like just because they were new and/or unexpected. Life is full of new things and we must help the child cope positively with them. Central factors in helping children with autism deal with new activities and events include giving them time to warm up to the idea and by putting a positive 'spin' on the idea of newness.

One successful way to help the child deal with change is a 'new is good' campaign. When I introduced this concept to a preschool, the staff just laughed and thought I was a little wacky. In this campaign, the adults around the child initially comment, the adults around the child comment on something about themselves, such as a new shirt, and say: "I have a nice new shirt. I like it. New is good!" After a couple of weeks of using the 'new is good' campaign, the adults comment on things the children had or did that are new. They might comment on a child's snack saying, "Oh look, Bobby has an orange today. He usually has an apple. New is good!" After the child gets used to the concept, try introducing something new for him. At first, you might try something small that he typically does not find objectionable. Over time, try more adventurous 'new' things.

Dealing with change and unplanned events

In life, plans and schedules may suddenly change because of unforeseen events. You may be on the way to shop for groceries and the car develops a flat tire. You have to stop, change the tire and, perhaps, abandon the idea of going to the store because there is no more time. A friend may drop by your house just after you promised the child you both would go to the park. You will have to delay or reschedule the trip to the park in order to visit with your friend.

These changes can cause huge meltdowns in children with autism. The child is focused on the plan or schedule and then, suddenly, it may not happen or is delayed.

Children with autism can be progressively introduced to the idea of 'changing one's mind'. Start off with something very familiar to the child where change is relatively inconsequential. Slowly help him become used to the notion that you can change your mind. Prompt him to 'change his mind' about familiar things (see the anecdote below). As he becomes more comfortable with this concept, make changes that are more important to the child such as altering a sequence of events or delaying an activity previously planned. Always be prepared to back out of the change if the child becomes overly stressed. You can just indicate you 'made a mistake' and then put things back as they were. Try again another time but keep trying.

A number of years ago, I was working with a boy with autism who took great comfort in consistent routines. Every time we worked together, I would put out four pictures and indicate to him we would do four things during our hour together. I then had him place the pictures on the hook-and-loop circles in the order he wished. I was concerned that he was becoming too deeply entrenched in this system. One day I looked at him after he had organized our plan and said, "I changed my mind." I then proceeded to switch the order of two of the pictures. He looked incredulously at the new plan. I explained that sometimes people change their minds and that is okay. I did this every time for the next three or four sessions until one day he turned the tables on me. After he finished setting out his plan, he stopped and said, "I change my mind [sic]" and switched the order of two items. I was thrilled. He had gotten the idea and was comfortable enough to use it on his own.

Checkpoint for dealing with uncertainty, newness and change: What *Learning Preferences and Strengths* did we challenge?						
	Introversion	Sensing	Thinking	Judging	Visual-Spatial	Musical-Rhythmic
Challenge:	Extraversion Intuiting Perceiving				Interpersonal Intrapersonal	

Notes: Introduction of uncertainty, newness and change stretches the *Learning Preferences and Strengths* in the following ways:

- *Extraversion* – people with an Introversion preference need time to warm up to new ideas and typically are uncomfortable with uncertainty. The introduction of uncertainty, newness and change emphasizes Extraversion where novelty is more positively viewed.

- *Intuiting* – people with Sensing preferences like detail and tangible facts. The introduction of uncertainty, newness and change pushes the child to look at the broader concepts like 'new is good' or 'I changed my mind' to deal with the uncertainty which is more natural for people with an Intuiting preference.

- *Perceiving* – people with Judging preferences like to have everything planned and decided. By bringing in uncertainty, newness and change, the child is learning to 'go with the flow' more and be more flexible like a person with a Perceiving preference.

- *Interpersonal* – the person with Interpersonal strengths maintains and forms cooperative relationships with others, adapting well in different situations. The introduction of uncertainty, newness and change helps the child with autism learn some beginning skills in this area.

- *Intrapersonal* – the person with Intrapersonal strengths has great awareness of himself, his needs and emotions. The introduction of uncertainty, newness and change challenges the child's ability to regulate his thoughts and emotions and develop a greater understanding of the relevance of uncertainty in his life.

Chapter 6

Program Content

Content of each child's program will typically follow the expected developmental sequence for young children for improving the child's:

- pre-academic knowledge

- speech production, receptive and expressive language skills

- fine motor development

- social skills

- gross motor development

- self-help skills

- behavior

With older children, the content will also reflect national, state or provincial educational standards. Subjects typically include:

- language arts
- math/maths
- social studies, history, geography
- science
- health and physical education

- art and design
- technology design, information and communication technology
- music

The educational and developmental areas noted above can be addressed within the structure and process described in this book.

For the present discussion, content will focus on the three main areas of need in children with autism:

A.   Learning/Cognitive skills (L/C)

B.   Social/Communication skills (S/C)

C.   Self-Regulation skills (S/R).

LEARNING FRAMEWORK

Content will follow an information-processing model, while honoring the Introversion-Sensing-Thinking-Judging learning preferences and the Visual-Spatial and Musical-Rhythmic learning strengths shared by many children with autism. The strategies will, unless otherwise noted, include the following *Learning Preferences and Strengths*:

- *Introversion* – people with an Introversion preference need extended time to process information. The child is provided the extended time to view and review the information presented to him before expecting him to respond.

- *Sensing* – people with Sensing preferences like to proceed in a step-by-step manner while focusing on detail and tangible facts. The child is helped to use his sensory systems to gather information and then note important and relevant facts.

- *Thinking* – people with a Thinking preference like to understand the logic and rationale for things they are expected to do. Reasoning is emphasized in the strategies presented in this chapter as is the child's preference for being analytical.

- *Judging* – people with Judging preferences like to have a clear beginning and end to a task and to approach things in a planful and orderly way. The approaches described in this chapter provide these within a productive and useful context.

- *Visual-Spatial* – people with Visual-Spatial strengths more readily understand and remember information they see. Strategies in this chapter are strongly visual and spatial and the child is helped to become more selective in his application of this learning strength.

At the end of each section in this chapter will be a Checkpoint. These will be used to summarize the *Learning Preferences and Strengths* incorporated within the strategies and provide any needed explanations. In addition, other preferences and strengths not typical to children with autism will be noted and described as Challenges.

Because of the strong emphasis on metacognitive awareness, or helping the child become aware of his thinking and reasoning, all strategies presented in this chapter prompt development of Intrapersonal strengths. Intrapersonal strengths involve understanding your personal assets and limitations and your ability to apply your thinking. Special focus is on the child's developing more self-awareness of his thinking processes.

WHERE TO START

When trying to determine where to start with any child, we must consider a number of factors, including:

- his skills in major areas of development

- his *Learning Preferences and Strengths*

- his likes and dislikes

- information from your observations of the child

- family priorities and needs.

This information must be carefully reviewed and blended to determine the child's main goals and strategies. Keep in mind that only so many things can be targeted at once. Briefer, well-planned Individual Program Plans or Individual Educational Plans typically are more do-able and usually more effective.

In terms of the *Learning Preferences and Strengths (LPS)* program, Learning/Cognitive skills are the foundation for many other areas of development. Work in this area should start early in the child's program. Even if you believe the child works systematically and notices only important and relevant information, he should practice these skills so that he becomes aware of them on an explicit level. This metacognitive awareness is critical to transfer and generalization to other tasks and settings and to the child's using the skills independently.

The early Self-Regulation skills, which focus on the child's controlling his own body, go hand-in-hand with many of the Learning/Cognitive skills. So, Self-Regulation can be worked on at the same time as Learning/Cognitive skills.

Social/Communication skills involve receptive and expressive language skills and dealing with verbal information in learning and social settings. Some of the more straightforward skills in this area should be progressively introduced into early programming.

More complex Social/Communication, Self-Regulation and Learning/Cognitive skills take longer periods of time to develop. They should be progressively introduced once the child is showing readiness for more complex levels of information processing.

A. LEARNING/COGNITIVE SKILLS (L/C)

The Learning/Cognitive skills section will focus primarily on visual information. An overview of the skills focused on and strategies taught within the Learning/Cognitive area is shown in Figure 6.1.

L/C.1. Intake of information

We have to help the child with autism learn to take in information more completely and accurately. We also have to help him focus only on what is relevant and important and not become overfocused on inconsequential details. The child must then learn to determine what he is expected to do and to remember important information.

L/C.1A. TAKING IN COMPLETE AND ACCURATE INFORMATION

Our main goal in this area is to make sure the child works systematically. The program structuring described in the previous chapter provides support for systematic work habits. Now, the child needs to learn this strategy for himself so he can apply it independently in any situation.

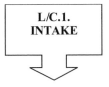

L/C.1.
INTAKE

Skill focus   *Strategies*

L/C.1a. Taking in complete and accurate   Working left to right/right to left
information
                                                 Working top to bottom/bottom to top

                                                 Using your 'finder finger'

                                                 Labeling

L/C.1b. Taking in relevant and important   Determining what is important
information
                                                 Ignoring

L/C.1c. Determining what is expected   Using signs and clues

                                                 Using models

L/C.1d. Retaining information   Rehearsing

L/C.2.
INTEGRATION &
ELABORATION

Skill focus   *Strategies*

L/C.2a. Connecting other knowledge   Grouping, categorizing

                                                 Finding and using patterns

                                                 Connecting past tasks and events

L/C.2b. Comparing and contrasting   Looking for similarities and differences

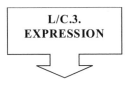

L/C.3.
EXPRESSION

Skill focus   *Strategies*

L/C.3a. Understanding other perspectives   Learning about perspective

                                                 Taking another's perspective

L/C.3b. Making a plan for clear and precise   Planning precise responses
responding

Figure 6.1 Learning/Cognitive Skills (L/C)

Strategies for taking in complete and accurate information

The rationale for these strategies is to help the child be systematic so he does not miss anything. The emphasis on left to right and top to bottom approaches to tasks provides foundations for more systematic English reading and printing. If the child's dominant language in educational settings operates from right to left and/or bottom to top, these orientations should be used instead.

1. *Working left to right or right to left*: In every activity or task, without fail, emphasize that the child must start from the left/right side and work toward the right/left. Set up tasks so the child is naturally guided to work left to right or right to left. Emphasize this systematic approach on schedules, plans and routines, when eating and when doing any task or activity.

    For learners with directionality problems and for young children just beginning their programs, use a visual reminder of where to start. Place a green 'go' dot at the starting point of the schedule, plan, routine, task or activity. Emphasize that "Green means go so that's where we start."

    Praise the child for being "systematic". Do not be afraid to use such a sophisticated word. It describes what we want the child to learn. Also, state the rationale: "We are systematic so we don't miss anything."

    This strategy not only helps the child learn careful intake of information but also coordination of vision with thinking.

2. *Working top to bottom or bottom to top*. After the left to right or right to left pattern is solidly established and the child is starting to use it on his own without prompting, introduce working from top to bottom or bottom to top dependent on the direction of the child's dominant language. Help the child understand that, once we finish the first row, we go to the next row just below/above it. Use sticky notes to cover up all but the first one row on a worksheet. Let the child complete it and then ask him where we should go next. If he points to the next row, praise him for being systematic and let him know "that way we won't miss anything".

    Reduce the use of sticky notes over time but give the child the option of using them or not. The majority of even older children will want to cover up the options; they have indicated that the other details 'bug' their brains and make it hard to concentrate.

3. *Using your 'finder finger'.* To help the child scan all information systematically, prompt him to use his 'finder finger'. Introduce this concept by telling the child he has something special on his hand that can help his brain: it is his index finger of his right hand. That is his 'finder finger' which helps his brain find all the important information he looks at. Practice together moving his 'finder finger' systematically across and vertically with pictures, worksheets or other activities.

    If the child talks about something that his 'finder finger' is not pointing to, draw him back to talk only about what his finger is finding.

    Praise the child for being "systematic" and state the rationale: "We are systematic so we don't miss anything."

    This strategy works on the child's systematic search strategy as well as use of pointing and coordinating vision with the pointing finger.

4. *Labeling.* In conjunction with the 'finder finger', prompt the child to name each important thing he sees. By stating the name of each object, action, location or person, he is more likely to maintain his focus of attention. It also prompts him to combine vision and language. This can also provide you with an opportunity to learn more about the depth and breadth of the child's vocabulary and where there may be gaps.

I worked with one child during his early elementary school years. We worked diligently on systematic work habits. I am sure that, at times, I sounded a bit tedious and repetitive when I prompted him, "What are you supposed to do when you look at a new task?" He responded positively and seemed to understand and use systematic search, his 'finder finger', labeling and the other strategies. When he was seven and a half, he needed a psycho-educational assessment for his school so one of the psychologists in my office administered the typical standardized measure. The boy and the psychologist allowed me to sit in during part of his assessment. As I watched the boy work, I was thrilled to see what he was doing. He used all of the strategies: he was *systematic, worked left to right and top to bottom, labeled important features* and *examined the whole task to determine what he was supposed to do.* I could see that whatever the final outcome of the testing, the psychologist was obtaining an optimal picture of his abilities.

When the boy was assessed at just under four years of age, he received quotients at 50, 'Extremely Low', from all therapists who worked with him. The parents were given the impression by the team not to expect a great deal in the future.

When he was assessed at seven and a half, he received an overall quotient within the High Average range; on some subscales, his scores were in the Gifted range.

When he was 18 years of age, he graduated with distinction from high school. He had attended regular schools since grade one and, even though there were occasional social 'glitches', he did very well academically. He is now enrolled in university.

Checkpoint for taking in complete and accurate information: What *Learning Preferences and Strengths* did we incorporate?

	Introversion	Sensing	Thinking	Judging	Visual-Spatial	Musical-Rhythmic
	✓	✓	✓	✓	✓	
Challenge:	Extraversion				Verbal-Linguistic Bodily-Kinesthetic Intrapersonal	

Notes: Teaching and guiding the child to take in complete and accurate information stretches *Learning Preferences and Strengths* in the following ways:

- *Extraversion* – people with an Extraversion preference like to think out loud. Having the child name each object and action he finds with this 'finder finger' presses him for greater amounts of Extraversion. This can cause him some stress because of the speed of processing required as well as coordinating vision and language so patience and perseverance are needed.

- *Verbal-Linguistic* – people with Verbal-Linguistic strengths use words to think and remember. Typically, children with autism do not have primary strengths in the Verbal-Linguistic area but naming objects and actions prompts them to use this modality.

- *Bodily-Kinesthetic* – people with Bodily-Kinesthetic strengths use their bodies or body parts to explore the world around them through touching and moving. Use of the 'finder finger' incorporates this modality to help the child focus his attention.

L/C.1B. TAKING IN RELEVANT AND IMPORTANT INFORMATION

Our main goal in this area is to make sure the child takes in only the information that is relevant and important to the task at hand. The program structuring described in the previous chapter increases the likelihood that the child will note the more relevant and important information. However, he needs to develop explicit knowledge of this strategy so he can apply it independently in any situation.

Strategies for taking in relevant and important information

The rationale for these strategies is to help the child focus on only the most relevant and important information in a task or situation. That means not only attending to specific things but also ignoring other unimportant and/or irrelevant details.

1. *Determining what is important.* Help the child determine what the task, picture or worksheet is about. As the learner is scanning and labeling each object and action, ask: "Is that important to what we are doing?" or "Is that what we are working on right now?" Respond as positively as possible: "That's right, that is important because we are looking at numbers and that is a number." If the child is distracted by something that is not relevant or central to the task, respond positively by saying: "That is interesting but we're not thinking about that right now. Can you think of something that is important right now?" For example, if the child is focusing solely on a dinosaur on the worksheet, we let him know that it is interesting but then redirect him to more central features.

    After some success on the child's part, select something 'silly' or absurd and model how to redirect your thinking. For example, "Oh, look, there's a hole in the paper…oh-oh, brain, that's not important right now. Find something important."

    After prompting and reinforcing the child's attempts, start asking him to explain: "Why do you think that is important?" Having him express his reasoning will help solidify the rationale for looking for and thinking about only what is important.

2. *Ignoring.* Teach the child the notion of 'ignoring' things that are not important. The rationale is: "If we ignore things that are not important right now, that can help our brains think better." For example, the ring of a telephone while we are working is not important. The child is prompted: "Tell your brain: don't get distracted, brain. I can just ignore it. It's not important right now." Use a visual cue like that shown to help remind him. If some aspect of a task is distracting the child, ask him what he could do to help himself. You can offer ideas such as covering up some things so they do not distract his brain. Place sticky notes on top of the distracting images. Prompt the child to make those decisions for himself.

Don't get distracted

Checkpoint for taking in relevant and important information: What *Learning Preferences and Strengths* did we incorporate?						
	Introversion	Sensing	Thinking	Judging	Visual-Spatial	Musical-Rhythmic
	✓	✓	✓	✓	✓	
Challenge:	Intuiting				Intrapersonal	

Notes: Teaching and guiding the child to take in relevant and important information incorporates and stretches the *Learning Preferences and Strengths* in the following ways:

- *Intuiting* – people with an Intuiting preference tend to see the big picture. By prompting the child with autism to determine if an object, event or person is important to what he is doing, he is being pressed to look at a broader scope.

L/C.1C. DETERMINING WHAT IS EXPECTED

Our main goal in this area is to help the child look at a task or situation and determine what may be expected of him. We all develop expectancies from our experiences. For example, if we are handed a sheet of paper, we can quickly determine with a brief glance whether it is a survey, test or request for information.

Strategies for determining what is expected

The rationale for these strategies is to help the child look for signs, clues and models in his environment that may help him understand what is expected.

1. *Using signs and clues.* Help the child understand that signs let us know where to go, what to do and what is happening. You may wish to use the word 'clues' if it sparks the child's imagination. Tell him that clues are like signs but they are 'sneakier'. Sometimes, clues are hiding things and we have to be detectives.

   Guide the child to examine the work presented to him. Ask him: "What do you think we are going to do here?" or prompt him with statements like, "I see N-A-M-E and a line. That's a sign telling us what to do." (print your name) or, "I see six people and only five chairs. That's a sign telling us to do something" (get another chair). Further guidance and practice may be necessary to help him notice the most important and relevant clues and signs.

   Once the child starts to identify clues and signs, praise his attempts. Since many formats for worksheets and independent tasks are similar, the child will have repeated opportunities for success. Once he experiences success, prompt him to explain how he knows. Use a surprised tone of voice and say, "Boy, your brain and eyes are really working! How did you know that?" This is really an attempt to prompt him to explain his rationale but it is said in a non-threatening and playful way. Having him state his rationale solidifies his understanding and use of the strategy.

2. *Using models:* Help the child understand: "Models show us what to do." Start with highly concrete examples like a simple craft or assembly toy. Prompt and praise the child for looking back and forth from his work to the model: "That's a good way to help your brain remember."

   As he shows that he is understanding the notion of a 'model', provide him with some materials and ask him how he can figure out what to do. Help him look for a model and praise him: "You're right, that is a model and that shows us what to do."

Checkpoint for determining what is expected: What *Learning Preferences and Strengths* did we incorporate?						
	Introversion	Sensing	Thinking	Judging	Visual-Spatial	Musical-Rhythmic
		✓	✓	✓	✓	
Challenge:					Intrapersonal	

L/C.1D. RETAINING INFORMATION

Our main goal now is to help the child learn specific strategies for holding information in his memory. For effective information processing, the child needs to hold on to the information long enough for it to enter into his memory system. Then it can be integrated with other information and/or elaborated to form new concepts.

Strategies for retaining information

The rationale for these strategies is to help the child hold information in his temporary memory bank. One strategy may work better than the others for particular children. It is best to try them out and see what facilitates his remembering. As the child's attention and/or language skills improve, other strategies may become helpful as well.

1. *Rehearsing.* Rehearsing means saying something over and over long enough to help short-term recall. As adults, we often use rehearsal to remember phone numbers long enough to dial the call.

    Prompt the child to: "Say the names over in your brain to help it remember." Start with simple things, such as when he needs a tissue, prompt him to say "tissue" in his brain all the way to the tissue box. Saying the name or phrase in a sing-song manner may help increase his retention. Rehearsal not only helps the child remember important information but also to stay focused.

Checkpoint for retaining information: What *Learning Preferences and Strengths* did we incorporate?						
	Introversion	Sensing	Thinking	Judging	Visual-Spatial	Musical-Rhythmic
		✓	✓	✓	✓	✓
Challenge:	Extraversion				Verbal-Linguistic Intrapersonal	

Notes: Teaching and guiding the child to retain information stretches the *Learning Preferences and Strengths* in the following ways:

- *Extraversion* – people with Extraversion preferences like to think out loud. Labeling and/or rehearsal strategies prompt the child to verbalize his perceptions and thoughts.

- *Verbal-Linguistic* – people with Verbal-Linguistic strengths use words to think and remember. The labeling strategy prompts the child to use this modality.

L/C.2. Integrating and elaborating information

Once the child has completed the intake phase of information processing, the information must be integrated with other things he knows. The information may also be used to elaborate or expand on his knowledge.

This is a particularly important phase of information processing for children with autism. Often, they appear to learn facts but the facts are often not well-organized or combined in useful ways with other things they know.

L/C.2A. CONNECTING OTHER KNOWLEDGE

The main goal in this area is to help the child form connections among pieces of information.

Strategies for connecting with other knowledge

The rationale for these strategies is to help the child notice clustering and grouping of facts and information and use this to integrate with and elaborate on what he already knows. The brain of a child with autism is like a clothes closet that has a lot of thoughts and ideas stuffed into it. When the child wants to find that other matching item, the search can be long and uncertain. If there was a good set of shelves and some drawers, it would be much easier to find the things he wants when he wants them. The following strategies are focused on helping the child develop such organizational systems.

1. *Grouping, categorizing:* Tell the child: "If we put things together, it is easier to remember them."

   Practice grouping objects by the characteristics shown in Table 6.1. Categorizing by color, shape and size are perhaps the 'easiest' groups to start with. It is best to start with one descriptor at a time and then begin combining them, such as color plus shape. Other concepts presented in the table are more complex and will require time and practice for the child to become proficient.

Use American Sign Language for the word 'together' as you note things that go together. The sign provides visual support for the concept and helps the child single it out. Children will often spontaneously self-cue with the sign while they think about how things go together.

Categorization worksheets and other tasks are quite easy to make using sorting activities with real or pictured objects. There are also many categorizing worksheets you can download from the internet. Look at Appendix I for suggestions.

American Sign Language for key concept 'together'.
Together

Table 6.1 Major categories for organizing information

color (red, blue, white)	size (big, long, huge, medium-sized)
number or quantity (one, first, full, some)	shape (round, square, rectangle, like a snake)
quality (clean, hungry, dry, thirsty, sticky, hard, fast, hot)	present or typical location (on the table, high, at the grocery store, in the sky)
parts of the object (wheels, windows, spots)	use (for cutting, riding, eating)
action (sleeping, running)	category (animals, clothes, adult)
social-emotional qualities (happy, bad, nice, mad, quiet, old)	material (wood, paper, cloth)

2.   *Finding and using patterns*: Help the child understand that patterns are things that repeat themselves and, if we look and think carefully, they can help us figure out what comes next.

   Patterns can involve colors, shapes, numbers, quantity or other features. Incorporate patterns into a variety of daily activities like calendar time where the date is printed on different shapes, colors or textures. Start with a two- or three-part pattern. Point to each part and rhythmically name its feature, giving different emphasis to the words so that the pattern becomes more obvious: yellow-*red*-yellow-*red*-(pause) what comes next? The calendar activity example shown here is a two-step pattern. It would be presented as "striped-grey-striped-grey-striped…what comes next?"

   Incorporate patterns into other activities such as placemats at the table or blocks in a tower. Point out patterns you notice: "I just saw a black car, then a blue, then a red, what should come next?" Helping the child learn time patterns, such as patterns in daily, weekly and monthly plans, is a potential stress-reducer for him.

3.   *Connecting the present with past tasks and events.* The child is asked to think of other things that are like the present task, object, person or event. Ask things like: "When else did you do something like this?" or "What does that look like?" Keep the comparisons fairly concrete initially, such as by asking when else he did a dinosaur activity or when he circled objects on a worksheet. Progressively, focus on the cognitive concepts, such as 'patterns', 'categories', 'clues' and 'models'.

Checkpoint for connecting with other knowledge: What *Learning Preferences and Strengths* did we incorporate?						
	Introversion	Sensing	Thinking	Judging	Visual-Spatial	Musical-Rhythmic
	✓	✓	✓	✓	✓	
Challenge:	Intuiting				Intrapersonal	

Notes: Teaching and guiding the child to connect current information with other things he knows stretches the *Learning Preferences and Strengths* in the following ways:

- *Intuiting* – people with an Intuiting preference tend to see the big picture. By prompting the child to group and interconnect ideas and concepts, he is being pressed to look more broadly at his learning.

L/C.2B. COMPARING AND CONTRASTING

Our main goal in this area is to help the child learn that objects, people, actions and events around him can be connected by similarities and differences. This helps him group and categorize – two functions that can facilitate his memory and recall.

Strategies for comparing and contrasting

The rationale for this strategy is to help the child learn to look for and notice how things are similar or different on varying dimensions.

1. *Looking for similarities and differences.* Start with simple tasks, like those suggested earlier for categorizing, to find out how features are the same. It is generally best to start with the concept of 'same' and solidify it before moving on to 'different'. When the child detects something the same, praise his response: "You're right, those are the same." Pair the word 'same' with the American Sign Language sign. Use of the sign helps highlight the concept for the child. Once the child seems to have a solid understanding of 'same', begin using synonyms like 'alike', 'like' and 'identical' and point out to him "that means the same".

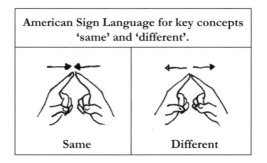

American Sign Language for key concepts 'same' and 'different'.	
Same	Different

For the concept 'different', start with simple tasks, like those suggested earlier for categorizing. As the child becomes more proficient, practice with simple pictures that the child can examine with his 'finder finger'. Take two similar pictures which you can alter by changing colors, shapes, sizes and objects and people and by adding or deleting objects. Have the child note differences, using one index finger from each hand to examine the two pictures simultaneously. Use the American Sign Language sign for 'different' to help emphasize that you are no longer looking for similarities.

Children with autism will often become confused by the terms 'same' and 'different' so the signs help reinforce distinctions between them. The signs can also help organize the child's thinking when used consistently. Typically, children will begin self-cuing by using the signs spontaneously.

Increasingly, ask the child to tell why the things are the same or different. Use a positive tone, like, "Wow, how did you know that, you sneaky guy!" This helps ensure that the child does not feel he is being interrogated or put on the spot while being prompted to express his reasoning.

In everyday life, draw the child's attention to things that are 'the same' or 'different' from other things he knows. Prompt him to explain how or in what way they are the 'same' or 'different'.

Checkpoint for comparing and contrasting: What *Learning Preferences and Strengths* did we incorporate?						
	Introversion	Sensing	Thinking	Judging	Visual-Spatial	Musical-Rhythmic
	✓	✓	✓	✓	✓	
Challenge:	Extraversion Intuiting				Bodily-Kinesthetic Verbal-Linguistic Intrapersonal	

Notes: Teaching and guiding the child to compare and contrast stretches the *Learning Preferences and Strengths* in the following ways:

- *Extraversion* – people with Extraversion preferences like to think out loud. This is not a natural preference for the child with autism but he is prompted to use labeling while noting similarities and differences and when explaining his reasoning.

- *Intuiting* – people with an Intuiting preference tend to see the big picture. Prompting the child to look for similarities and differences presses him to examine broader concepts.

- *Bodily-Kinesthetic* – people with Bodily-Kinesthetic strengths use their bodies or body parts to explore the world around them through touching and moving. Use of the 'finder finger' incorporates this learning strength to reinforce other preferences and strengths.

- *Verbal-Linguistic* – people with Verbal-Linguistic strengths use words to think and remember. Typically, children with autism do not have primary strengths in the Verbal-Linguistic area but naming similarities and differences prompts them to use this modality.

L/C.3. Expressing information

The final phase in information processing requires the child to plan and express his thoughts and ideas. It involves considering the perspective of other people and then planning and forming clear and precise responses.

L/C.3A. UNDERSTANDING OTHER PERSPECTIVES

Our main goal in this area is to help the child understand that not everyone sees things the way he does and that those other perspectives can be valid.

Strategies for understanding other perspectives

The rationale for these strategies is to help the child experience increasing success in expressing his thinking as well as communication breakdown.

1.   *Learning about perspective.* One creative teacher I worked with used a visual, concrete way to help children with autism learn that their perspective is not the only one. The teacher decorated a box where each surface was covered with a different color of paper. She sat the children in a circle and, in turn, asked each child what color the box was. Each child, as expected, said the box was the color he could see. She then rotated the box and asked again. By repeating this process, the children learned that what they see is not necessarily what everyone sees. Use the term 'perspective' with the children so they can learn the correct word for the phenomenon they are learning.

   Barrier activities, described in the Social/Communication section, are other ways of helping the children learn about perspective.

2. *Taking another's perspective.* Once the children have some understanding that what they see is not necessarily what someone else sees, begin activities that press them to use that information to adjust their responding.

Role-playing is one strategy that helps the child take different perspectives. Allow the child opportunities to be 'teacher' so he can assume a 'safe' but different perspective. This type of reciprocal teaching also reinforces the child's sense of control and competence.

Role-playing can be expanded to include characters from a familiar book. This can be done with young children's books as well as more advanced novels. In our preschool, I have used a literature-based approach where one key book was chosen for each month of the year. All needs identified on individual plans were integrated into the literature theme. The children found comfort in the repetition of the same book and, after becoming familiar with it, were willing to play different roles. For your interest, a sample literature-based theme is included in Appendix III. An extensive book database which can be searched by concept, theme or other key word is included in Appendix I.

Checkpoint for understanding other perspectives: What *Learning Preferences and Strengths* did we incorporate?						
	Introversion	Sensing	Thinking	Judging	Visual-Spatial	Musical-Rhythmic
		✓	✓		✓	
Challenge:	Intuiting Feeling				Interpersonal Intrapersonal	

Notes: Teaching and guiding the child to understand other perspectives stretches the *Learning Preferences and Strengths* in the following ways:

- *Intuiting* – people with an Intuiting preference tend to see the big picture. By prompting the child to understand and take someone else's perspective, he is being stretched to go beyond the details that may be visible or apparent to just him.

- *Feeling* – people with Feeling preferences value others' needs and want to meet them. The issue of perspective-taking is a largely

Feeling concept because sensitivity to other people and their perceptions is central to being successful.

- *Interpersonal* – the person with Interpersonal strengths has the ability to understand the feelings and thoughts of others. In perspective-taking, the child has to ensure he is sensitive to similarities and differences in what other people experience.

L/C.3B. MAKING A PLAN FOR A CLEAR AND PRECISE RESPONSE

Our main goal in this area is to help the child plan and provide responses that are clear and understandable to others. In addition, we strive to ensure that the child's responses are a more precise representation of his thinking and abilities.

Strategies for making a plan for a clear and precise response

The rationale for this strategy is to help the child reduce impulsive responding or reticence to respond.

1. *Planning precise responses.* The child is helped to determine different ways he might respond. He may balk at responding, respond imprecisely or dive right in without reflecting on what he should do.

   If the child does not want to respond, ask him if he has a problem. Point out clues or models that can help him determine how to respond. For example, if he is having difficulty forming letters or numbers, you can model those letters or numbers or point out models, such as the alphabet on a placemat. If he continues to be reticent, remind him of similar work that he has done before. If he continues to balk, it is time to negotiate. Negotiation starts with "How about…?" and includes things like, "I do the first one and you do the next one?" or "You do two and then you can be done?" Try to avoid coming to an impasse or battle of wills with the child; see Chapter 8, **Behavior in Children with Autism**, for more discussion on approaches to behavior.

   If the child responds imprecisely, keep in mind that some children are just learning so there is an acceptable level of imprecision initially. If he is capable of more precise and accurate work, ask him to judge for himself if that is his best work or if that is what he was supposed to do. Guide him to more precise work by providing models, clues and other visuals.

   If the child tries to respond impulsively, prompt him to stop and think. Remind him: "That way you can do your best work," and/or "That gives your brain a chance to do good thinking." Ask him to tell his brain to slow down and think really hard before responding. A visual reminder may be helpful.

Over time, the child needs to begin self-monitoring his work and judging the accuracy and adequacy of responses without adult prompting. Help him learn to use a visual checklist, like that shown below. The checklist sets out a process the child should use to review his work. In the example, the child is prompted to ask himself if he took in all important information, knew what was expected of him, retained that information, responded as accurately and precisely as he could and then double-checked his work. The content of the checklist can include whatever is important for individual children to produce more precise and accurate responses. The child can put an 'X' through things he has checked or remove the picture from the list.

Did I...?				
look at all of the important information?	understand what I was supposed to do?	remember all the important parts?	do my best work?	check my work after I finished?

Figure 6.2 Example of visual checklist for self-monitoring

Checkpoint for planning precise and accurate responses: What *Learning Preferences and Strengths* did we incorporate?						
	Introversion	Sensing	Thinking	Judging	Visual-Spatial	Musical-Rhythmic
	✓	✓	✓	✓	✓	
Challenge:					Intrapersonal	

B. SOCIAL/COMMUNICATION SKILLS (S/C)

Before starting to work on social and communication skills, the child's skills and knowledge must be well understood. Standardized assessments are helpful for receptive and expressive language skills but generally less helpful for social skills. Children with autism are often able to acknowledge and/or recite social rules but not use them spontaneously.

Gather information about social and communication skills using a form such as the *Communication Skills Checklist* included in Appendix III. This form should be completed by the child's parents, teachers, support workers and other caregivers who know the child well. These will provide multiple viewpoints. The information can then be blended to look for the trends and determine which areas are most important to different people and/or in different settings.

Before developing goals, watch other children in the same age group as your target child. See how they behave and what they do and say. We well-meaning adults must be careful to teach the child with autism to act and speak in ways that will help him 'blend' with his peer group.

Narrow down the child's social/communication goals to three or four. When developing strategies, look at what the child may be comfortable doing. Some of our children do not mind standing up in front of others and taking risks. Many others, however, need prompting, rehearsal and more subtle ways of accomplishing their social and communicative goals. Look at each situation and setting from the individual child's point of view – look through his eyes and his heart.

I worked with a team of therapists and teachers who wanted a child with autism to walk up to another child and say, "Can I play with you?" It looked a little awkward but I was not sure why. I spent the morning in a regular kindergarten class and found out why. As I watched the children, I noted how nonverbal they were. If a child was interested in playing with a toy another child was using, he typically just stood near the other child and looked on. If he did not receive an invitation, the child continued to watch but added a smile. If he was still not invited, the child would comment on the toy, usually with a compliment like: "That's a cool car!" If that did not work, the final strategy was for the child to ask directly to play.

**S/C.1
INTAKE**

Skill focus   *Strategies*

S/C.1a. Taking in complete and accurate   Attending to specific words
information
                                                                Developing specific listening behaviors

S/C.1b. Taking in relevant and important   Ignoring
information

S/C.1c. Retaining information   Rehearsing

                                                                Visual frames

                                                                Recalling object descriptions

                                                                Constructing meaning from longer paragraphs
                                                                and passages

                                                                Visualizing

**S/C.2
INTEGRATION
&
ELABORATION**

Skill focus   *Strategies*

S/C.2a. Determining if the information is   Monitoring comprehension
understood
                                                                Asking for repetition and/or clarification

**S/C.3
EXPRESSION**

Skill foucs   *Strategies*

S/C.3a. Making a plan for responding   Using visual frames

S/C.3b. Considering other perspectives   Playing 'teacher'

                                                                Using barrier tasks

                                                                Developing situationally-appropriate
                                                                communication

                                                                Developing situationally-appropriate behaviour

Figure 6.3 Social/Communication Skills (S/C)

S/C.1. Intake of information

Children with autism often do not know when they are supposed to pay attention to things said to them. They are also expected to take in and remember all of the relevant and important information. This is particularly difficult with spoken directions for a number of reasons. Unlike visual information which can remain visible to you, once something is said, it is gone. Also, the processing of verbal information is typically slow and inconsistent for children with autism.

S/C.1A. TAKING IN COMPLETE AND ACCURATE INFORMATION

Our main goal in this area is to make sure the child focuses his attention on the information being presented. The visual supports and structures described in Chapter 7 provide assistance to the child. He must, however, develop strategies for dealing with verbal information in a variety of settings.

Strategies for taking in complete and accurate information

The rationale for these strategies is to help the child learn basic behaviors and attitudes associated with listening to verbal information.

1. *Attending to specific words.* Once the child has become familiar with a story, you can use it to develop his attending and alerting to specific words. Every so often, stop at a key word and prompt the child to fill it in. You may start this type of listening with pictures that support recall of the key words. If the child does not immediately fill in the missing word, you can then point to the picture to help him.

    Songs that require actions also help the child to learn to attend to spoken language. Action songs, such as "If You're Happy and You Know It" can be found on the internet; see Appendix I for suggestions. As you sing the song, slow down and wait for the child to fill in the action before you join him.

2. *Developing specific listening behaviors.* The child with autism needs help in becoming aware of 'good listening' behaviors. By this point, the child has begun to develop listening skills but he must now become explicitly aware of them. Ask the child: "How can you help yourself listen?" Make a visual reminder list with the child, like those shown here, and then practice the strategies with him. Practice should be done playfully and positively. You can start by calling his name when he is looking elsewhere. Prompt him to provide an exaggerated response, such as by rapidly turning his head toward you. Keep the visual reminder available at all times. If the child forgets to look or listen, tap your finger on the appropriate picture to remind him.

An activity that can help the child learn that looking is important when others are speaking to him is to use directions that require visual attention. Such directions involve paying attention to the speaker's words and nonverbal cues. A list of example directions is included below. These should be done with a 'watch out, I might trick you' attitude which is fun-filled and enjoyable.

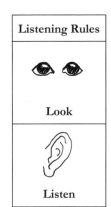

Figure 6.4 Example of visual reminder for beginning listening skills

Directions requiring visual attention

1. Put that (object you point to) in my hand.

2. Put this (object in your hand or close to you) over there (point).

3. Put that (object you point to) over there (point).

4. Put three of these (object in your hand or close to you) on the floor.

5. Walk over there (point) and then come back.

6. What color is this (object in your hand or close to you)?

7. Give me one of those (objects you point to).

8. Tell me what shape this (object in your hand or close to you) is.

9. Wait over there (point).

10. Make your face look like this (any facial expression).

11. Do this (wave, nod, wink, blink, fold your arms, stick out your tongue).

12. Tell me where to put this (object in your hand or close to you).

13. Put this (object in your hand or close to you) in your pocket.

14. Look at this (point to object close to you).

15. Tell me what this (object in your hand or close to you) is called.

16. Do you want this (object in your hand or close to you)?

The child may need direct teaching of nonverbal cues before he is able to respond consistently to directions requiring visual attention. Most children with autism do not know to look for nonverbal cues and they do not easily interpret them. I developed the Do-Say What-Say© game to help children learn nonverbal cues in social gestures and pantomimed actions. The game uses a set of "Say What" cards that direct the player to demonstrate an action, like throwing a ball or cutting, for other players to interpret. The "Do" cards ask each player to show how to say things 'with your body', like how to say "stop" or "look". Each person gets a chance to act out an action for other players to guess. One child discovered that, by pointing, he could induce people to look where his finger directed them. It was such a powerful revelation to him; he did not want to stop.

When children with autism reach school age, they often have little idea of when to listen to the teacher and when that is not necessary. They need help in understanding that teachers typically 'mark' important information in specific ways. The teacher may say "class", "children", "this is for homework", "please don't forget", "there are three main things", all of which should signal the child to pay attention. The child with autism should be taught these 'signal' words and phrases so he will know when to stop and pay attention. Visit the child's current and/or prospective classroom so you can learn the teacher's typical 'signal' words and phrases. Then practice them with the child so he is well-prepared for success. Consider printing them on a list of 'signals' for the child.

Note on eye contact: The type of 'looking' we are emphasizing at this phase is to have the child make at least a momentary glance in the direction of the speaker. Demanding more than brief eye contact can overload the child's ability to process any information. The goal is to have the child let the speaker know he is listening by looking in the direction of the speaker. Praise any eye gaze or eye contact with: "Wow, you looked at me. That tells me you are listening. Good job!" Place more emphasis on helping the child understand why we make eye contact, such as to let the other person know we are talking to him or her, than on commanding eye contact. Typically, the child's eye contact will increase naturally once he relaxes, trusts you and understands the situational expectations. Also, when he learns the specific reasons and rules for looking, he is more likely to use consistent, meaningful eye contact.

Checkpoint for taking in clear and complete information: What *Learning Preferences and Strengths* did we incorporate?						
	Introversion	Sensing	Thinking	Judging	Visual-Spatial	Musical-Rhythmic
	✓	✓	✓	✓	✓	
Challenge:	Intuiting				Verbal-Linguistic Interpersonal Intrapersonal	

Notes: Teaching and guiding the child to take in clear and complete information challenges the *Learning Preferences and Strengths* in the following ways:

- *Intuiting* – people with an Intuiting preference tend to see the big picture. By prompting the child with autism to determine and use broader concepts involved in listening, he is being pressed to look at the bigger picture.

- *Verbal-Linguistic* – people with Verbal-Linguistic strengths use words to think and remember. Prompting the child to attend specifically to verbal language focuses him on this modality.

- *Interpersonal* – the person with Interpersonal strengths has the ability to understand the feelings and thoughts of others. The strategies presented in this section help the child learn some beginning skills in being more responsive to other people.

S/C.1B. TAKING IN RELEVANT AND IMPORTANT INFORMATION

Our main goal in this area is to make sure the child determines and focuses only on the information that is relevant and important to the task or situation at hand. The structures described in Chapter 5, **Program Structure,** increase the likelihood that the child will note the most relevant and important information. However, the child needs to learn strategies he can use in any situation to help himself deal effectively with verbal information.

Strategies for taking in relevant and important information

The rationale for these strategies is to help the child focus on the most relevant and important information in a task or situation. That means not only attending to important things but also ignoring the unimportant and/or irrelevant details.

For a child with autism, distractions can be external, such as things that happen in the environment around him, or internal, such as thoughts, songs, jingles, or scripts that keep running through his head. We need to help him deal with both external and internal distractions.

1. *Ignoring.* The child is taught not to let his brain get distracted. A new picture is added to the "Listening Rules" as shown on p.123. To practice this, engage the child in a task and produce a noise or have another person enter the room. If the child becomes distracted, prompt him with: "Is that important right now? What do we need to tell our brains?…Don't get distracted, brain!" After a few practices with the verbal prompt, try just tapping your finger on the picture of 'Don't get distracted' to remind him. Promote the child's use of self-talk to remind himself "don't get distracted, brain".

    Once the child has a fairly solid understanding of what 'don't get distracted' means, you can introduce the notion of 'ignoring'. Help him learn that he can tell his brain to ignore things that are not important and/or that 'bug' him. The rationale we use with the child is: "We can ignore things so they don't bug us."

    An important area to address is listening in 'noise' . Children with autism have tremendous difficulty listening when there is background noise. This does not bode well for classroom and other group settings. Practice listening to and following directions in background noise, like people talking and sounds from streets, cafeterias, malls, bus depots, train stations and anywhere the child may frequent. You can record these sounds and play them during listening practice so that the child learns how to tune them out.

    Be careful with the concept of 'ignoring'. The child needs to learn he can ignore some things and not others. You might write a short Social Story™ with the child or make up a social rule about when he cannot ignore what is said. The list could include such things as when his parents say it is time for bed, when his teacher says it is time for snack and when the fire bell is sounded.

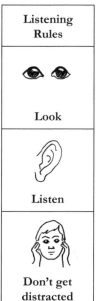

Listening Rules / Look / Listen / Don't get distracted

Figure 6.5 Example of visual reminder for developing listening skills

Children with autism often need more concrete support to ignore external and internal distractions. Table 6.2 lists strategies that can provide that support.

Table 6.2 Examples of strategies for dealing with external and internal distractions

Visual support	Type of distraction	Strategy
	Internal	Using Social Tickets.
		Make ticket-shaped cards like that shown. They are approximately 2 by 3 inches.
		Practice helping the child say "stop that please" while holding the card to cue him. Then, when he encounters a situation, give him the card to prompt use of the words on his own or show the other person what he wants. Have the cards available to the child at any time. As he becomes accustomed to the use of Social Tickets, praise him when he uses them on his own or prompt him to get the ticket to "help his brain".
	External	Making a shield to "protect us".
		Make a cardboard shield and let the child decorate it. Tell him that shields protect people so other things and/or people cannot 'bug' him. With some children, gluing small plastic bugs to the shield can be a fun physical reminder of what they are fending off.
		Practice helping the child put the shield in front of his face when something or someone bugs him.
		This strategy will appeal to those children who are interested in knights, ninjas and other 'warriors'.
	External	Marking a force field around our bodies so "nothing can get in to bug us".
		Use a hula hoop or another prop to mark a 'force field' around the child and/or his desk or other work area. Help him understand that this can protect him so other things and people cannot 'bug' him.
		Practice helping the child sense 'power' in his force field. Then put it to use when something bugs him.
		This strategy will appeal to those children who enjoy *Star Trek* and other science fiction programs or books.

Table 6.2 continued

Visual support	Type of distraction	Strategy
	Internal	The Brain Box©. This is a small box with a picture of a brain on it. It is used to put things in that are "bugging your brain". The Brain Box© is used prudently and very sincerely. If the child appears to be bothered by some internal song or script that keeps running through his mind, indicate that we need to put it in the Brain Box©. Very sincerely pretend to take the thoughts from his forehead. Either place the 'thoughts' directly in the box or write them on a piece of paper and then put it in the box. Announce to the child: "now we took them out of your brain so they don't bug you anymore. They can stay in the Brain Box©". If you do not have your Brain Box© available, you can write the thought or idea on a sticky note. Show the child how you have taken it from his brain, put it on paper and then place it out of sight so it does not 'bug' him anymore. You can give the thoughts back to the child by taking them off the paper or out of the box and putting them back into his head. This can be done at the end of his work, session or day.

An example of the effect of the Brain Box© concept will help you understand how powerful it can be.

One day, a child arrived at school repeatedly singing the chorus lines from Robert Munsch's book *Mortimer Be Quiet*: "Clang clang rattle bing bang. Gonna make my noise all day." He repeated and repeated the chorus until finally the teacher said, "Wow, that really seems to be bugging your brain. How about if we take it out?" She proceeded to sincerely remove it from his brain and put it in the Brain Box©. He immediately stopped singing the chorus. For the rest of the afternoon, he did not sing the chorus. Then his bus ride came. The child started screaming. The teacher ran over to him and asked what the problem was. The child said: "I need my words back!" The teacher opened the Brain Box© and put the invisible words back into his brain. He trotted off happily singing the chorus once again.

	Introversion	Sensing	Thinking	Judging	Visual-Spatial	Musical-Rhythmic
Checkpoint for taking in clear and complete information: What *Learning Preferences and Strengths* did we incorporate?						
	✓	✓	✓	✓	✓	
Challenge: Intuiting					Interpersonal Intrapersonal	

Notes: Teaching and guiding the child to take in relevant and important information challenged the *Learning Preferences and Strengths* in the following ways:

- *Intuiting* – people with an Intuiting preference tend to see the big picture. By prompting the child to determine if an object, event or person is important to what he is doing, he is being pressed to look at the bigger picture. The child is helped to learn what should be attended to and what should not.

- *Interpersonal* – the person with Interpersonal strengths has the ability to understand the feelings and thoughts of others. The strategies presented in this section help the child learn some beginning skills in learning to deal with other people.

S/C.1C. RETAINING INFORMATION

Our main goal in this area is to help the child learn specific strategies for holding spoken information in his memory. From an information-processing point of view, the child needs to hold on to the information long enough for it to be entered into his memory system so that it can be integrated and elaborated.

Strategies for retaining information

The rationale for these strategies is to help the child to hold information he hears in his temporary memory bank. One strategy may work better than the others for different children. It is best to try them out and see what facilitates each child's remembering. Other strategies may become more helpful at different points in his development, such as when the child's attention improves or his language skills expand.

1. *Rehearsing.* Rehearsal means saying something over and over long enough for us to accomplish what needs to happen. The child should be prompted to use rehearsal as one strategy to assist retention. Prompt him: "Say it over in your brain to help it remember." Add a

'say it over in my brain' picture to the listening rules as shown in the
Listening Rules below. Prompt the child to say the words out loud. It
takes a lot of practice before he will be able to use silent rehearsal. It
is helpful to hear what he is saying to himself: sometimes what the
child repeats may be different from what was said or intended.
Rehearsal is effective for relatively short statements or simpler pieces
of spoken information.

2. *Visual frames.* This involves using categories of information which
    can extend the amount of information the child retains. The intent is
    to set up an expectancy in the child that this information is going to
    be coming his way. The frame also shows the child that only a certain
    number of pieces and kinds of information are important.

    Visual frames can include pictures and/or printed lists of details
    and story outlines. These can help the child construct meaning from
    information he hears. Construction of meaning is the process of
    putting together the pieces of information and making a complete
    picture from them.

    Recalling object descriptions. A visual framework of
    important features should initially include *the name
    of the object* ("what is it?"), *the number* ("how many
    are there?"), *the shape* ("what shape is it?"), *the size*
    ("what size is it?") and *the color* ("what color is it?").

    Show the child the visual framework and use it
    while you describe an object. Prompt him to
    "remember in his brain" each feature as you
    describe it. Tap each square on the picture strip as
    you describe the object. Then ask the child to tell
    you what you described. Tap on a picture if he
    forgets to tell that feature.

    Over time, add more features to descriptions,
    like what parts the object has, where it is or where
    you find it, what you use it for, what it is doing and
    what kind of thing it is.

Listening Rules
Look
Listen
Don't get distracted
Say it over in my brain

*Figure 6.6 Example of visual reminder for more developed
listening skills*

What is it?	How many are there?	What shape is it?	How big is it?	What color is it?
	6 3 1 2 5 4		△ △	

Figure 6.7 Example of visual framework to help retention of descriptions

Constructing meaning from longer paragraphs and passages. Visual formats are described below for improving retention of information from longer paragraphs and passages.

The 'Story Hand' is used for constructing meaning from stories or experiences. Each finger of the child's left hand is associated with a major component of a simple story structure. They include *when* ("once upon a time"), *who* ("there was a boy named Jack and a girl named Jill"), *where* ("who went to the well"), *what happens* ("they climb the hill to the well, Jack falls down and cracks his head and then Jill falls down") and *how it ends* ("they were both sad"). Add symbols to each part of the Story Hand if necessary to help the child understand.

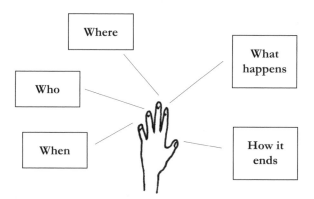

Figure 6.8 Story Hand for retention of simple stories

Start with a relatively short, familiar story, rhyme or real event from the child's life. Make sure not to have too many characters or events in the story during the early stages of learning. Tap each finger on the Story Hand as you tell that part of the story.

Once the child demonstrates an understanding of the Story Hand format, add a feelings statement at the end. The feelings statement is a traditional part of stories like "…and they lived happily ever after." Initially, keep the feelings statement fairly simple, like "and they felt happy". Then expand the feelings statements with a wider range of emotions and the reason why the characters felt that way.

Next, add more events to the stories: use the first joint on the index finger for the first event or the problem that gets the story going, the middle joint for what happened next and the knuckle for the third major event.

Once the child has demonstrated success using the Story Hand, introduce the Story Format in Figure 6.9. The Story Format is a linear form of the Story Hand.

When – setting (time)
Who – main characters
Where – setting (place)
What happens - three main events: 1. Beginning   2. Middle   3. End
How does it end?
How do the main characters feel? Why?

Figure 6.9 Story Format for retention of simple stories

The Story Format can be used for longer and more complex stories and can be combined with other strategies, like note-taking. Even fairly young children, five and six years of age, can be taught to jot down in pictures or words the main pieces of information in each category of the Story Format. Note-taking can enhance retention of the information greatly if it is taught carefully and practiced frequently. The simple and complex Story Formats are included in Appendix III.

Title/topic
Meaning/connection to other things I know
Main idea
Important details: 1. 2. 3. 4. 5.
What's most important to understand about this topic?

Figure 6.10 Story Format for retention of more complex stories

A more advanced format for retaining information through note-taking is shown in Figure 6.10. The note format prompts the child not only to determine the main idea but also to tell how the information relates to other things he knows. He then notes important details from the information he hears. He must also summarize the information to determine the main idea. He is also expected to decide what is most important for him to understand.

Visual or graphic organizers can be introduced as the child becomes more able to deal with multifaceted and less linear information. Visual organizers can be used to arrange a hierarchy, as shown in the first diagram on p.130 for dinosaurs, a sequence or cycle, as shown in the second diagram for butterflies, and relationship, as shown in the third (Venn) diagram for food preferences. Visual organizers can also be used to depict a time-line, comparison, cause-effect, story details, concepts, characteristics or attributes and decision making or problem solving. Bar graphs can be used to display frequency or magnitude of characteristics, like hair and eye color, height and gender. Web resources for visual organizer templates are included in Appendix I.

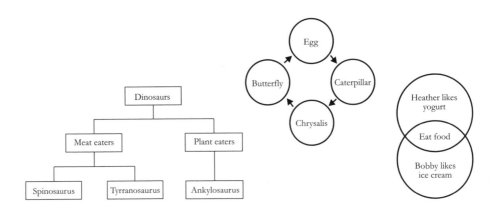

Figure 6.11 Example of visual information organizers

3.   *Visualizing.* This strategy requires a little more sophistication on the child's part but it can be tremendously effective. Prompt the child: "Let's make a picture in our brains to help us remember." Sometimes, it helps to associate the picture with a camera or video in his brain if that is meaningful to him.

Start out with descriptions of common objects or simple stories for him to remember. Use the same format for description of objects and story construction described earlier. This time, the emphasis is on making a picture. Prompt the child to draw a picture on paper. Even children with fine motor difficulties can be convinced to draw a picture. Stress to them: "The picture's just for your brain so it doesn't matter what it looks like, it just has to make sense to your brain."

Checkpoint for retaining information: What *Learning Preferences and Strengths* did we incorporate?						
	Introversion	Sensing	Thinking	Judging	Visual-Spatial	Musical-Rhythmic
	✓	✓	✓	✓	✓	
Challenge:	Intuiting				Verbal-Linguistic Bodily-Kinesthetic Intrapersonal	

Notes: Teaching and guiding the child to retain information stretches the *Learning Preferences and Strengths* in the following ways:

- *Intuiting* – people with an Intuiting preference tend to see the big picture. By prompting the child to look at categories or structure of information, we are prompting him to look at a broader scope.

- *Verbal-Linguistic* – people with Verbal-Linguistic strengths use words to think and remember. Typically, children with autism do not have primary strengths in the Verbal-Linguistic area but using language to help retention prompts them to use this modality.

- *Bodily-Kinesthetic* – people with Bodily-Kinesthetic strengths retain information more readily when they can associate a body movement. By teaching the child to sketch or print information he hears, the movement patterns are likely to help him remember.

S/C.2. Integrating and elaborating information
S/C.2A. DETERMINE IF THE INFORMATION IS UNDERSTOOD

Our main goal in this area is to ensure that the child knows when he understands something and learns what to do when he does not.

Strategies for determining if the information is understood

The rationale for these strategies is to help the child monitor his understanding of spoken information and learn how to help himself. These same strategies can be extended to reading.

1.   *Monitoring comprehension.* The child is prompted to follow the 'Good Listening' rules and to reflect on his comprehension of information he hears. Most children with autism have minimal to nonexistent comprehension monitoring. They need clear and concrete opportunities to learn these skills.

   Requests versus comments. Some children need the chance to understand the difference between a comment and a direction. For example, if you said "that's a neat car", the child might go and pick it up and/or start playing with it. We have to help him understand that a comment does not require a physical response. If you said, "Can you give me that cat?", you expect a physical response from the child. A child with autism can often tell you words a teacher or other adult said but he does not realize that he is supposed to do something with them. One mother told me that, by careful questioning, she was able to help her child recall what the teacher told 'the children' to do; her child, however, did not understand that she was part of the group being addressed.

   Make up a list of comments and directions in relation to a worksheet, picture or objects. In a playful and positive manner, like "I am going to try to trick you", use a variety of comments and requests in relation to the material at hand. Help the child understand the difference between the two types of statements so that he acts only after a request is made. If he acts on a comment, ask him, "Did I tell you to do something? I think I tricked you. Let's listen again."

   Incomplete requests. With these activities, the child is helped to determine when he hears enough information to be able to respond. Start by practicing in a situation where it is not possible to hear all of the information. This provides a clear opportunity for the child to experience communication breakdown and where you can be certain that he does not know what to do. While working with objects, a worksheet or picture, produce a noise, like a cough, sneeze or book hitting the floor, or whisper when a key word is said. For example, "color the (cough instead of the object name) yellow" or "put the (whisper the object name) in the cup". Let the child attempt to deal with the dilemma before you help him. Ask him, "Do you know what to do?" If he attempts to act on the incomplete information, ask him: "Do you really know what to do? I said… (repeat the direction with 'obscured' information)." Keep the practicing positive and playful but our goal is to help the child develop clear 'on-off' responses.

Unknown words. Before starting this type of request, be sure the child is responding consistently to incomplete requests.

Our goal with requests containing unknown words is to have the child determine if he understands all of the words stated. This is a large increase in complexity from the previous step because the child now has to decide whether he knows what each word means.

The child is provided alternately with directions that contain words you are certain he does not know, for example "color the stifle he hurt" or "put the spatula on the floor". Wait for the child to respond. If he tries to respond to a request he did not understand, probe his knowledge of all of the words you stated (e.g. "What are you supposed to do? Do you know what…is?"). If he stops himself and does not attempt to follow the direction, tell him that was a really smart thing to stop himself because that is a weird word.

Lengthy requests. The goal with this type of request is to have the child develop a clearer understanding of when he is not able to remember all of the words. Use reasonable requests and ones that are longer than the child can retain. Start with requests that are nine or more words in length, shortening or lengthening the statements as needed. If the child attempts to follow a request when he is truly uncertain about what to do, prompt him: "That was a good try but do you remember everything I said?" Make sure the child knows that he should always use his 'good listening' rules but sometimes we cannot remember everything someone says.

2. *Asking for repetition and/or clarification.*

Incomplete requests. Once the child understands when he cannot hear all of the direction, prompt him to say "say again please" or: "Can you say that again, please?" dependent upon his expressive language skills. These are referred to as requests for repetition. Setting the requests to a melody can make it easier for the child to say. The intonation pattern helps 'glue' the words together into a simpler melodic stream.

Unknown words. Asking for clarification is typically used when you do not understand specific words. Once the child learns to stop when he hears a word he does not know, prompt him to ask: "what does…mean?" or "what's…?"

Lengthy requests. When the child cannot remember all of the request even though he used his good listening skills, prompt him to request repetition or clarification. For example, have him say: "Can you say that again, please?" or "did you say…?"

Checkpoint for determining if information is understood: What *Learning Preferences and Strengths* did we incorporate?						
	Introversion	Sensing	Thinking	Judging	Visual-Spatial	Musical-Rhythmic
	✓	✓	✓	✓	✓	
Challenge:					Verbal-Linguistic Interpersonal Intrapersonal	

Notes: Teaching and guiding the child to determine if he understands information stretches the *Learning Preferences and Strengths* in the following ways:

- *Verbal-Linguistic* – people with Verbal-Linguistic strengths use words to think and remember. Prompting the child to monitor his understanding of information and requesting repetition or clarification prompts him to use Verbal-Linguistic strengths.

- *Interpersonal* – the person with Interpersonal strengths has the ability to understand the feelings and thoughts of others. Requesting repetition and clarification presses the child to be responsive to others.

S/C.3. Expressing information

The final phase in information processing requires the child to plan and verbally express his thoughts, ideas and experiences. It involves organizing the response, considering the perspective of the other person and then forming a clear and precise statement or story.

S/C.3A. MAKING A PLAN FOR RESPONDING

Our main goal in this area is helping the child put his thoughts and ideas together to form coherent and understandable responses.

Strategies for making a plan for responding

The rationale for these strategies is to help the child learn some basic forms of response. Once the child can use the basics, he can be assisted to extend these into longer and more complex explanations. The idea is not to stifle ideas but help the child figure out how he might express them more precisely. Initially, the child may experience frustration. With repeated practice, he will become accustomed to and more facile with the strategies.

1.   *Using visual frames.*
      Description of objects. Use a visual frame like that shown in Figure 6.7 to guide the child in organizing and expressing his descriptions. Once the child is successful with the basic categories, add further information like parts the object or animal has, where it is or where you find it, what you use it for, what it is doing and what kind of thing it is.
      Games like *Go Fish* can be used to practice describing. Cards can be made up so they follow a progression from 'simpler' to more complex:
      ○ pictures of objects or animals that vary by color and number ("Do you have three brown dogs?" versus two brown dogs or three black dogs)
      ○ pictures of objects or animals that vary by location ("Do you have a squirrel in a basket?" versus a cat in a basket or a squirrel behind a basket)
      ○ pictures of objects or animals that vary by color, size and features ("Do you have a medium-sized cup with green spots on it?" versus a large cup or one with pink hearts)
      ○ pictures of objects or animals that vary by fine details ("Do you have a blue car with a black top and three green stripes on the side?").

Initially, you will find some children provide lengthy and highly detailed descriptions. To help decrease this, examine the deck of cards with the child before starting the game and help him note which things are the same on each card. Then, prompt the child that the 'same' things are ones that we do not have to talk about because we know they are there. For example, if all of the pictures are of squirrels, then we do not have to use the word 'squirrel' in descriptions.

Games like Guess Who™, Headbanz™, and I Spy™ are also fun ways to practice describing objects.

Another 'twist' to describing can be teaching the child how to form riddles. Use the visual frame, shown in Figure 6.7, fold over the "what is it?" square and prompt the child to use the other categories to describe an object. Most children will need the concrete prompt of folding the "what is it?" category away to suppress their desire to provide the label. An example activity could involve placing an apple in a 'riddle bag' so others cannot see it. Using the visual frame, the child could give the following clues: "There is one, it is round, it is sort of small and it is red." Other people must guess what it is he is talking about.

Construction of stories. Practice using the Story Hand, in Figure 6.8, and Story Frames, in Figures 6.9 and 6.10, for organizing ideas. Start with simpler tasks like describing a picture sequence of a familiar story or activity. An example including all major components is as follows: time ("one day"), place ("at home"), main character ("a boy"), major events ("mixes", "rolls", "cuts out cookies") and how the main character felt ("happy").

Then progress to a scene from a familiar story or real-life experience for the child to describe. Over time, introduce made-up or imaginary stories. Imaginary stories can prove extremely difficult for some children so you can set up the Story Hand or Story Frame with a variety of pictured options for each major category. The child selects one or more pictures from each category: time, characters, place, actions, and ending. Then, he can construct a story based on the cards he selected.

Checkpoint for making a plan for responding: What *Learning Preferences and Strengths* did we incorporate?						
	Introversion	Sensing	Thinking	Judging	Visual-Spatial	Musical-Rhythmic
	✓	✓	✓	✓	✓	
Challenge:	Intuiting				Verbal-Linguistic Intrapersonal	

Notes: Teaching and guiding the child to make a plan for responding stretches the *Learning Preferences and Strengths* in the following ways:

- *Intuiting* – people with an Intuiting preference tend to see the big picture. By prompting the child to plan his response from main information categories, he is pressed to determine the broader concept.

- *Verbal-Linguistic* – people with Verbal-Linguistic strengths use words to think and remember. The strategies described in this section prompt the child to use language skills to plan and think ahead.

S/C.3B. CONSIDERING OTHER PERSPECTIVES

This is a major area of difficulty for children with autism. They have significant ongoing problems considering that other people may see or understand things differently from them. This then greatly impairs their ability to adjust their behavior in appropriate ways.

Our main goal in this area is to help the child with autism understand that other people may have a different perspective and see things in another way. Then he needs to learn to adjust his message to improve the other person's understanding.

Strategies for understanding perspective

The rationale for these strategies is to help the child experience success in communicating his message as well as communication breakdown. Communication breakdown occurs when a person misunderstands or misinterprets your message.

1. *Playing 'teacher'.* Provide the child with opportunities to be 'teacher'. This gives the child a chance to role-play and take on the perspective of the adult. Use activities and tasks that are familiar to the child and that have been successful in the past. Then prompt him to be the 'teacher' for you.

    Playing 'teacher', also referred to as reciprocal teaching, can be increasingly extended to include other children. This allows the child an opportunity to use familiar content in face-to-face interactions with peers where he can give feedback and acknowledge their successes.

2. *Using barrier tasks.* One of the best ways I have found to help the child understand how others interpret his words is with barrier tasks. These activities involve two people with a barrier between them that obscures their view of each other's task. Both people have the same task but one person must clearly and precisely tell the other person

Figure 6.12 Example barrier task setup

what to do. The 'barrier' makes sure that only verbal information is used to complete the task.

Start with simple coloring tasks. Construct a barrier between the child and you using a binder or file folder. Make sure that each person has the same picture and his own set of crayons or markers. Model instructions for the child: "Color the boy's hair black." Then compare your pictures and provide verbal feedback to the child, like: "Wow, you listened really well and I used clear words so you could understand." Then the child has a turn. Introduce more complex materials by using pictures that depict multiples of the same objects so the child has to describe distinguishing features and/or the locations.

Other activities include dressing dolls and building structures. A popular activity is constructing monster faces with different patterns and shapes of hair, hats, eyes, noses and mouths. The various features for the monster face provide opportunities not only for using precise language but also for using comparisons, such as: "Use the nose that looks like a pear."

3. *Developing situationally appropriate communication.* A child with autism must be taught social cues that signal the need for changes in what he says or how he says it. The first stages should include helping him learn common social phrases and nonverbal cues.

    Develop a list of social situations and emotions the child will likely encounter. Make up statements and/or nonverbal actions that would typically be used in those settings and to express those emotions. Practice social phrases with the child by using prompts, such as: "Say what you say when someone is mad," or, "Say what you say when someone has done a good job." Help him use key phrases and incorporate different tones of voice to go with each statement, for example, praising versus reprimanding. Phrases most useful to the child can be put onto Social Tickets, as described in Table 6.2 in daily situations. The child will get a chance to use verbal and nonverbal communication skills, including changing his tone of voice for angry versus happy tone.

For social cues, practice nonverbal gestures with the child, prompting him: "Show how to say 'look there' with your body," or "Show how to say 'I don't know' with your body." Use reciprocal teaching so that the child begins to recognize nonverbal gestures in other people. In real-life situations, ask the child questions, like: "What is the other person's body saying?"

Reader's Theatre can provide more opportunities to role-play. Reader's Theatre is minimal theatre: there are no stage sets, no costumes and no memorizing parts. The children are given copies of the scripts, parts are selected and then the children read the scripted lines for their individual roles. Reader's Theatre is a good way to develop responsiveness to others' comments and statements within a preset context. Repeated readings improve each child's speed of response as well as their reading fluency. Scripts for Reader's Theatre are available on the internet; some sites are listed in Appendix I.

4. *Developing situationally appropriate behavior.* Understanding other people's feelings and emotions is an area of significant difficulty for children with autism. One way to help the child interpret emotions in others is to develop a Feelings Book. This is an analytical approach to learning the main distinguishing facial characteristics of different emotional states.

    Find photographs of people expressing different emotions and organize them into side-by-side comparisons. Start with happy, angry and sad. Try to have a range of intensity within each group, such as simply smiling versus grinning. Help the child identify a few key facial features and cues that help us know how a person feels. Start by working on three major cues, including eyebrows, eyes and mouth, to narrow down what the child should look for. Try out the different emotions in a mirror so the child can see his own eyebrows, eyes and mouth. Compare different emotions in relation to the physical cues as shown in Figure 6.13.

Eyebrows: raised a little
Eyes: open wide
Mouth: corners turned up

Eyebrows: down in the middle
Eyes: a little bit closed
Mouth: corners turned down
a little bit

Figure 6.13 Example of Feelings Book page comparing features of two emotions

Checkpoint for understanding other perspectives: What *Learning Preferences and Strengths* did we incorporate?						
	Introversion	Sensing	Thinking	Judging	Visual-~ Spatial	Musical- Rhythmic
		✓	✓	✓	✓	
Challenge:	Feeling				Verbal-Linguistic Interpersonal Intrapersonal	

Notes: Teaching and guiding the child to understand other perspectives stretches the *Learning Preferences and Strengths* in the following ways:

- *Feeling* – people with Feeling preferences value others' needs and want to meet them. In perspective-taking, the child must consider other people and their perceptions to be successful.

- *Verbal-Linguistic* – people with Verbal-Linguistic strengths use words to communicate clearly with others. The strategies described in this section prompt the child to use language skills to express his thinking in precise and appropriate manners.

- *Interpersonal* – the person with Interpersonal strengths has the ability to understand the feelings and thoughts of others. Perspective-taking is a strongly interpersonal concept because the child has to ensure that he responds to others' cues and perceptions.

S/C.3C. PROVIDING CLEAR AND PRECISE RESPONSES

Our main goal in this area is to ensure that the child's intended message is what the listener understands. This means that the child provides well-organized information, includes enough information but not too much and considers the other person's perspective.

Most people working or living with a child with autism learn to 'fill in the blanks' in order to understand what he is trying to communicate. If you know his history, recent events in his life and how he typically refers to things, places and people, you can piece his comments together and figure out what he is trying to say. We need to learn how to stand back and objectively determine what a stranger may need to know from the child in order to understand him. This means that, as the child develops, we need to continually re-adjust our expectations of him as a communicator and decrease the amount of 'work' we do as listeners.

Strategies for providing clear and precise responses

The rationale for these strategies is to help the child use words and organization that help ensure his intended message is received by the listener.

1.   *Using visual frames.* Use the visual framework for descriptive information, Figure 6.7, the Story Hand, Figure 6.8, and the Story Frames Figures 6.9 and 6.10 to guide the child in expressing his ideas and experiences. If he forgets a feature, tap your finger on the picture or word on the visual framework to remind him to include that information.

     Written expression can also be developed by using these visual frames. The child can use them like checklists to ensure that all information is included. For one school-aged child, I made these frames in miniature on the back of cardboard rulers from McDonald's®. This meant he could keep them on his desk and not look 'odd'.

2.   *Using barrier tasks.* Barrier tasks, described earlier, help the child use more precise language that is understandable to his listener. When communication breakdown occurs, the child begins to understand the information needs of other people.

     While engaged in a barrier task, stop every so often and compare the child's work with the listener's. This provides concrete evidence of the clarity and precision of the child's directions. At these times, any differences can be discovered and the confusion discussed. This will help the child learn more about how to shape his expressive language to help others understand what he wants them to do. For children who provide lengthy and detailed descriptions, they can learn what is important for them to communicate and what is not critical to the task.

Checkpoint for providing precise and clear responses: What *Learning Preferences and Strengths* did we incorporate?						
	Introversion	Sensing	Thinking	Judging	Visual-Spatial	Musical-Rhythmic
		✓	✓	✓	✓	
Challenge:	Extraversion				Verbal-Linguistic Intrapersonal	

Notes: Teaching and guiding the child to provide precise and clear responses stretches the *Learning Preferences and Strengths* in the following ways:

- *Extraversion* – people with Extraversion preferences like to think out loud. With these strategies, the child with autism is prompted to verbalize his thoughts, ideas and experiences.

- *Verbal-Linguistic* – people with Verbal-Linguistic strengths use words to think and remember. The strategies described in this section prompt the child to use language skills to express his thinking.

C. SELF-REGULATION SKILLS (S/R)

Self-regulation is the ability to control your own body, perceptions, thinking and emotions in situationally appropriate ways (see Figure 6.14). It involves deliberate inhibition of undesired behavior in the service of achieving goals.

The focus of this content area is helping the child understand the requirements of a situation and then adjust his efforts. In order to do this, the child must learn to determine his arousal/excitement level and adapt his behavior. He must also learn to monitor his body, perceptions, thinking and emotions and then control them.

The ultimate goal is for the child to be able to do this on his own without adult intervention or prompting. The child must learn to manage his thoughts, feelings and actions flexibly. Part of this entails learning where and when he can lower his self-control level or take off the brakes and become 'dis-regulated' if he wishes.

Skill focus	Variation	Activities
S/R.1a. Controlling hands	Location Speed Intensity Manner	Imitating the adult Imitating a pictured model Imitating a peer Self-Direction
S/R.1b. Controlling feet	Location Speed Intensity Manner	Imitating the adult Imitating a pictured model Imitating a peer Self-Direction
S/R.1c. Controlling whole body	Location Speed n/a Manner	Imitating the adult Imitating a pictured model Imitating a peer Self-Direction

Skill focus	Strategies
S/R.2a. Maintaining focus	Look and/or listen for only the most important information Tell myself: "don't get distracted" Ignore things that are bugging me Think about if I understand or hear all of the information presented to me
S/R.2b. Internalizing thoughts	Talk to my brain Thought bubbles

Skill focus	Strategies
S/R.3a. Interpreting states and cues	Feelings book
S/R.3b. Remaining calm	Emotions dial
	Video modeling
S/R.3c Determining appropriate times and places	Relationship diagram
	Visual cues

Figure 6.14 Self-Regulation Skills (S/R)

Helping the child learn self-regulation

The child's control of his body is the first area of focus in self-regulation. Then control of thinking is addressed. This area involves the child's learning to self-regulate how and when he uses his cognitive resources. The final area is emotional control where the child learns how to modulate his feelings. The main skills and strategies or activities are outlined below.

S/R.1. Body control

Body control is perhaps the most straightforward area to teach. Start first with body parts and then with the whole body. This order is used because it is much easier to have the child sitting on the floor or on a chair and moving parts of his body before attempting whole body control. If you try for whole body control first, it could result in a chaotic situation with children scattering everywhere.

Each activity is practiced with the body parts or whole body in different locations. Then different speeds, intensities and manners of movement are introduced.

The continuum for activities within each of these areas follows a specific sequence of decreasing adult intervention and increasing conceptual complexity. The first step is to imitate the adult, a live model. This is followed by imitating a pictured model which is slightly more 'complex' because it is two-dimensional, inanimate and 'frozen' in time. The third step is imitation of a peer. Learning how to do this has important implications for future social learning since children with autism do not readily imitate peers. The final step is for the child to internalize the skill and begin to monitor and adjust his own behavior.

All of the activities can be done to songs and rhymes, making them more fun and more memorable for the child. Songs like "Head and Shoulders Knees and Toes" or "If You're Happy and You Know It" are good examples. Further examples can be found in Appendix I. Actions can also be incorporated into stories. Use the book database included in Appendix I to search for appropriate material.

During these activities, avoid having the child touch other people until he gains consistent control of his body.

S/R.1A. CONTROLLING HANDS

A. *Location* – this refers to where the child puts his hands.

  (i) *Imitating the adult.* The action and location are modelled by the adult. As shown in Chapter 5, **Program Structure**, you may wish to start work on imitation in a side-by-side position with the child. Prompt him: "make your hands do the same" or "do the same" as you put your hands on your knees, tummy, head, feet and on the floor, table, chair and such like.

(ii) *Imitating a pictured model.* Present pictured models to the child, like those in Figure 6.15, one at a time. Prompt him: "make your hands do the same thing" or "you do the same".

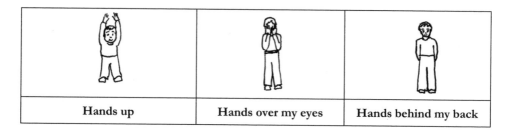

| Hands up | Hands over my eyes | Hands behind my back |

Figure 6.15 Examples of pictured models for the child to imitate

(iii) *Imitating a peer.* Use the pictures from *Imitating a pictured model* to prompt the child chosen to act as 'teacher'. He may also make up new locations but, typically, children need the pictures to prompt them.

(iv) *Self-direction.* Praise the child when he puts his hands in appropriate places, like on the table or on his own toys. Indicate to him: "Wow, look at your hands. You controlled your hands really well!" If he is about to attempt some action, like grabbing another child, intercede as quickly as possible with: "What do you need to tell your hands?" Prompt the child to tell his hands: "Hands, you need to be (location)." Then remind him that he can control his own hands.

Control of the hands is an important focus in the child's using his 'finder finger', presented earlier in this chapter. When the child uses his 'finder finger', praise him for controlling his hand.

B.   *Speed* – this refers to how quickly the action is done.

(i) *Imitating the adult.* The action and speed are modelled by the adult. Pair the various speeds with visual cues, like those shown in Figure 6.16, and the verbal prompt: "Make your hands go slow/fast/in between."

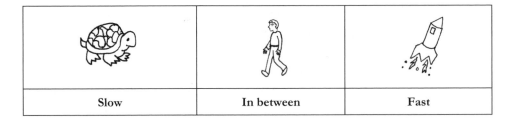

| Slow | In between | Fast |

Figure 6.16 Example picture cues for prompting different speeds

(ii) *Imitating a peer.* The child chosen as 'teacher' can determine the speed and/or ask other people to choose.

(iii) *Self-direction.* Remind the child that he has control to make his hands go "fast" or "slow" or "in between". For example, when he is speeding through an activity, he can be prompted: "What do you need to tell your hands?"

C.   *Intensity* – this refers to how hard or gently the hands are used.

(i)   *Imitating the adult.* Actions, such as clapping hands, hitting the floor with hands or clapping your thighs, can be used in this activity. Pair the different intensities with visual cues, like those shown in Figure 6.17, and the verbal prompt: "Make your hands (action) hard/gentle/in between."

| 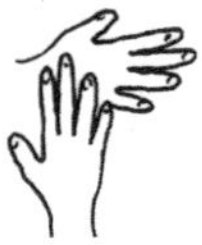 Gentle |  In between |  Hard |

Figure 6.17 Example picture cues for prompting different action intensities

(ii) *Imitating a peer.* The child chosen as 'teacher' can determine the intensity and/or ask other people to choose.

(iii) *Self-direction.* Remind the child that he has control to make his hands be "gentle" or "hard" or "in between". For example, if he is about to grab something or someone, he can be prompted: "What do you need to tell your hands?"

D.   *Manner* – this refers to the way in which the hands are used. Comparison is used to determine manner, for example "like a butterfly" or "like an elephant". The comparisons used in this activity also serve a cognitive function since the child must use less concrete thinking ("We all know your hands are not bears!") and use his imagination.

   (i) *Imitating the adult.* Present the notion of doing an action like different animals. Use your voice to reinforce the idea of light and fluttery (higher pitched, softer voice) or big and stomping (lower pitched voice).

Butterfly	Elephant	Rabbit	Bear	Fairy	Spider

Figure 6.18 Example picture cues for prompting different manners of action

   Actions such as wriggling the fingers like a spider, hopping hands on the floor like a rabbit, stomping hands on the floor like an elephant, tickling one hand with the other like a butterfly or flitting fingers through the air like a fairy can be used in this activity. Pair the different manners with visuals, like those shown in Figure 6.18, and the verbal prompt: "Make your hands (action) like a (animal)."

   (ii) *Imitating a peer.* The child chosen as 'teacher' can determine the manner and/or ask other people to choose.

   (iii) *Self-direction.* Remind the child that he has control to make his hands be "like a butterfly" or "like a bear".

S/R.1B. CONTROLLING FEET

A.   *Location* – this refers to where the child puts his feet.

   (i) *Imitating the adult.* The action and location are modeled by the adult. Put your feet up in the air, on the floor, one foot up and such like and prompt the child "make your feet do the same" or "do the same" while you do the action.

(ii) *Imitating a pictured model.* Show the child a picture like one of those in the diagram below. Prompt him "make your feet do the same" or "do the same".

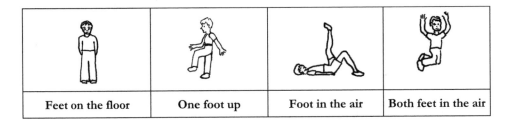

| Feet on the floor | One foot up | Foot in the air | Both feet in the air |

Figure 6.19 Example picture cues for prompting different action locations

(iii) *Imitating a peer.* Use the pictures from *Imitating a pictured model* to prompt the child chosen to act as 'teacher'. He may also make up new locations.

(iv) *Self-direction.* The child is reminded when he is about to attempt some action, like putting his feet on someone else: "What do you need to tell your feet?" Prompt the child to tell his feet: "Feet, you need to be (location)." Then remind him he can control his feet all by himself.

B.   *Speed* – this refers to how quickly the action is done. See Figure 6.16 for visual prompts.

(i)   *Imitating the adult.* The action and speed are modeled by the adult. Pair the various speeds with the visual cues, shown earlier, and the verbal prompt: "Make your feet do slow/fast/in between."

(ii) *Imitating a peer.* The child chosen as 'teacher' can determine the speed and/or ask other people to choose.

(iii) *Self-direction.* Remind the child that he has control to make his feet go "fast" or "slow" or "in between". If he is running indoors or at the swimming pool, stop him and ask: "What do you need to tell your feet?"

C.   *Intensity* – this refers to how hard/loudly or soft/quietly the feet are moved. See Figure 6.17 for visual prompts.

(i)   *Imitating the adult.* Stomp your feet, dance lightly on your toes, and such like for "gentle", "hard" and "in between". Pair the different intensities with visual cues, shown in Figure 6.17, and the verbal prompt: "make your feet (action) hard/gentle/in between".

(ii) *Imitating a peer.* The child chosen as 'teacher' can determine the intensity and/or ask other people to choose.

(iii) *Self-direction.* Remind the child that he has control to make his feet be "gentle" or "hard" or "in between". If he is about to kick an object or person, prompt him: "What do you need to tell your feet?" Remind him to tell his feet to be gentle.

D. *Manner* – This refers to the way in which the feet are used. See Figure 6.18 for visual prompts.

   (i) *Imitating the adult.* Present the notion of doing an action like different animals. Use your voice to reinforce the idea of light (higher pitched voice) and fluttery or big and stomping (lower pitched voice). Pair the different manners with visual cues, like those shown earlier, and verbal prompts like: "Make your feet (action) like a (animal)."

   (ii) *Imitating a peer.* The child chosen as 'teacher' can determine the manner and/or ask other people to choose.

   (iii) *Self-direction.* Praise the child when he demonstrates control of his feet. If he forgets to control how he uses his feet, ask him: "What do you need to tell your feet?" Remind the child that he has control to make his feet be "light like a butterfly" or "heavy like a bear" or "in between".

S/R.1C. CONTROLLING THE WHOLE BODY

A. *Location* – this refers to where the child puts his body.

These activities provide excellent opportunities to work on location words, such as "put your body on the floor", "under the chair", "under the table", "beside the chair", "behind the chair" and such like. Be sure to use inanimate (not alive) objects, like furniture, for the child to orient his body to. Children with autism tend to have difficulty determining which object to focus on in terms of location. The child may say either "the chair is under the boy" or "the boy is on the chair". The natural tendency in typical language users is to talk about the animate (live) thing first, that is, "the boy (animate) is on the chair (inanimate)". Use this 'animate-first' strategy in presenting different options to the child.

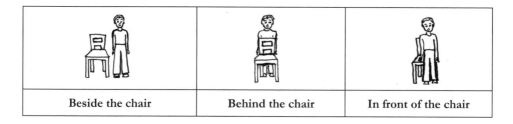

| Beside the chair | Behind the chair | In front of the chair |

Figure 6.20 Example pictures for prompting different lociations for the body

(i)   *Imitating the adult.* Put your body on the floor, under the chair, under the table, beside the chair, behind the chair and other locations. Prompt the child to do the same thing as you.

(ii) *Imitating a pictured model.* Show the child a picture, like in Figure 6.20, and prompt him to imitate.

(iii) *Imitating a peer.* Use pictures like those shown above to prompt the child chosen to act as 'teacher'. He may also make up new locations.

(iv) *Self-direction.* If the child is in a place he is not supposed to be, ask him: "Where does your body need to be?" Be sure also to praise him when he is in the correct location or position, such as when he sits during a group activity or during supper.

B.   *Speed* – this refers to how quickly the action is done.

(i)   *Imitating the adult.* The action and speed are modeled by the adult. Pair the various speeds with visual cues, shown in Figure 6.16, and appropriate verbal prompts.

(ii) *Imitating a pictured model.* Show the child a picture, like one of those above, in combination with the visual cues for speed. Prompt him to imitate.

(iii) *Imitating a peer.* The child chosen as 'teacher' can determine the speed and/or ask other people to choose.

(iv) *Self-direction.* Remind the child that he has control to make his body go "fast" or "slow" or "in between". He should be prompted to remind his body. Incorporate games like "Red Light-Green Light" and "Simon Says" to practice self-regulation with the child. A "Stop-Go" game can also be used where a red 'stop' light or green 'go' light can be held up to prompt body control.

C.   *Manner* – this refers to the way in which the child uses his body.

   (i)   *Imitating the adult.* Prompt the child to move his body like different animals using pictures like those shown in Figure 6.18.

   (ii) *Imitating a peer.* The child chosen as 'teacher' can determine the manner and/or ask other people to choose.

   (iii) *Self-direction.* Remind the child that he has control to make his whole body move "light like a butterfly" or "heavy like a bear" or "in between".

Yoga can readily be incorporated into the child's program as a means of learning self-regulation. We have used yoga successfully in helping children with autism learn to center and calm themselves. There are a number of books, for example *Integrated Yoga* by Nicole Cuomo (2007), and videos intended for children that can provide guidelines and examples. Some picture models that can also be used are shown in Figure 6.21.

Figure 6.21 Example yoga positions for incorporation into self-regulation activities

During a summer camp, we wanted to help the children understand that they could control their own bodies. One of the workers developed the "Stop and Think" song (shown opposite).

The "Stop and Think" song became a sort of mantra for both the adults and the children. If any one of us was feeling like we were about to 'lose control', we would break into the song. If a child was at a distance, we could simply point to our wrist, the 'control' position, as a reminder to him.

Another song that can be used effectively to help children calm themselves is "Take a Rest" from Sesame Street®. While quietly singing this song, the children are encouraged to lie down or put their heads down and "take it slow, take it easy".

The Stop and Think Song

Stop, think, control my body

(hold hand straight out from your shoulder for "stop", touch your temple for "think", touch your left wrist where you typically wear a watch for "control")

Stop, think, control my body

(same actions as above)

Stop, think, control my body

(same actions as above)

I am in control

(point to your chest with your index finger for "I")

Checkpoint for body control: What *Learning Preferences and Strengths* did we incorporate?						
	Introversion	Sensing	Thinking	Judging	Visual-Spatial	Musical-Rhythmic
		✓	✓	✓	✓	✓
Challenge:					Verbal-Linguistic Bodily-Kinesthetic Interpersonal Intrapersonal	

Notes: Teaching and guiding the child to control his body stretches the *Learning Preferences and Strengths* in the following ways:

- *Verbal-Linguistic* – people with Verbal-Linguistic strengths use words to think and remember. The concepts of location, speed, intensity and manner are incorporated into the strategies with the expectation that the child will learn to understand and use these concepts. In addition, the child is prompted to use self-talk, or verbal mediation, to help himself gain control of his body.

- *Bodily-Kinesthetic* – the person with Bodily-Kinesthetic strengths can use his body in skilled ways. The central focus of the skills in this section is on helping the child learn how to control and regulate his body movements.

- *Interpersonal* – the person with Interpersonal strengths has the ability to understand the feelings and thoughts of others. By pressing the child to imitate others, he must learn to respond to requests and directions by others.

- *Intrapersonal* – Intrapersonal strengths involve understanding your strengths and limitations and your ability to apply your thinking. The focus on self-direction helps the child develop more self-awareness of his body and body parts.

S/R.2. Control of thinking

Control of thinking refers to the child's being able to focus his attention selectively, ignore unimportant distracters, plan and generally control his thinking. These have received specific focus in the activities presented earlier within the Learning/Cognitive skills and Social/Communication skills. Among them are:

- I can look and listen for only the most important information.

- I can tell myself: "don't get distracted".

- I can ignore things around me that are bugging my brain.

- I can think about if I understand or hear important information.

- I can talk to my brain to help my body and brain work better.

One child exhibited that he truly began to understand the notion of the power of his brain. He announced one day that he wanted to see this thing called his 'brain'. He tried looking into his mouth with a mirror and really pondered how he might get to see it. We finally convinced him to settle for a picture because his head/skull has to be closed to protect his brain.

It is important to prompt the child while pointing to your head: "Think in your brain," and "tell your brain…" This should be done in any situation where it might be important for the child to be cautious and/or decrease impulsive responses. Over time, the child will begin to understand the concept and use it spontaneously.

Initially, the child is prompted to talk to his brain out loud. This will give people around him a chance to monitor what he is saying to himself. It is an opportunity to shape and prompt his self-talk as necessary. Over time, the child needs to learn to internalize this self-talk, otherwise he may be perceived as 'odd'. Two strategies to help children use inner-speech include:

- prompting the child to "just say it in your brain" when he uses self-talk.

- helping the child use an erasable 'thought bubble'. Draw a thought bubble on card stock, cut it out and laminate it. The child can then draw or print his thoughts on it.

In a social skills group of eight- and nine-year-old children, I introduced the thought bubbles and received some amusing results. We were working along on a concept when suddenly one of the children held his thought bubble over his head; on it was written "Bobby really is bugging me". Another child then responded on his 'thought bubble': "just ignore him".

These strategies can be effectively applied in group situations so the child's self-talk will not interrupt or annoy others. Also, there are social implications to 'say it in your brain': the child is taught that it is okay to think some things but not say them out loud.

Checkpoint for control of thinking: What *Learning Preferences and Strengths* did we incorporate?						
	Introversion	Sensing	Thinking	Judging	Visual-Spatial	Musical-Rhythmic
		✓	✓	✓	✓	
Challenge:	Intuiting				Verbal-Linguistic Intrapersonal	

Notes: Teaching and guiding the child to control his thinking stretches the *Learning Preferences and Strengths* in the following ways:

- *Intuiting* – people with an Intuiting preference tend to see the big picture. By prompting the child to think about his brain and thinking, he is being pressed to look at broader concepts.

- *Verbal-Linguistic* – people with Verbal-Linguistic strengths use words to think and remember. The child is prompted with these strategies to use self-talk to mediate and modulate his thinking and thought processes.

- *Intrapersonal* – Intrapersonal strengths involve understanding your strengths and limitations and your ability to apply your thinking. The child is being helped to develop more self-awareness of his thinking and thoughts.

S/R.3. Control of emotions

The concept of controlling emotions means helping the child understand and modulate his feelings. It is not intended to have the child stifle his feelings. The child is expected and prompted to experience a full range of emotions but he needs help learning to:

- interpret cues for emotional states in himself and others

- remain calm

- determine the appropriate times and places for certain emotions and behaviors

- use consistent approaches to problem solving.

Each of these areas will be addressed individually in the following sections.

S/R.3A. INTERPRETING EMOTIONAL STATES AND CUES

1. *Feelings Book.* Interpreting emotions was introduced earlier in the Social/Communication section of this chapter. One activity in that section was the Feelings Book where the child was helped to identify the major physical features of different emotional states. Extend the emotions and their distinguishing features into everyday life. Point out the emotions and, over time, ask the child to identify how others are feeling. Then prompt him to explain how he knows the person is feeling that way, attempting to elicit the main characteristics from him.

Emphasis should then to shift to the child. He needs to start identifying his own emotional state. Use the categories from the Feelings Book and help the child identify them in himself. Include other body cues as well, such as tightened tummy, head or shoulders. These should be investigated with each individual because emotional states physically express themselves differently in different people. Take photos of the child prompting him to demonstrate these different emotions for you. A Feelings Book of the child's own emotions can be compiled with him. These can be enjoyable activities that help the child identify how his body and face look and feel.

S/R.3B. REMAINING CALM

1. *Emotions dial.* Our goal is to help the child remain calm so that he is more able to learn and to use strategies to assist himself.

    The first step in remaining calm is to learn about a range of emotional states. One powerful strategy is to develop an 'Emotion Dial' that visually displays a range. The zone to the left, typically shown in green for 'go', is the place where "my body and my brain feel calm". Model 'calm' for the child and help him try it out for himself. Working with him, help him to identify how his eyebrows, eyes and mouth look and how his body feels when he is calm. Take a photograph of the child demonstrating 'calm' and write down the face and body features he identifies. Associate the feeling of 'calm' with the left-hand zone of the Emotion Dial.

    The zone in the middle, typically shown in yellow for 'caution', is associated with the feeling that: "My body and my brain are starting to feel tight and stressed." Model this state for the child. Have the child demonstrate it for himself and help him identify the main features on his face and in his body. Take a photograph of the child

Figure 6.22 Example emotion dial

demonstrating 'stressed' and write down the face and body features he identifies. Associate the feeling of 'stressed' with the middle zone of the Emotion Dial. Have the child go from 'calm' to 'stressed' repeatedly so that he can feel and see the different cues in his face and body.

The zone on the right, typically shown in red for 'stop', is connected with strong emotions where "my body is tight and my brain feels like it is buzzing" or whatever the child reports or seems to be experiencing. With most children, it is recommended that you do not model this state because it is simply something that needs to be controlled. Associate the 'buzzing' feeling with the right-hand zone on the Emotion Dial and help the child relax his face and body and resume a feeling of 'calm'. Demonstrate resumption of 'calm' by telling yourself to "be calm", shaking out your hands and then taking a deep breath. You can put these three steps into a picture format to help prompt the child as shown in the self-calming techniques in Chapter 8, **Behavior in Children with Autism**.

The Emotions Dial is used on a daily basis with the child. Use it to point out and praise him for being "calm". If the child begins to show signs of stress, move the dial out of the left-hand (green) zone to whatever degree you observe in his stress level. Over time, the child will assume increasing control over his emotional state and spontaneously use strategies to help himself.

A four-year-old with autism was at a shopping mall with her mother. As they proceeded along, her mother noticed that the little girl became more distracted and tense. The child stopped and told her mother she wanted to sit down. She then took her mother to a quiet corner of the mall and remained there for five to ten minutes. This child had successfully learned to identify when she was becoming stressed and how a break could help her regain her composure.

---

2.   *Video modeling*. Videos or DVDs are compelling to many children with autism and, thereby, provide a potent means for teaching social and behavioral skills. They have a particularly appealing feature for children with autism: they can be viewed repeatedly.

If you are going to use video modeling, carefully plan what you wish to accomplish. Set out the main concepts clearly and precisely. Behaviors modeled in the video should be presented as simple steps. Optimal length is between five and ten minutes.

I developed a video, entitled *Dealing with Frustration*, produced by a professional film production company. In it, frustrating situations were described and a simple three-step process for remaining calm (stop, think, make a plan) was presented. The video, intended for children from three to ten years of age, has been very powerful in teaching children with autism. They enjoy watching it repeatedly and generalize the strategies to everyday settings.

S/R.3C. DETERMINING APPROPRIATE PEOPLE, TIME AND PLACE

One of the most difficult areas to help children with autism sort out is how to show affection to others in appropriate ways. We do not want to frighten the children, such as by saying strangers are dangerous, or make them unwilling to show affection but it is critical that they understand appropriate affection. One way to do this is a Relationship Diagram. This is a visual 'map' of how to relate to different people in the child's life. An example is shown below.

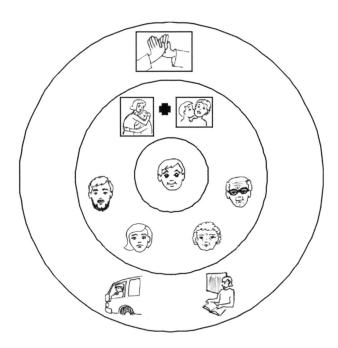

Figure 6.23 Example Relationship Diagram

In the center is the child himself. In the next circle are pictures, showing people the child can 'hug and kiss'. They include pictures of Mom, Dad, Grandpa and Grandma. Dependent upon the family makeup and the family's ways of showing affection, people and behavior should be changed. For example, if Grandpa is rather fragile and arthritic, he would probably not enjoy being hugged.

In the next circle is a picture of 'high five'. High fives can be given to important people in the child's life who should not be hugged and kissed. People in this circle may be friends, teachers and bus drivers.

Other circles can be added to include people you might just say "hi" to, such as people you see all the time at the pool or in the grocery store. Another circle could be added for places where you need to use your 'quiet voice', such as church or the library. People who could help the child in emergency situations, like firemen and police officers, should be included in a circle to assist the child in understanding their roles.

Checkpoint for emotion control: What *Learning Preferences and Strengths* did we incorporate?						
	Introversion	Sensing	Thinking	Judging	Visual-Spatial	Musical-Rhythmic
		✓	✓	✓	✓	
Challenge:	Intuiting Feeling				Verbal-Linguistic Interpersonal	

Notes: Teaching and guiding the child controlling his emotions stretches the *Learning Preferences and Strengths* in the following ways:

- *Intuiting* – people with Intuiting preferences are able to see the larger scope of an issue and the over-riding concepts. Problem solving and other strategies for controlling emotions stretch the child to look beyond the details of a situation and begin to understand the wider implications.

- *Feeling* – people with Feeling preferences value others' needs and try to meet them. Helping the child learn appropriate time and place for emotions, he is beginning to understand the impact he may have on others.

- *Verbal-Linguistic* – people with Verbal-Linguistic strengths use words to think and remember. The child with autism is prompted with these strategies to use self-talk to mediate and modulate his thinking and feelings.

- *Interpersonal* – the person with Interpersonal strengths has the ability to understand the feelings and thoughts of others. With the strategies described above, the child is being helped to understand and control his own emotions.

INCORPORATING ALL STAGES OF INFORMATION PROCESSING AND MULTIPLE SKILLS

Learning conversation and small talk

In conversation, the listener has to take in relevant information completely and accurately. Then he must retain it long enough to make sure he understands what was said. After that, he needs to plan his response, take into consideration who his conversational partner is and then respond back. In day-to-day adult conversations, all of this occurs within less than five seconds.

Once we have worked on all of the Social/Communication foundation skills described in the previous section, we can help the child with autism incorporate them into conversational skills and 'small talk'. Small talk is not easy for a lot of people, particularly people with autism. There are a number of reasons for this. Among them are the speed and accuracy of information processing required and the planning and formulation of a response. Another important issue is also that most people with autism see no real need to chat with others, particularly if it is about topics in which they have no interest.

Table 6.3 Basic topics of conversation with examples

Topic	Example
Books	Have you ever read…?; What's your favorite book?
Clothes	I really like you…; What kind of jeans do you like?
Computers, Games	What's your favorite software?; Do you have a computer at home? What kind?
Family	How many people are there in your family?; Do you have any brothers or sisters?

Food	What's your favorite food?; Do you like…?
Friends	Do you know…?; What's your favorite thing to do with friends?
Health	How are you?
Movies, TV	What's your favorite movie/TV show?; Do you like…?
Plans	What are you going to do this weekend/summer?
Restaurants	What's your favorite restaurant?; Do you like…?
School, Work	How was school/work today?; Do you like…?
Shopping	What's your favorite place to go shopping?; Do you like…?
Sports	What's your favorite sport?; Do you play…?
Vacations	What's your favorite place to go for a vacation?; Where did you go on your last vacation?
Vehicles	What kind of car does your family have?; What's your favorite car/truck?
Weather	How do you like the weather today?

The first issue that needs to be discussed with the child is the rationale for conversation and 'small talk'. Explain to him that we chat with other people so (a) we can learn things about them, (b) we can see if they like some of the same things we do, and (c) other people will think we are more friendly.

For children with autism, it is important to present broad concepts, like conversation and small talk, in concrete logical ways. I spent considerable time trying to figure out what people do during 'light' conversational small talk. I found that there is a relatively small set of topics. The main topics, with examples, are shown in Table 6.3 above.

I made up game cards with each of these topics depicted on them. Because children with autism tend to focus on specific topic areas that interest them, I included a card that says "Favorite" so the child can have a chance to talk about his favorite topic every so often.

The next step was to set up the game with different levels of complexity for initiating or continuing the topic of conversation. The 'easiest' and most straightforward way to prompt the child was to ask the question: "What's your favorite…?" This question is used a great deal by young children and requires only that the child determine the main topic. I made up a gameboard, like that shown in Figure 6.24, which included all major question forms, including what, who, where, when, how and why.

What		**When**
Who		**How**
Where		**Why**

Figure 6.24 Small Talk gameboard setup

Knowing that open-ended tasks are stressful for children with autism, further structuring was needed. I added a timer so that the child would understand that there was a clear beginning and end to small talk. The timer also 'forces' the child to keep the conversation going and prevents him from providing just single-word answers.

Before playing the game, it is important to develop a Social Rule for small talk, like that shown. To construct a Social Rule, the child and adult work together to define small talk, when, where and with whom he can use small talk, what the child can say and do and why people engage in small talk.

The rule spells out for the child the basic rules and rationale for chatting with others. By including the "with whom" section, we can exclude 'strangers' or other people the child should not engage in conversation.

To start the game, one person selects the first topic card on the pile. The timer is set to one minute; increase the time as the child becomes more proficient at staying on topic. The first person makes a comment or asks a question about the selected topic. Each person who responds and asks a question is given a token so that there is a tangible indicator of success. The person with the most tokens at the end of the game wins; try, however, to keep the game as equal as possible so small talk does not become too competitive.

Social skill: how to do small talk

Definition: small talk is chatting with other people about everyday things

When: when I talk to people I know

Where: at home, on the playground, at school

With whom: my friends, my family and other people I know

What to say and do:

1. listen to what the other person says

2. talk about the same topic so we both talk for one minute about it

3. ask the other person questions about the topic

4. I can change the topic after we have talked about the topic for one minute

5. I can talk about any of the small talk topics

6. I need to remember not to talk just about my favorite topics.

Reasoning: I do this because other people will learn something about me and I will learn something about them. They will learn that I am friendly too.

As the child becomes more proficient at small talk, introduce the use of comments in addition to questions. You may consider giving out one token for questions and two for comments in acknowledgement of their increased 'complexity'.

Once the child shows some proficiency with the game, include more people so he can learn to maintain conversation among three and four people. Also, introduce a variety of people like siblings, friends and other adults. Encourage families to use the game when they are having a quiet family-only supper. The game format can help ensure that everyone at the table gets an opportunity to speak and listen, even younger siblings.

Checkpoint for conversation and small talk: What *Learning Preferences and Strengths* did we incorporate?						
	Introversion	Sensing	Thinking	Judging	Visual-Spatial	Musical-Rhythmic
		✓	✓	✓	✓	
Challenge:	Extraversion Intuiting Feeling				Verbal-Linguistic Interpersonal	

Notes: Teaching and guiding the child to engage in conversation stretches the *Learning Preferences and Strengths* in the following ways:

- *Extraversion* – people with Extraversion preferences like to think out loud. The child is prompted to verbalize his questions and thoughts on each topic which requires increased speed and accuracy of processing the information.

- *Intuiting* – people with an Intuiting preference tend to see the big picture. By prompting the child to engage in small talk, he is pressed to look at the broader concept of conversation.

- *Feeling* – people with Feeling preferences value others' needs and try to meet them. Conversation presses the child to consider others' needs in engaging and continuing small talk.

- *Verbal-Linguistic* – people with Verbal-Linguistic strengths use words to think and remember. The child is prompted with these strategies to engage in a verbal exchange with others.

- *Interpersonal* – the person with Interpersonal strengths has the ability to understand the feelings and thoughts of others. Conversation and small talk are strongly interpersonal concepts because the child has to ensure that others can understand his message.

Dealing with figurative language

A great deal of figurative language is used in everyday conversation, especially in descriptions and humor. For children with autism, this can be quite confusing because they tend to interpret language literally. That is, when you say, "Oh my goodness, she is going to hit the roof!", the child might find it odd that the person is going to reach up and strike the ceiling.

Children with autism need a clear strategy for dealing with figurative language because it can be the source of apparently 'inappropriate' behavior and/or replies. Sometimes, the literal interpretation of figurative language can cause children with autism to become upset. For example with "I could eat a horse", the child with autism may become upset and say, "You're not supposed to eat horses!"

Tackling the issue of figurative language is complex and should start with the child's learning to detect instances of it. Then the child needs to learn basic ways of responding to figurative language. Most people do not understand the exact meaning of idioms and other figurative language but can get the gist of it from the context. This is what the child with autism needs to learn. Later on, work can be done with the child to understand the actual meaning of common figures of speech, using a book such as *What Did You Say? What Do You Mean?* by Jude Welton (2004).

I was running a social skills group with nine- to ten-year-old boys. We were sitting in a circle and the boy beside me was squirming and had his arm out the neck of his t-shirt and the other arm out the bottom. I turned to him and said, "Bobby, you are an octopus today." Two boys across the circle looked serious and intense. One boy said, "Oh, Bobby couldn't possibly be an octopus because they are invertebrates and Bobby is not an invertebrate." The other boy agreed and added, "And octopuses have tentacles and Bobby only has arms." I finally turned to the boys and told them I was just making a joke. I also put figurative language on our schedule for the

---

The main types of figurative language are shown in Table 6.4. Clichés are a special class of figurative language. They do not lend themselves well to direct analysis because their meaning tends to become obscured through repeated use. It is usually best to teach them to the child directly. There are some excellent books on clichés and idioms written for children that can help the child understand their meanings.

Table 6.4 Basic types of figurative language with examples

Type	Definition	Examples
Cliché	A word or phrase that has become overly familiar or commonplace that cannot be interpreted literally. It usually has been used excessively and has become a bit meaningless and even irritating.	No pain, no gain. A penny for your thoughts. Over the hill. That was a no-brainer. Don't get your knickers in a knot. That's pretty hard to swallow. Please don't upset the apple cart. Be sure to mind your manners.
Hyperbole	Deliberate exaggeration to emphasize a point, commonly used with humor.	Mile-high pie. I nearly died laughing. I tried a thousand times. I could eat a horse.
Idiom	A word or phrase that is an expression whose meaning cannot be figured out from the individual words; it often becomes common to a language, group of people or culture.	My mom is going to hit the roof. It's raining cats and dogs. We don't see eye to eye. I've gotta keep my nose to the grindstone. Please stop your clowning around. Make sure you keep your cool.
Metaphor and Simile	A word or phrase is applied to something it usually is not related to; the relationship is symbolic. Similes are often introduced by "like" or "as".	I'm drowning in money. He's a diamond in the rough. He's pretty green. The sun is like a yellow ball of fire in the sky. That's east as pie. He's as gentle as a lamb.
Personification	Giving a non-human thing human qualities.	The stuffed bear smiled as the little boy hugged him. The rain kissed my cheeks as it fell. The car engine coughed and sputtered.

The child is helped to use a 'filter' for detecting figurative language. It is an analytical flowchart to help the child respond to yes/no questions to identify the presence of figurative language and then respond appropriately to it. The flowchart is shown in Figure 6.25.

The first stage is intended to signal to the child if the words or phrase might be an instance of figurative language. The simple question is: are there some words that do not seem to fit with what the person is talking about? If the answer is "no", just keep the conversation going. If the answer is "yes", then move on to the next question.

The next stage in the filter asks if the idea seems stupid or unlikely. If the answer is "yes", then it is likely an instance of figurative language which should not be interpreted literally.

The next stage will help the child deal with the figurative language more appropriately. It asks if the child knows the meaning of all of the words in the phrase. If he does not know what a word or words mean, he is prompted to request clarification. For example, if he hears "mind your manners" and is not sure what "mind" means or what exactly the word "manners" includes, he needs to ask what the other person means.

In the next stage, if the child understands all of the words, he is asked to make a picture in his head. This will help him visualize the relationship amongst the words. Then, the child needs to determine if most of the words refer to something positive or negative. In the example of 'hitting the roof', hitting anything is probably not a positive thing. This will lead the child to respond with something like "oh dear" because the analysis showed that the figurative language referred to something negative that was going to be done by the person. Examples of these analyses are shown in Table 6.5.

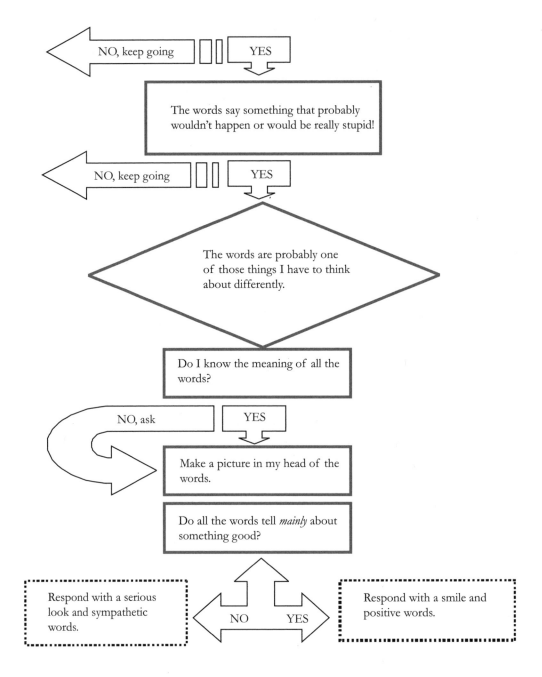

Figure 6.25 Decision filter for detecting and responding to figurative language

Table 6.5 Examples of figurative language and analyses

Examples of figurative Language	Stage: Make a picture	Stage: Mainly good?
Hyperbole: Mile-high pie.		Some people really like pie. The pie is huge so some people would be happy. That's a good thing.
Idioms: It's raining cats and dogs.		That's weird to have cats and dogs falling from the sky. They would break my umbrella. I don't think I would like that so it's not a good thing.
Metaphors/Similes: He's as gentle as a lamb.		Lambs are just babies. They are pretty cute and playful. They probably wouldn't hurt anybody. Gentle as a lamb is probably a good thing.
Personification: The car engine coughed and spluttered.		When I have a cough, I feel really bad. I bet the car is sick. That's not a good thing.

Checkpoint for dealing with figurative language: What *Learning Preferences and Strengths* did we incorporate?						
	Introversion	Sensing	Thinking	Judging	Visual-Spatial	Musical-Rhythmic
	✓	✓	✓	✓	✓	
Challenge:	Intuiting				Verbal-Linguistic Interpersonal	

Notes: Teaching and guiding the child to deal with figurative language stretches the *Learning Preferences and Strengths* in the following ways:

- *Intuiting* – people with an Intuiting preference tend to see the big picture. By prompting the child to determine if a statement is an instance of figurative language, he is being pressed to look at a broader linguistic concept.

- *Verbal-Linguistic* – people with Verbal-Linguistic strengths use words to think and remember. The child is required to process verbal information selectively, retain it and then analyze it in order to determine if it is an instance of figurative language. Then he uses this information to adjust how he responds.

- *Interpersonal* – the person with Interpersonal strengths has the ability to understand the feelings and thoughts of others. By the child's trying to determine if the other person's statement is an instance of figurative language, he is being pressed to understand the other person's thinking and/or intention.

Learning to detect and respond to real friends

One large concern about children with autism is their potential to be victimized by others. Children with autism tend to be very honest and fair-minded people and they typically assume others will be the same. Therefore, it is critical that we help the child understand the difference between a real friend and someone who may try to 'use' him or hurt him. The original idea was presented in a workshop by the Geneva Centre for Autism from Toronto, Canada.

Table 6.6 Detecting real friends

Real friend	Pretend friend	NOT a friend
Acts the same way with you as he does with all his friends.	Acts differently with you than he does with other people.	Ignores you most of the time.
Acts like he is happy to see you.	Sometimes acts like he is happy to see you but other times he does not want to talk to you.	Talks about mistakes you made and tells other people about your mistakes.
Asks you to do things with him and to help out.	Asks you to do things he doesn't want to do.	Asks you to do things you should not do.
May try to protect you from problems.	May say he doesn't want to be your friend if you don't do or say what he wants.	May try to make fun of you and say mean things about you to other people.

Carefully review each characteristic in Table 6.6 with the child. Make sure the child understands the words and concepts. You may wish to change some of the wording to help the child understand. Act out different scenarios that are examples of each characteristic but be cautious about depicting negative behaviors as some children will become overfocused on them.

Once the child has learned about real friends, pretend friends and not-a-friend, he needs to learn how to deal effectively with each type. Table 6.7 sets out some guidelines. Discuss and define each feature with the child. The notion of paying attention to your real friend will need to have clear guidelines of how much attention is enough and how much is too much. That is, help the child understand the difference between being friendly versus what might appear to be 'stalking'. It is usually best to spell out very specifically what the child should do, such as in terms of how many times to call them on the phone each day. For the "Pretend friend" and "Not a Friend", the child should be coached to try ignoring them as the first step rather than running immediately to an adult. The goal in all of the child's programming is to help him become as self-sufficient as possible. However, if the other child continues to 'bug' him, he should be encouraged to seek adult assistance.

Table 6.7 How can I act with a...

Real friend	Pretend friend	NOT a friend
Pay attention to him the same way he pays attention to me. Listen to him.	Tell him if he said something that is unfair or mean.	Ignore him and talk to an adult if the not-a-friend keeps trying to bug you.
Say "thank you" to his compliments and for helping me.	Say "no thanks" and ignore him.	Ignore him and walk away. Talk to an adult if the not-a-friend keeps trying to bug you.

Checkpoint for detecting and responding to real friends: What *Learning Preferences and Strengths* did we incorporate?							
	Introversion	Sensing	Thinking	Judging	Visual-Spatial	Musical-Rhythmic
			✓	✓	✓	
Challenge:	Intuiting Feeling				Interpersonal	

Notes: Teaching and guiding the child to detect and respond to real friends stretches the *Learning Preferences and Strengths* in the following ways:

- *Intuiting* – people with an Intuiting preference tend to see the big picture. By prompting the child to determine if a person is a real friend or not, he is being pressed to look at broader concepts.

- *Feeling* – people with Feeling preferences value others' needs and try to meet them. The issue of real friends prompts the child to consider others' intentions for interacting with him.

- *Interpersonal* – the person with Interpersonal strengths has the ability to understand the feelings and thoughts of others. In determining if the other person is a real friend or not, the child is being pressed to try to understand the other person's thinking and/or intentions.

Chapter 7

Program Process

MEDIATED LEARNING

The over-riding goal of the *Learning Preferences and Strengths (LPS)* program is to help children with autism develop the skills and strategies needed to continue learning on their own. The program enhances the child's cognitive growth and his ability to adapt to changing situations and demands. The self-limiting learning style of the child with autism is well-recognized. Our job is to engage him, draw him out and extend his abilities.

The process used for instruction is one of mediating learning rather than simply 'teaching.' Mediation of learning is a strikingly different dynamic process, compared to teaching for the simple transfer of information, facts and skills. Mediation activates learners and teaches them how to learn so they become increasingly self-motivated and autonomous.

When I was first introduced to the Mediated Learning Experience, developed by Reuven Feuerstein, a visionary Israeli psychologist, I experienced a large cognitive stretch. I was not used to thinking in terms of the 'big picture' of learning. I struggled with the concepts and assumptions of mediated learning but, with time and experience, I improved in my ability to mediate effectively. The empowerment and growth I was able to activate in the children was striking.

Through mediated learning, the adult strives to help the learner understand and deal more effectively with the world and with other people. Mediators within the *LPS* model include all adults helping the child develop and learn. Older siblings and other children can also develop skills for mediating learning. Mediated learning is a natural part of typical interactions between parent and child but here it is made more intensive, intentional and explicit. The mediator acts as:

- a filter who helps sift through and select important information

- an interpreter, guide and elaborater to help the child derive rules and principles beyond the 'here and now'

- a catalyst to help arouse curiosity and interest in the child

- a bridge to connect new learning with current knowledge and to other situations and tasks.

Noting and understanding regularities, patterns and predictability in the world are central to a mediational approach to teaching. The adult helps the child filter and select meaningful and understandable information, interpret that information and elaborate on it. The child is an active participant who is consistently challenged at a level that prompts him to develop new knowledge and skills. The child is enticed to explore and learn and he is 'stretched' from what he typically does to what he is capable of doing. Such a relationship between child and mediator requires both careful selection of tasks as well as a trusting relationship with the adult.

(in effective learning environments) Children's curiosity and persistence are supported by adults who direct their attention, structure their experiences, support their learning attempts, and regulate the complexity and difficulty levels of information for them. (Bransford *et al.* 2000, p.101)

The mediator is also a 'bridge' between the child and the world. Generalization is made explicit in mediated learning such that the child is guided to determine other settings and tasks where concepts, rules and strategies can be used. Bridging helps the child understand how learning principles can be extended into daily situations.

Mediation is a highly verbal process in which key elements and features are labeled. Mediators talk about the important features and processes, the rules and regularities and the connections. However, this does not mean that the child is bombarded with talking. The amount of talking is geared to the needs and tolerance of each child. Key messages are supported by visual cues, such as printed symbols and words when and where needed. In the early stages, short simple phrases are used with the child. As the child grows and develops, these key phrases are extended to more complex discussions. Mediators do not have 'cognitive secrets'. They make explicit what the child is experiencing and what learning processes are taking place.

At the end of this chapter will be a Checkpoint. This will be used to summarize the *Learning Preferences and Strengths* incorporated within the strategies and provide any needed explanations. In addition, other preferences and strengths not typical to children with autism will be noted and described as Challenges.

SEVEN PILLARS OF MEDIATED LEARNING

Over the years, I developed a set of seven features or pillars of the mediated learning experience that are critical to advancing development in children with autism. These pillars form essential underpinnings to the child's learning experience.

When using the Seven Pillars of Learning, the mediator takes on the following major roles:

- designing tasks and the learning experience

- leading and facilitating the learning process

- enhancing the child's awareness of himself and of the process of learning

- building on or neutralizing prior knowledge and experience

- nurturing and engaging the child's preferences, strengths and interests.

The Seven Pillars of Learning include those shown in Figure 7.1: Shared Participation, Reciprocity, Meaningfulness, Feeling of Competence, sense of Mastery and Control, Metacognition and Learning Processes.

The first five pillars center on social-emotional aspects of learning, acknowledging the importance of the affective side of education. Cooperation, sense of belonging and self-confidence are central to Shared Participation and Reciprocity. Meaningfulness provides the 'hook' for learning to help intrigue and engage the child and make learning more fun. Feeling of Competence and Mastery and Control provide the child with a sense of power and competence in ways that support educational and developmental goals. The remaining two pillars are more cognitive in nature. Metacognition helps the child develop autonomy and self-evaluation which ultimately lead to a sense of freedom and competence in learning. He is helped to develop problem-solving, critical thinking and creative thought. Learning Processes focus on the child's

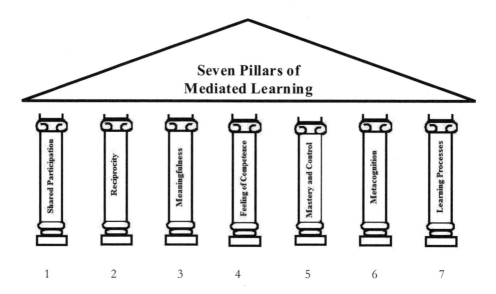

Figure 7.1 Seven pillars of mediated learning

understanding of the need for effort in learning and tolerance for repetition in order to achieve mastery.

All seven pillars work to enhance and extend the typical *Learning Preferences and Strengths* of children with autism. The role of the mediator and of the child will be defined for each of the pillars. A description of how the implementation of each of these features should feel, sound and look is also included.

1. Shared Participation

Shared Participation refers to the greater equality the child plays in the teaching/learning process using a mediational approach. Through Shared Participation, the child is drawn into the center of the learning process. The child is prompted to be an active participant and not just the passive recipient of information and knowledge. This helps the child develop a sense of cooperation, belonging and connection with the mediator and the learning process. The child also learns to trust his own abilities and develop a sense of optimism about learning.

Mediator role. Before attempting Shared Participation, the adult must carefully observe the child's verbal and nonverbal 'messages' in order to identify how the child typically exhibits participation. This is the starting point from which to grow and expand.

The mediator engages the child directly to think about and solve problems on his own and to draw on previous experiences and knowledge. He helps the child focus and maintain attention to the task or experience, enticing the child into the center of the learning process. The child is helped to persist with tasks and to overcome obstacles; that is, develop frustration tolerance. The child must sense that there is nothing he can say or do that will make you reject him; you may disagree but he can always trust you. He is provided with an environment that permits the dignity of risk.

Child role. Through Shared Participation, the child learns to trust the adult and feel comfortable in 'guessing' or giving a 'stab' at a task. He begins to view the adult as someone who is consistently willing and able to assist him. He knows the adult will encourage and assist him if and when needed. The child must clearly understand that he is expected to participate and be receptive to other people's ideas and to new experiences.

Feel. The adult provides social, cognitive and emotional support to the child. The 'feel' of the relationship is that both people are on a quest together, with neither having 'the' answer or solution to the present situation. The child must be consistently given the message that he is accepted and valued as a human being and as a learner. He must also know that he is safe and that you will not just leave him hanging. You will help him overcome obstacles and feel supported in his learning. On the other hand, the child must be given the message that he is expected to participate in the learning activities.

Sound. The term "we" is used a great deal to ensure the notion of sharing is consistently incorporated. For example, the adult says, "Oh my gosh, look what we've got here!" which are words to focus and engage the child. The adult then can proceed to: "What do you think we're supposed to do here?" and perhaps "That looks pretty tricky but we've got good brains." If you see other possible solutions to a task, use statements such as: "We seem to disagree on how we see the problem. Maybe we could look at it this way?" These last statements engage the child and give him a sense of competence while prompting him to try different approaches when needed.

Look. In order to achieve Shared Participation, the learning environment needs to be predictable and well-organized. Once the child has become familiar with the expectations and activities and he learns to trust the adult, his participation will increase dramatically. The 'look' of Shared Participation is the mediator and child head-to-head puzzling over a task, activity or experience.

2. Reciprocity

Reciprocity refers to the dynamic back and forth connection between the mediator and child. The adult–learner relationship is a dynamic one where both influence each other and learn from each other. One person can influence more than the other at times and they balance each other at other times.

Mediator role. The adult's goal is to stretch the child's thinking and learning beyond the present point. Sometimes, it means backing up a bit to re-establish important underpinnings, including a trusting relationship with the child. The adult must consistently make judgements about the child's learning in order to ensure that his experience is neither too easy nor too difficult.

The adult must also help the child reduce impulsiveness and sustain his effort with a task or experience. This means that the adult will help the child reduce defensiveness and negative feelings as well as to model self-reflection when approaching and attempting a task.

The adult must be open to new experiences or new 'twists' on experiences. Be prepared to answer questions from the child even if they are unexpected. This is an opportunity to model self-reflection like, "Gee, let me think a minute about that." It is also a chance to ask the child for more information and to provide feedback to him.

Child role. The child develops a sense of his own ability to influence others within a 'true' reciprocal relationship. The child also continues to learn that the adults will support his attempts; he is not in a 'sink or swim' relationship. At the same time, he must learn that he is expected to strive for the best he can do.

Feel. There should be a calm sense of action–reaction. The adult must form a positive trusting relationship with the child. The child must sense that the adult will gently stretch his thinking as well as support him. Careful observations of the child will allow you to develop an understanding of his signs and signals of learning versus stress.

The 'feel' of Reciprocity is also one of expectation. Each participant is expected to be engaged, providing and seeking information where and when necessary. The child should learn also that his actions influence others and he is an agent of change.

The child should feel a sense of competency and self-determination as learning proceeds. In addition, the child develops an understanding of the amount of effort he needs to provide in order to learn.

Sound. The majority of sounds emitting from a reciprocal relationship are positive and joyful. Reciprocity can be totally nonverbal or highly verbal, dependent on the child, the task or activity and the setting. For example, when playing in a sand or rice table, children are typically quite silent and are often not interested in others' talk.

Look. The 'look' to Reciprocity is that of a finely choreographed dance. The adult and child become partners within the learning/teaching process where the adult leads the child some of the time but changes directions or motions in response to the child. The 'look' also is one of rapt attention where both partners are concentrating to the exclusion of everything else.

3. Meaningfulness

Meaningfulness refers to helping the child understand the purpose, importance and value of a task or activity and how the concepts, ideas or information may relate to his interests and experiences. The child's personal interest areas are included in the curriculum whenever and wherever possible. This process helps make the learning personally relevant to the child as well as fun. Meaningfulness acts as a 'hook' to draw the child into a task or experience. Then the application of the curriculum is stressed so that the child can see the real-world connections.

Mediator role. The adult tries to inspire wonder and curiosity in the child. The child's interests and preferences are incorporated into learning situations and tasks so that they are more meaningful to him. The adult asks questions to encourage the child to think and prompts the child to ask questions. The child is also asked to provide his own thoughts about why it is important to learn about the task or experience.

The adult must help the child understand the reasoning behind learning. The adult acts to make the information, concepts and ideas explicit. Statements like "we work systematically so we don't miss anything" and "We can learn to count so we can figure out how many dinosaurs you have" are examples of making the process and content explicit and meaningful to the child.

Bridging is critical to the mediated learning experience. The adult systematically helps the child connect learning to other situations at school, at home, in other important settings as well as into the future. Bridging is one of the most important ways to promote transfer of learning.

Child role. The child should have a sense of adventure and excitement about the task or experience. It is important for the adult to know the level of stimulation needed by and tolerable to the child so that an optimal level is reached and maintained.

Feel. The 'feel' is positive forward-moving energy and interest on the part of both individuals. The child is comforted and alerted by the inclusion of his high interest areas.

Sound. The child is always given a rationale for the task and the way it is approached. The adult 'hooks' the child by including areas of keen interest and helps him understand why he should be interested in the learning aspect of the task. This needs to be imparted explicitly to the child as well as eliciting from him how he thinks the information could be helpful.

Look. The 'look' of Meaningfulness is relaxed focus on the task or experience and motivation to engage in the activities.

4. Feeling of Competence

Feeling of Competence refers to ensuring the child thinks positively about himself as a learner and feels he is good at what he is trying to do. He must develop a sense of his own power and competence as a learner. The child is more likely to develop actual competence in learning by reinforcing these feelings. If the child develops a sense of personal competence, he will be more willing to approach new and more difficult tasks where success may not be immediate. He will develop a sense of joy and satisfaction in learning.

Mediator role. The mediator must explicitly support and acknowledge the child's competence and abilities. Statements such as "you really thought hard about that one" and "you have a really good brain" are examples. As the child proceeds with learning, the adult should ask the child how well he thought he did and prompt the child to rate his own performance. Both accurate and less accurate performance should be gently challenged with questions, like: "That was a good idea, how come you did it that way?"; you will note that the statement gave the child positive feedback first so that he does not become defensive. Through this process of asking the child to explain his approach to tasks, we learn more about his thinking and he will begin to rely more on his own thoughts and feelings.

Errors by anyone should be looked at as opportunities for learning. The adult could say things such as "I think I made a mistake. We won't worry. Let's see how it happened," and seize the chance to learn from the error. The adult must be willing to admit his own ignorance about some things and/or his own errors. If the child's idea does not 'fit' with the adult's, the adult needs to provide positive feedback (e.g. "that's an interesting idea") and then pursue the child's thought processes. More often than not, the child did make some connection to the lesson or topic at hand but it was not initially apparent to the adult. If, indeed, the child was completely off-topic, he is still viewed as competent but his brain may have gotten 'distracted'. The child himself is not in error but parts of him (brain, eyes, hands, ears) can go astray.

Child role. The child must learn to respect and trust both his own and the adult's judgement. We want him to be motivated toward achieving personal competence and not just by completing tasks or being rewarded for his work.

The child must also learn to trust himself and be willing to try more difficult and new tasks. An important issue is for the child to learn that mistakes mean that he and his brain are learning. This optimism should pervade every aspect of learning.

An occupational therapist was working with some children with autism on riding bicycles. Over time, the children increased in their independence but still experienced occasional tumbles. Any time a child wobbled or bumped himself, the therapist would exclaim, "Oh, you are learning. When you have an accident that means your body is learning how to ride the bike." One of the boys took a little tumble a few days later and, over tears and a proud smile, announced "I'm learning!"

Feel. The 'feel' is one of mutual trust and open and honest feedback among participants.

Sound. On a frequent basis, the child needs to hear exactly what he did well and that he has the ability to do many things in this world. There are simply no 'wrong' or 'bad' answers or ideas. To children with autism, praise should state specifically which aspect of their performance was done well. Using sweeping statements like "you are wonderful" without specific information about his performance could arouse distrust in the child.

Look. Increasingly, the child should exhibit more relaxed approaches to tasks and willingness to try things by himself. The child looks like he is alerting himself and approaching tasks with greater confidence and self-assurance.

5. Sense of Mastery and Control

Sense of Mastery and Control refers to the child's developing an understanding of his own learning strengths and preferences and how he has the ability to master a task and an area of learning. He also learns that he has power to make good learning choices and begins to develop a sense of responsibility for himself and his learning.

Mediator role. A sense of Mastery and Control is achieved by setting up a learning environment that supports the child's learning preferences and strengths, including those described in Chapter 5, **Program Structure**. The adult–child relationship helps stretch and challenge the child's abilities and knowledge. The adult provides the child with a sense of control by arranging schedules and tasks so that the child can have some 'say' about the tasks and activities he will be doing and/or the order in which he does them. The 'actual' control the child is allowed to have is up to the adult. For example, I typically indicate to the child that I would like us to do three things. I then lay out three picture or word cards and ask the child to decide the order of activities. This really constitutes a minor concession to the child but it provides him with a positive sense of control.

An important role of the adult is to help the child strive for mastery and to develop a sense of the effort needed to achieve it. We want to develop a sense of 'there, it's done! I did it all by myself!' in each child. This will start with relatively small, 'easy' tasks but, over time, the complexity and difficulty will increase and the child will be helped to rise to the challenge.

Child role. The child should feel that he has some 'say' in what is done and how it is done. As described above, the 'say' can be in making small decisions but the child must have a sense that what he does and says can have an impact.

The child must also learn to strive for mastery. Mastery occurs where, after effort and practice, the child's knowledge and skills come together. If the child is provided with well-organized and sufficiently challenging tasks, he will begin to learn the amount of effort that is needed for learning. The child will come to enjoy complexity and greater challenges, viewing them as hurdles he can surmount rather than barriers.

The child should become increasingly aware of the improvements he is making in learning and ascribe these changes to his own knowledge and effort. Interestingly, people with learning disabilities often perceive learning in others as 'magical' and requiring no effort. They do not realize that others use strategies to help themselves learn. The person with learning disabilities does not recognize this and assumes learning is effortless for everyone except him. Children with autism are likely to have the same misconception if we do not help them develop a sense of the effort, precision and knowledge needed for learning.

Feel. The 'feel' in this situation is one of 'I can do it' and 'wow, I did it!' Initially, the accomplishments may be small but the feeling of Mastery and Control is strong.

Sound. The sound arising from this learning process is one of shared effort and joy. The child is encouraged with statements such as: "It's a little bit tricky but you can use your good brain," and "I saw you stop and think about that one and you did it! Well done, you worked and thought hard and you did it."

Look. The 'look' of Mastery and Control is independence and pride. The child takes over increasing responsibility for his learning and does so with confidence.

6. Metacognition

Metacognition refers to understanding your own thinking in terms of what it means to learn. It includes planning, monitoring and revising your approach. Metacognition also involves reflecting on your learning strengths and needs, what works for you and when and where you need to use strategies. Thinking is emphasized throughout all programming and interactions within the *LPS* model to help each child learn to direct his own cognitive efforts. The goal is to help the child develop more autonomy and freedom in learning.

Mediator role. The adult's job is to help the child understand the overall thinking and learning that he has gained from an experience or task. That means that we make the child's thinking explicit so that he can learn to evaluate and manage his own learning. The adult prompts the child to understand that he has control over his thinking and that he can control the processes necessary for learning such as remembering, concentrating, memorizing and guessing.

The adult explicitly models and discusses the thinking that is happening and the processing required. These can start off with very simple language and actions like: "Okay, brain you need to think," while pointing to your temple. Increasingly, the language and concepts become more complex like: "Wow, I really got distracted there. I need to tell my brain just to ignore that silly noise and keep thinking," and "That's too hard for me. Oops, just a minute, I've got a good brain. I just need to take my time and think hard." The child will pick up on these models and start imitating your words and actions.

Child role. The child is initially expected to attend to your modeling and then attempt to imitate your words and actions. With enough consistency on the adult's part, children typically start imitating within a short period of time. They also will start generalizing to other settings and tasks. Over time, the child will internalize the metacognitive strategies and use them spontaneously.

Incrementally, the child learns to reflect on what he knows, what he does not know, what he needs to learn and what the task demands are. He becomes aware of what he learned, how easy or difficult a task was, how he could do better next time, whether he needs some help and how he felt about his learning. The child will learn to ask himself questions like "What am I doing?", "Why am I doing this?", "How does it (this approach) help me?" and "How could I do better next time?"

The child learns to understand his own abilities and mental processes. He also begins to attribute success or failure to his own actions, intentions and beliefs. The child starts to understand he can control the conditions needed for learning by practising, rehearsing, participating actively and using his learning strengths.

Feel. The 'feel' is one of the child's sensing the power of his own brain and his ability to learn. It is a positive and directed energy, like when a forward gear is engaged in a car.

Sound. The 'sound' is highly verbal during introduction and practice of the concept and strategies. If the child is low verbal, many of the metacognitive strategies can be depicted visually for him to select and use.

Look. The 'look' is one of confidence and increasing autonomy. The child is seen to plan and sequence his own work, monitor his progress, assess his own performance and seek help when needed. He is also observed to apply the strategies he has learned in different settings and with different tasks.

7. Learning Processes

 Learning Processes are the mental activities we use to help make our learning more effective and efficient. The framework for learning is an information-processing model. This model is useful for depicting the multiple factors involved in learning and in higher-order thinking skills. Like a computer, a person's mind is depicted as taking in information, performing operations on it to change its form and content, storing and locating it and generating responses to it. The three main phases of information processing are shown in Figure 7.2.

Skills discussed in this section will focus on helping the child's:

- *intake* of information, including perceiving it through the senses or modalities, such as sight, hearing, feel and movement

- *integration and elaboration* of the information, connecting it with other things he knows and storing the information, and

- *output* or expression of knowledge which involves retrieving the information and planning and expressing thinking and reasoning.

For example, at the Intake phase, children with autism tend to have difficulty shifting attention and in determining what information is most relevant and important. They may try to take in all of the information available and become overloaded. On the other hand, the child may take in a piece of information that is not central to the present task and respond based on that information. Challenges are also found at the stages of Integration and Expression. Because of this, Learning Processes are consistently targeted and emphasized during activities and experiences with the child. The goal is to help the child develop more effective modes of thinking, learning and problem solving. A form for observing how a child approaches tasks and activities is included in Appendix III. This form will help you determine areas that need attention in terms of program content. It can also be used to monitor the child's progress in developing learning skills.

Mediator role. The adult helps the child learn how to manage his thinking, efforts and time in order to persist with tasks and to use flexible approaches. The child's learning experiences are mediated so he can 'extract' the main principles. The adult models statements about the principles and learning strategies to help the child learn and solidify them and their rationale.

The child is exposed to a balance of specific examples and general principles during tasks and experiences. The adult does not use directive approaches to 'teaching' the child; instead, she provides guidance to aid the child's understanding of his taking in, integrating and expressing information and ideas as described in Chapter 6, **Program Content**.

Child role. The child is closely engaged in the process so that his depth of understanding of learning principles and strategies is enhanced. He develops an understanding of his own learning preferences and strengths and his challenges. He also learns to identify central and secondary information and what may be confusing to him. The child is helped to monitor his progress and persist with or change his approach.

The child is engaged in discerning ways of thinking and learning that can be used in a variety of different settings. The child is armed with ways to continue on his own to learn new things. He can then apply the processes to different content in a variety of subjects and to a wide range of settings.

Feel. The 'feel' of Learning Processes is consistently cognitive and factual. Emphasis is placed on the learning and cognitive resources needed to deal effectively with tasks and experiences and to derive strategies and principles from them. There is no sense of 'failure'; not being able to complete a task accurately is viewed by both participants as an opportunity for learning.

Sound. The 'sound' is positive information sharing between the participants, focused on advancing the child's understanding of himself as a learner.

Look. The 'look' of Learning Processes is a shared quest of both the child and mediator trying to understand how to tackle a learning task or experience.

WAYS TO BEGIN MEDIATING

The Seven Pillars of Mediated Learning are an integral part of interactions with the child. The previous section provided overviews of participant roles and how the mediation feels, sounds and looks. If you review Chapter 6, **Program Content**, you will note the inclusion and integration of the pillars in the procedures and strategies described. The 'art' of mediational learning requires not only these procedures and strategies but also careful attention to the concepts described in the present chapter.

You will begin including mediational approaches as you implement program content. It is not until you become comfortable and fluent in both program structure and content that you will be able to start focusing on refining your skills in creating a mediated learning experience for the child. Be patient with yourself. You cannot expect immediate facility at being a mediator of learning. When you watch an expert, like Reuven Feuerstein mediation looks so easy and simple. When you try it yourself, you will find that it is much more complex and multi-faceted. A great deal of practice, thought and feedback is needed to become an effective mediator.

As noted previously, the majority of the pillars focus on the affective side of learning for the child. An essential part of mediation is gaining and maintaining the child's sense of trust in the adults helping him learn. This requires the adult to demonstrate acceptance of the child for who he is, solid reliability, openness and honesty and careful alignment between his actions and beliefs. These features were captured in the preceding discussion of the pillars and are incorporated into all interactions with the child.

Supporting adult–child interactions

In the early stages of working with a child with autism, ensuring trust within mediational interactions is critical. The child must learn that he is expected to respond to comments and questions but that the adult will support his efforts. A framework for doing this is presented in Table 7.1.

After the adult asks a question or makes a comment to which the child is expected to respond, the most important 'gift' to the child is time. Allow the child extended time to process the information.

If the child does not respond at all or responds in an incomplete or inaccurate manner, the adult takes responsibility by repeating the question or comment. The child is provided with positive encouragement for any attempts. It is heartbreaking to see any child 'shut down' by an adult who does not give the child a chance to respond and does not attempt to engage the child and make sense of his attempts.

Give him credit for attempts and praise him for any positive aspects of his response. Find any part of what he did that even indicated he was engaged. For example, you may comment on how he seemed to be thinking hard or looking carefully.

The expected response is then modeled for the child and practiced with him so he can experience greater success next time. Support for his sense of Mastery and Control, feelings of competence and shared participation is crucial to his learning and his development of trust.

Table 7.1 Ways to develop and support child interactions

Adult asks a question or makes a comment	Explanation
1. Provide time for the child to process the information and formulate his response.	Pause to allow the child time to answer. Humans typically expect a response within three to five seconds and become restless after that.
	Protect the child by simply waiting, sometimes up to several minutes. You may also protect his place in conversation by reminding others whose turn it is: "It is Bobby's turn right now." This provides a good opportunity for others to learn patience and respect while the child is given a sense of acceptance and that he can rely on you to help protect his rights.

If the child does not respond within 10 to 15 seconds or does not respond in a complete and accurate manner, move to Step 2.

Table 7.1 continued

2. Restate the question.	Ask the question a second time, giving the child the benefit of re-hearing what was said as well as the benefit of longer processing time.

If the child still does not respond or does not respond in a complete and accurate manner, move on to step 3.

3. Rephrase the question.	Use different words and shorter sentences that might help the child understand and may increase the probability of a response or more complete answer.

If the child still does not respond or does not respond in a complete and accurate manner, move on to step 4.

4. Provide guidance.	Give the child direct hints and clues. This can include pointing to the object he is supposed to name, reminding him of a previous response or experience or providing him with the first sound of the word.

If the child still does not respond or does not respond in a complete and accurate manner, move on to step 5.

5. Provide a model for imitation.	Provide a model for the child so he can learn what is expected. Phrasing the model in the form of "you could say …" allows him to preserve some dignity. Then ask him to say all or part of your model and praise him for his effort.

Asking questions to stretch learning

A central mediational approach for developing metacognition and learning processes is asking questions of the child. By asking questions, the adult can help the child take in new knowledge, assimilate it into things he already knows and change his knowledge with the addition of the new information.

The mediator's role is also to elicit evidence of the child's thinking as well as to help the child develop new rules. One of the best ways to do this is with 'process' questions. They are questions that cannot be answered with a simple "yes" or "no" or other brief responses. Process questions act as 'thinking starters' that enhance and solidify learning.

The step from reinforcing any attempts at responding to expecting the child to answer process questions is large. There are important steps in between that can support his sense of trust while stretching his thinking and verbal language skills. Below and in Table 7.2 is a continuum of different adult mediational responses that can progressively elevate the child's learning to higher levels of abstraction.

At Level 1, the child's learning is confirmed and continues to be at a concrete level. For example, the child is told "That's right. That is a dog."

Level 2 responses from the adult raise the child's learning from the immediate concrete experience to thinking about and expressing his knowledge. Process questions that facilitate this type of learning include:

- How did you do that?

- How did you know it's right?

- Why is that important?

- Why is this one not okay?

Level 3 elevates this further by prompting the child to think and express his ideas about the important characteristics of an entire category of information. Example process questions are:

- How is that the same as/different from…?

- What should you do after…?

- How did you know that is the best one?

- Why is this better than that one?

Level 4 responses prompt the child to think analytically and creatively. The child is asked to think hypothetically in a 'what-if', 'how-else' manner. Sample process questions include:

- Where else would you…?

- How else could you…?

- When else might you…?

- Why do we…?

At Level 5, the child is prompted to think at a higher level which involves more global analysis. He is asked to determine overall rules, strategies and principles involved in the learning. Sample questions are:

- What if we…?

- How else could you…?

- What would happen if…?

- What else could you…?

Table 7.2 Continuum of levels of learning and abstraction based on adult responses

Level of child learning and abstraction	Adult response to child's comments of question	Child learning
Level 1	Acknowledge and/or summarize what the child says. Example: "That does look like a British Rail Class 153 DMU."	The others are listening to me and what I say is important. He may learn no new information but is encouraged in his attempts at communicating.
Level 2	Encourage the child to elaborate on his response. Example: "How do you know that is a British Rail Class 153 DMU?"	Learns others are interested in his knowledge. Learns to think beyond the 'here and now' and to justify and solidify his knowledge by verbalizing it.
Level 3	Encourage the child to generate alternatives and think of ways to compare them. Example: "What makes that train different from other ones?"	Learns others are interested in his knowledge and to think beyond the 'here and now'. Learns about important features of different alternatives.
Level 4	Encourage child to form hypotheses. Example: "What would happen if we changed the colors of that train?"	Learns to think beyond the 'here and now'. Learns how to think analytically and creatively by hypothesizing, generating alternatives and evaluating them.
Level 5	Encourage child to derive overall rule or principle. Example: "When else would you...?"	Learns to look at the process he is using to learn and extend it to other settings or situations.

Checkpoint for program processes: What *Learning Preferences and Strengths* did we incorporate?							
		Introversion	Sensing	Thinking	Judging	Visual-Spatial	Musical-Rhythmic
			✓	✓	✓	✓	
Challenge:	Extraversion	Intuiting	Feeling		Verbal-Linguistic Interpersonal Intrapersonal		

Notes: Teaching and guiding the child through mediating his learning experiences challenges *Learning Preferences and Strengths* in the following ways:

- *Extraversion* – people with an Extraversion preference tend to think out loud and respond more quickly to others. By prompting the child to share participation in tasks and experiences and to explain his thinking and reasoning, he is being pressed to become more immediately responsive to others around him.

- *Intuiting* – people with Intuiting preferences are able to see the larger scope of an issue and the over-riding concepts. The mediation process stretches the child to look beyond the details of a situation or task and begin to understand the wider implications and principles.

- *Feeling* – people with Feeling preferences value others' needs and want to meet them. Expecting shared participation and reciprocity from the child presses him to consider and respond to others' actions and interactions.

- *Verbal-Linguistic* – people with Verbal-Linguistic strengths use words to think and remember. The child is prompted to respond to others during interactions with them and express his thinking and reasoning.

- *Logical-Mathematical* – people with Logical-Mathematical strengths enjoy forming hypotheses, developing paradigms and building arguments. As the child is prompted to be a more active and analytical learner, Logical-Mathematical abilities are emphasized.

- *Interpersonal* – the person with Interpersonal strengths has the ability to understand the feelings and thoughts of others. By pressing the child to participate in interactions with others, he is being prompted to try to understand the other person's thinking or intention.

- *Intrapersonal* – Intrapersonal strengths involve understanding your strengths and limitations and your ability to apply your thinking. The child is helped to develop more self-awareness of his learning preferences, strengths and challenges within interactions with the mediator.

Chapter 8

Behavior in Children with Autism

WHAT IS BEHAVIOR IN CHILDREN WITH AUTISM?

Behavior is an action or reaction to internal and/or external events, people, objects or stimulation. It is a function of the interaction between the person and the situation.

In all children, behavior is typically either internalized or externalized. Children with autism often experience extreme patterns of internalization you may not notice initially. There may be a lengthy period of time during which the child's internalized behavior builds up. The child may exhibit small changes or symptoms, like adhering more rigidly to routines or increased sucking or chewing of his clothes. Usually, in retrospect, caregivers who know the child well can put the pieces together and recognize when the build up started. With such a protracted time-line, determining the cause or causes can be challenging.

Externalized behavior is usually either self-directed or directed to other people or objects. In children with autism, self-directed behavior can include 'odd' mannerisms, such as handflapping, humming, shrieking or pacing. Some self-directed behaviors can be harmful, such as when the child bites himself or bangs his head.

Externalized behavior can be toward objects or people. Object-related behavior can include throwing things or damaging them, such as tossing a chair or tearing a book. People-related behavior can include scratching, hitting out, pulling the other person's hair or biting them.

After observing and working with many children with autism over the years, I see behavior as neither 'good' nor 'bad' – it is communication. That is, if a child is showing internalized or externalized behaviors, he is telling us something about how he feels or about what is happening around him or what he perceives to be happening.

We, as the adults in the child's life, need to be sensitive to these indicators because he is trying to let us know something is awry.

WHAT IS PROBLEM BEHAVIOR?

When should we consider a behavior to be problematic enough that something should be done? I believe that a problem behavior is one that:

- interferes with the learning and development of the child himself
- interferes with the learning and development of other children
- causes a potentially unsafe situation and/or
- is socially and/or culturally inappropriate or unacceptable.

This definition is much broader than is typically used. It allows the child to behave in 'unconventional' ways so long as they do not meet any or all of the four criteria above. If the child wants to stand while doing a task rather than sitting, it would not meet any of the criteria above and it would be permitted at least in early learning situations. If the child wants to work under his desk or a table, it would be allowed because it does not meet any of the criteria. A child who walks the perimeter of a room on first entering it and then settles to work would be given the opportunity to do so. There are very likely sensory reasons for all of these behaviors. However, if a child is overfocused on chewing his shirt or on loudly singing his favorite song and cannot move on to doing an expected task, these would be considered problem behaviors. Children who grab other children's materials or who scratch other children are considered to have problem behaviors because they interfere with the learning and development of both him and the other children.

In terms of socially-appropriate behavior, it is not up to the therapist, adult, support worker or other hired caregiver to decide what this is. In different cultures, appropriate and/or acceptable behavior is defined quite differently. It is critical that these issues are addressed with the child's parents and they help delineate what is acceptable in different situations within their family life. For example, an issue of major importance may be that the child sit quietly at temple or church or say "please" and "thank you". In other families, these may be of little importance.

The main focus in defining problem behavior is not on the adult's preferences, desires or perceptions. It is of utmost importance in dealing with children with autism to keep your cool and your objectivity. Dr. Carl Haywood (1990), from Vanderbilt University, warned: "recognize that the child's behavior is neither random nor malicious but is motivated by some need, wish or impulse on the part of the child that might be worth considering" (p.8).

Many times I have heard teachers, parents, and caregivers state that a child is being 'manipulative' or 'stubborn' or is 'trying to make my life difficult'. I recall one teacher who told me I should not bother observing a seven-year-old client in her classroom because his only problem was that "he lacked a work ethic". These words were clear indicators of adult frustration.

The behavior is the child's attempt to communicate some need or feeling. It is our role to consider what the child is trying to express. We need to recognize that there is some legitimacy to the child's needs and/or feelings that motivated the behavior. Haywood (1990) stated it very well: "behavior is seldom just plain bad but is more often ill-timed or set in the wrong place or directed inappropriately" (p.8).

One boy I worked with for a few years said to me, "okay, Heather, you f***ing b****" after I asked him to do something. I did not respond other than by moving on to the next task. I had a feeling that, given his family and their values and also the manner in which the child said the words, he had no idea what they meant. Discussing the incident with his mother later, she knew immediately where her son had learned the words. She also agreed with me that her son could have substituted the words "cutie pie" and have intended the same thing as his 'swears'.

It still surprises me sometimes when a child with autism does not understand appropriate situations for different language forms. Caution is required when attempting to use typical society norms for judging behavior in children with autism.

THE RELATIONSHIP BETWEEN BEHAVIOR AND STRESS

The word 'stress' has a negative connotation for most people. Stress is anything that thrills us, worries us, scares us or threatens us. Stress can be a strong motivator and energizer at the appropriate intensity.

With too little stress or energy, a person may feel 'bored'. For the child with autism, if the arousal drops below an optimal level, he will likely seek stimulation from other sources to keep himself alert. It may be in appropriate or inappropriate ways, for example, he may withdraw, start chewing on his shirt or poke another child.

We all learn most optimally when there is a certain amount of stress, stimulation and energy. Optimal levels of stress are dependent on a number of factors, including the following:

- *Child's physical state* – is he well-rested, did he eat within the last two to three hours, is he feeling well, is he wearing comfortable clothing, is he warm or cool enough, is he thirsty, did he have a change in medication or start a new medication? If the child is not feeling comfortable and well, his optimal range is reduced and he more readily enters into distress. Children with autism are especially likely to fall apart if they do not have adequate sleep or food.

- *Adult's physical state* – if the parent, teacher, therapist, or caregiver is tired, hungry, thirsty, or overly warm or cold, this discomfort can be sensed by the child with autism and set him off.

- *Child's emotional state* – this may be related to past history or current events such as if his home life is disrupted or if he woke up feeling 'grouchy'.

- *Adult's emotional state* – children with autism are often 'emotional sponges' who absorb but do not necessarily understand emotions around them. Is the parent, teacher, therapist or caregiver stressed, angry or anxious? All of these will be absorbed by the child and cause him to be agitated.

- *Learning environment* – is it relatively quiet, is it calm? In a calm and secure environment, the child's optimal energy range is expanded.

- *Learning task* – is it new to the child, is it something he has done many times in the past, is it challenging in terms of content or process, does it prompt him to use verbal or fine motor skills that are more difficult for him, is the task too lengthy, does the child fully understand what is being expected of him? If the child has enjoyed and been successful with this sort of task in the past or it is a topic area of interest, the optimal energy range is extended.

With too much stress or stimulation, the child may enter a state of distress which leads to anxiety. Performance and learning will then take a down-turn. Distress is the point at which the child perceives that the demands of the situation exceed his personal resources in terms of time, experience and abilities or skills. The child with autism may shut down, internalize his concerns or act out when he experiences distress.

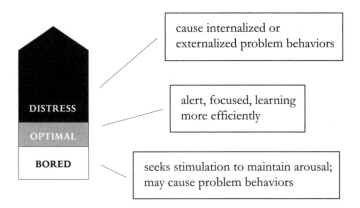

Figure 8.1 Continuum of stress and related behaviours

For individuals with autism, the amount and type of stress and stimulation needed to reach an optimal level is, at least initially, a fairly narrow range as seen in Figure 8.1. That means the transition from under-stimulation to over-stimulation and distress can happen quickly and without much forewarning.

Our goal in working with the child with autism is to help him:

- modulate the amount of stimulation he needs before reaching an optimal level. Some children require intense stimulation, such as motor or sensory activities, in order to alert them for optimal learning. Other children require calming and centering activities to prepare them for learning

- expand his range for optimal learning. This entails reducing both the 'bored' and 'distress' ranges by teaching the child metacognitive strategies for self-regulation

- increase the consistency of his being able to attain and remain within the optimal learning range.

While working with the child with autism, you cannot expect to hold him at the optimal level of performance and arousal for long, at least in the early stages. I use a rule of thumb: initial goals should be to maintain the child's optimal learning level for as many minutes as he is old. With two- to three-year-olds, this is two to three minutes in the early stages of intervention. You may have to start with his remaining on task for a matter of seconds, however.

After each increasingly longer work period, the child needs an opportunity to 'breathe out'. This means the child is helped to cycle through arousal and centering for optimal learning up to the edge of stress and back to a lower arousal level where he can take a breather. During the 'breathing out' period, he can engage in an enjoyable preferred activity before he is expected to work again.

When we work to expand the child's optimal range of learning, there will be frequent times when you have him 'hovering' on the edge of distress. This is often a delicate balance that requires careful sensitivity to things that may 'push him over the edge'. Processes for helping maintain the child within the optimal range are well described in the previous chapter on mediated learning.

STRESSORS IN CHILDREN WITH AUTISM

Stressors are those things that push the child from optimal arousal with high levels of performance and learning to distress and decreasing performance. Optimal arousal is the state in which the child's alertness and focus are such that learning is more effective and efficient. Distress is the state at which the child becomes over-stimulated and/or overwhelmed.

Naomi Quenk (1993, 2000) has performed extensive research into 'type dynamics'. She looked at each of the 16 personality types of the *Myers-Briggs Type Indicator®* and found how different types react to stressors, what their distress reactions are and what resources help them regain a state of equilibrium.

For people with Introversion-Sensing-Thinking-Judging (ISTJ) preferences, like children with autism, stressors tend to be those things that violate their need for clarity, precision, planfulness, logical decision-making and time to warm up to a situation. Strikingly, the stressors Quenk found for ISTJs parallel what I have observed repeatedly in children with autism. They are summarized in Table 8.1 with examples for children with autism.

Individual children will vary in relation to which stressors are their personal 'distress buttons'. Observe the child in different settings to determine which stressors are most likely to trigger him. A form for observing the child is included in Appendix III.

DISTRESS REACTIONS IN CHILDREN WITH AUTISM

Once the child with autism has gone beyond an optimal level of stimulation and has begun to experience stress and anxiety, it is usually not a long way to a 'distress' reaction.

Quenk (1993, 2000) found that typical responses of people with Introversion-Sensing-Thinking-Judging (ISTJ) preferences to high levels of stressors include 'overdoing' their sensing function, either diving into detail or becoming

Table 8.1 Typical stressors for people with Introversion-Sensing-Thinking-Judging preferences

Typical stressors for ISTJ preferences	Examples of stressors for children with autism	
	School	Home
environment is poorly organized	materials, tasks and activity areas are not clearly organized or delineated	personal belongings are not consistently in the same location
tasks are vague with poorly defined standards, expectations, goals, priorities	many options for activities are available; approach and/or goals for tasks are left open-ended; materials for a task are simply laid out in front of the child in no particular order	there is no clear order to tasks or daily life, no agenda
decisions and methods are based on opinion or conjecture rather than reasoning and logic	"I just want you to do it this way."	"do this" (without explanation)
other people's incomplete or imprecise work impacts the quality of his work	part of a craft is not cut out carefully, a word is misspelled or missing	sibling or parent helps with a task but does not do it exactly as the child expects or had in mind
sudden change without forewarning and/or good rationale	"I changed my mind." "We aren't going to do that today after all." A substitute teacher or worker just shows up with no forewarning	adult tells the child they will go shopping later but the car tire is flat or the adult decides to shop another day or at a different store
child is asked to 'wing it' and the reality and facts of the situation are ignored	"Don't worry, it'll be okay this way." "That's good enough." "It doesn't need to be perfect."	the child's shirt is wet or his hands are dirty and he is told to ignore it
new possibilities are presented to the child after he has already made up his mind	"You already started but how about we do it this way?"	"Let's do it tomorrow." "Let's go swimming instead of skating."
too many details or a great deal of data are presented to him all at once	"then we can do this and this and this"	"get your ___, then ___, then ___, then ___"
working too long or too hard	child has spent a long time on one task and still has not completed it to his satisfaction	child has expended a great deal of energy on an activity and is expected to do more
high level of competition	pressing the child to complete a task faster or within a very short time limit	sibling or peer is trying to induce the child to engage in competition for accuracy or speed

overwhelmed by it. They may become highly emotional and begin to panic and 'catastrophize'.

Again, the distress reactions found by Quenk are remarkably similar to those found in children with autism. The child's first response is often overdoing sensing where he mouths or chews objects, spins or paces, flaps his hands, or becomes overfocused on small details. The thinking preference may take a downturn and feelings, often in their rawest forms, emerge with the child's melting down, becoming increasingly rigid and extremely fearful. Quenk's distress reactions for ISTJs are summarized in Table 8.2, along with examples for children with autism.

Individual children will vary in their distress reactions. Observe the child in different settings to determine how he typically reacts to the stressors identified earlier. The form used for observing stressors, distress reactions and calming strategies is included in Appendix III.

REGAINING EQUILIBRIUM IN CHILDREN WITH AUTISM

Quenk (1993, 2000) discovered that people with Introversion-Sensing-Thinking-Judging (ISTJ) preferences tend to become calm again with certain types of help or actions. Quiet, calm assistance, reassurance and quiet time can soothe them. Sometimes, however, they have to play out the stress reaction and 'hit bottom' before being able to regroup and re-emerge.

The calming strategies from Quenk, presented in Table 8.3, are ones we commonly use with children with autism. The strategies help the child regain control of his Sensing function and his ability to deal with details. They involve his using his Introversion function to stop and take some time by himself. There are also attempts to help him see the bigger picture and use his strong Thinking function to consider the situation rationally and objectively.

We developed the acronym RESTORE to help us remember how to assist the child in restoring his equilibrium after or during a stress reaction. The RESTORE process encompasses most of the calming strategies noted above and provides a specific sequence for both the adult and child. The process is summarized in Table 8.3.

Table 8.2 Typical distress reactions for people with Introversion-Sensing-Thinking-Judging (ISTJ) learning preferences

Distress reaction in ISTJ preference	Examples of reactions by children with autism
focus on any act or action that involves touch, taste, smell, movement, hearing or vision	chew clothing, flap hands, suck toys or other objects, pace, bang head
focus doggedly on details and facts	organize and re-organize toys; over-focus on detail or lack of detail on schedule or plan
distrust his understanding of details and have difficulty focusing on relevant information	become upset over trivial things, such as the wrong kind of pencil or crayon; worry about his ability to finish a task
become impulsive and act without thinking	hit, kick, or bite someone else; make hurtful comments to others
experience confusion, anxiety and panic even if appearing outwardly calm and unperturbed	child may appear calm but may start chewing an object, his body may tighten up, his pupils may dilate
become negative, unwilling to tolerate the unknown or the unfamiliar, sometimes being unwilling to accept even known, familiar and enjoyable activities	child does not want to get an ice cream cone that he normally enjoys; refuses or becomes upset at the mention of favorite or familiar things
erupt into extreme, harsh reactions	child has a total melt down
imagine disastrous outcomes and see previously safe places as being dangerous or frightening; 'catastrophizing' like Chicken Little	child fears there are monsters under his bed or bees are everywhere
resist even minor changes in routine, procedures and goals	rejects even fairly innocuous suggestions like: "How about if we color this first?"; "How about we put on your shirt first?"
begin to lose things, blame others for the loss	"I can't find my shoes. They're gone. Somebody took them!"
obsess about things causing stress and be unable to switch off and relax	"it'll never get better"; "he will take my toy again tomorrow"
become very silent and unwilling to talk about stresses	"nothing's wrong"; "let me alone"; hide
try to avoid a stressful situation or task	"I don't want to go to the gym."; run away and hide
blame other people or objects for the difficulty; become suspicious about other people's intentions	"he keeps taking my toys"; "he just wants to take my favorite dinosaur"; "the monster will eat me"; "Heather said I can't do that."

Table 8.2 continued

Typical calming strategies for ISTJ preferences	*Examples for use with children with autism*
unobtrusive help with some of the details and facts that are overwhelming him; organizing and accomplishing small projects or steps	"How about if we do this part tomorrow?"; "How about if you do that part and I'll do the other part?"; covering up or removing parts of a task
time to recognize connections between a new event or activity and other experiences he has had	"The last time this happened, it worked out in the end." "Remember how much fun we had last time?"
getting away from the stressful situation	quiet time in corner, library, tent or his bedroom
time alone in a pleasant sensing environment	swinging on a swing or hammock, playing in a rice table or ball bin; chewing gum or other textured food
specific and concrete validation of his competence and worth	"You have a really good brain but sometimes your eyes forget to look/your hands forget to be gentle."
reminding him of previous positive outcomes	"Remember the last time this happened, you fixed things up really well and did great work."

Table 8.3 The RESTORE process

R	**Relax**, rid yourself of any preconceptions for what reason the child may or may not have for what he is doing or just did – **reframe** the child's behavior in neutral, observable terms.
E	**Empathize** with him and **express** your concern for the child and his feelings.
S	**Soothe** him silently, say little or nothing, hug him, rub his back or whatever soothes him; **sense** his heart and breathing rates to remind yourself about the child's stress reaction.
T	**Time** alone is given to the child to calm down; allow him to do nothing or do something that is not too stimulating; make sure it is also not too much fun for him because we want him ultimately to get back to work.
O	**Organize** the task or activity into smaller and/or more 'do-able' pieces; do this out of the child's line of vision as much as possible so sight of the task or object does not set him off again.

Table 8.3 continued

R	**Reinforce** his feelings of competence, telling him briefly about how he has done something similar before and/or how he has a good brain; prompt self-talk about his own ability to control his thinking and actions; identify his positive characteristics or contributions the child makes.
E	**Entice** him to the task or activity, such as by expressing or showing your own uncertainty about how to do it correctly, stating its positive or interesting features and/or by trying it out yourself with or without other people; encourage him to think about what happened and why and how he could behave differently next time in positive terms.

One example of how you apply the RESTORE process is shown in Table 8.4.

Table 8.4 Applying the RESTORE process

EXAMPLE: A task is placed in front of Bobby and immediately he melts to the floor and starts thrashing around. He whines "no, no, don't want to".	
R	Your immediate response is: "Well, fella, you can do it and you're just trying to avoid work today!"
	STOP – take every judgement about the child's behavior and reason about why he might be behaving this way out of your mind. Look at Bobby objectively as a person in distress who is trying to communicate something. Children with autism often grin and smile when excited. They may appear to be enjoying something because of this facial expression but it does not necessarily mean pleasure. If someone falls down, the child may smile not because he thinks it is funny; he is exhibiting an expression of excitement.
	DO NOT start thinking about what you may or may not have done correctly – this is not the time.
	Take a deep breath, count to five and calm yourself. Remember that children with autism tend to be 'emotional sponges' so, if you become agitated, it is likely just to add to Bobby's state.
	Also, if he is thrashing around, remove any objects or people from the immediate area that may be in the 'line of fire'.
E	Exhibit some empathy by saying things like, "Hey, big guy, what's the problem?" or "I'm sorry you are so upset."
S	Sit back and let Bobby calm down a little.
	If he is a child who responds to back rubs, rub his back.
	If he is a child who responds to joint compression, use strategies learned from your occupational therapist.

T   Leave him alone now that he has calmed somewhat. You could offer him some water or juice or a piece of gum.

     If his presence is interfering with other children's work, you could usher him gently to a quiet corner and set a timer to two to five minutes, explaining to him: "You can calm your body for 2 (5) minutes."

O   Now is the time to look at the task you wanted him to do and decide what could constitute 'done'.

     This is where you have to do some quick problem solving about what may have triggered him.

     You may decide to cut the task into smaller parts. Children with autism are highly visually oriented and prefer to finish what they start so it could just upset him more if you handed him back the worksheet and said, "just do three". He can see that there are many more items on the sheet and seeing them may trigger another reaction. You could simply cut the worksheet in half.

     If he has difficulty with fine motor skills, you may think about having him tell you the answers and you write them for him or you do every second item for him.

R   Bobby is calm by now and it is your time to draw him back into learning.

     Your statements may be something like, "I am so glad you are calm now. You did a very good job of telling your body to relax." Then, "You have a really good brain and I know you can do this work really well – sometimes it's a little bit hard but you can just tell your brain to think and your body to be calm."

E   Now you can entice him back to the task.

     You may decide that the work is just too much for him that day, especially if it is a new concept or something more difficult. At that point, say something like, "Oh man, I guess I got confused. This silly worksheet is for another day. Here is the one we were supposed to do."

     You may work at enticing him back by pointing to something he knows or likes on the sheet: "Hey, look at this, this is your favorite number over here."

     You may also entice him by noting what he gets to do once he has finished the current task. Even if it is not one of his favorite things, you can make it sound really desirable. For example, you could say, "Wow, after this you get to go and wash your hands!"

THE 'CRISIS PLAN'

Sometimes, you simply do not have the time or you are not in a reasonable location to try these techniques. You may be in a time crunch and not have the time or resources available to restore the child's equilibrium. You may be in the middle of a shopping center or at church and do not want to embarrass your child or receive advice and judgement from people around you. The child's behavior may also be causing distress in other children around him.

That means you should always have a 'crisis plan'. In the middle of a shopping center or church, you may simply pick up the child, put him under your arm and go to the car. If you cannot pick him up, you might just clear the area as much as possible of anything he could hurt himself with or hurt others and let him go for it until it blows over. Try your best to ignore well-meaning 'critics' and 'advisors' in the form of passers-by who feel compelled to give you advice or criticize your child and you. Just tell them the child has special needs and you know what you are doing.

It is of no use whatsoever to try to talk or reason with him when he is in a state of distress. Your words and actions may simply aggravate the situation and cause the child more distress. When children with autism are in a state of distress their ability to process information is severely compromised and adding information to his distress can make it worse.

WAYS TO AVOID DISTRESS REACTIONS

There are a number of ways to help the child avoid and deal with sources of stress and anxiety that can cause problem behavior. Strategies of choice are proactive and focused on preventing problems.

Use the information you obtained on stressors, distress reactions and calming strategies from observing the child. This information will help you determine the type of strategies needed and when and where they are necessary.

Below are seven major types of strategies used to prevent problem behaviors.

1. Form rules about desired behaviors

Formation and use of rules was presented in the "Plans and routines" section of Chapter 5 and in the "Control of emotions" section of Chapter 6. The present discussion will focus on establishing rules to proactively define desired behavior. They may involve undesirable behaviors such as screaming, whining, calling others names or hitting.

Follow these steps:

- Identify behaviors that are key issues to the family and others concerned with the child.

- Select one behavior to work on at a time.

- Define the desired behavior and find a positive label for it, if at all possible. Some children can become over-focused on the negative behavior if it is mentioned. To them, the most salient information in a statement like "don't hit your brother" is "hit your brother". If the behavior is exhibited at specific times or in particular locations, define them.

- Engage the child in forming the rule so that he feels part of the decision-making in your relationship. Pair a visual reminder with the rule.

- Practice the rule by acting out scenarios with the child. Ensure there are opportunities for both you and the child to remind each other of the rule.

One day a teacher showed me a Social Story™ written for one of her students by a well-meaning support worker. The teacher was concerned about how the story was written. I took one look at it and saw the title was "I should not run away." Knowing the child, my immediate response was "I bet he got quite excited about that story and it really backfired." The teacher said that, when the child looked at the story, he indicated excitedly, "Look, there's me running away!"

Introduce it into daily life once the child seems to have a solid understanding of the rule and its application. Acknowledge whenever the child uses the rule with statements such as: "Wow, you used your gentle hands! Good remembering!"

If the child forgets, you can remind him and vice versa. Remain positive and treat any errors as 'forgetting'.

If the child ignores the rule or purposely violates it, sit down with him, discuss the issues and try to reach a renewed understanding or a compromise. Remind him of the social consequence of forgetting to use the rule, like "other people will not want to be your friend".

Provide sufficient time for the child to achieve automaticity with the rule before introducing a new one. See Table 8.5 for examples of desired behavior rules.

Table 8.5 Examples of the desired behavior rule strategy

Example	Visual Reminder
"We use gentle hands" – to remind the child that we do not grab objects or push others. Help the child understand what "gentle" means by modeling with your hand. Then help him gently stroke your hand and arm and his own. Repeatedly label those actions as "gentle".	**We use gentle hands**
"We use kind words" – is a reminder not to use "mean words" that hurt other people. The term "kind words" can also be associated with the physical reference to "gentleness". Provide the child with examples of kind words, like "please" (versus just grabbing), "silly" (versus "stupid") and "thank you".	**We use kind words**
"We use an inside voice" – is a reminder about self-regulation of voice volume. Pair voice volume with pictures to show "inside voice", "outside voice" and "quiet", like those shown. Practice different loudness levels while singing familiar songs. For the loud "outside voice", the time should be relatively brief because "that is the voice we use when we are outside". Pair different voice volumes to locations, such as a quiet voice at the library, temple or church.	**Quiet voice** **Inside voice** **Outside voice**
"No whining zone" – can be used to help the child learn where he can and cannot do certain things. Help the child understand the meaning of the word "whining" and the visual reminder by play-acting with him. It is important to remember that, whenever the child is told he cannot do something, he needs to have a time and/or place where he can exhibit the behavior (see Channeling below).	**No whining zone**

"Please do not interrupt" – interrupting busy people is a frequent
problem area for children with autism. For example, they do
not easily understand the cues when Mom is on the telephone
or when two people are talking. Make a 'please do not
interrupt' crown for the adult to wear at times when it is
critical for the adult to be undisturbed, such as for an
important telephone call or conversation. An example of the
crown is shown.

The parent of one child indicated that the child's whining was driving her
around the bend and she was concerned about blowing up at her daughter.
I suggested making signs that said: "No Whining Zone' and "Whining
Zone'. The 'Whining Zone' sign was put up in her bedroom but everywhere else in the house was a 'No Whining Zone'. The signs were put up at
home by the mother and child. The next time the child whined, Mom
calmly tapped on the 'No Whining Zone' sign and escorted her child to the
bedroom where she was told she could whine as much as she wanted. After
a couple of trials, the child automatically took herself to her room if she
felt like whining.

2. Optimizing the child's energy level

Help the child learn ways he can calm or alert and center himself before he
reaches a level of distress. Some children with autism appear scattered and high
energy. Others seem to have low energy levels and tend to shut out people
and/or activities. Review the information on calming strategies you obtained
from observing the child. This will help you determine if quiet time away or
engaging in sensory activities are more effective for optimizing the child's
energy level. Table 8.6 presents examples of ways to optimize a child's energy
level.

3. Establishing routines for transitions

Transitions or changes from one activity to another are very difficult for
children with autism. They need to be helped to remain calm during changes to
recess, group gathering times, lunch, going home, going to bed, stopping a
favorite activity and other changes during the day. Table 8.7 presents examples
of ways to establish transition routines.

Table 8.6 Examples of strategies for optimizing energy

Example

'break' or '*quiet time*' – to help the child learn that he can take a break or quiet time to regain his optimal energy level. When you notice that the child appears to be increasingly agitated, state something like: "It looks like your brain and your body are getting excited/upset. It is probably a good idea to take a little break. Why don't you come over here and have two minutes of quiet/break time?" Then give him a 'break' or 'quiet time' card and help usher him to a quiet spot like a tent or other area. Start a timer and let him be. Remind him when he is calm that, if he feels his body or brain get upset or excited, he can get a card on his own and take a break. Soon, he will start initiating getting the break card and taking a break. If it appears that he is using break time as an excuse to avoid work, you will have to help him re-define the parameters for when breaks or quiet time can be taken such as when his body feels tight.

I need a break

self-calming techniques – to help the child learn to relax his brain and body. When the child is calm, he should be taught basic strategies for self-calming. They can be relatively simple, including "stop-think-take a breath", or more complex relaxation techniques, like progressively tightening and then releasing major muscle groups in the body.

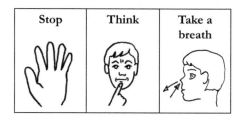

Stop	Think	Take a breath

regular sensory breaks – used with children who are just learning self-regulation and who need regular alerting or calming to maintain optimal energy levels. Work with an occupational therapist to determine how frequently sensory breaks should occur, how long they should be, what types of sensations should be included and in what order. With 'heavy work' the child is expected to do some activity that encourages deep joint compression to help center and calm him. 'Movement' can give him a chance to alert and activate his body.

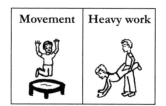

Movement	Heavy work

Table 8.7 Examples of strategies for easing transitions

Example	Visual reminder

pictures – were described in the schedules, plans and routines section of Chapter 5, **Program Structure**. Picture calendars, schedules and plans forewarn the child about what is going to happen. Knowing what will occur can help the child stay calmer.

Calendar	Thinking	Science center	Computer center	Snack

songs and rhymes – can smooth movement from one activity or location to another. Children with autism typically respond positively to music and rhythm. Associating a transition with a song or rhyme can ease the child's stress.

Twinkle, twinkle little star, stop and clean up where you are.

warnings with timers – provide objective visual information. Timers, as discussed in the clear expectations section of Chapter 5 **Program Structure**, serve as a physical indicator of activity termination that can help the child remain calmer.

Two minutes are up – we need to shut the computer down now.

transition objects – can be helpful for some children. Large transitions, such as home to school or school to home, can be eased by having one special, desirable object designated as the transition object. The child gets to hold and play with that object only during the time between locations. At both ends of the trip, the object is put away.

Now Teddy gets to go home with you.

4. Channeling

This involves helping the child channel his energy and learn appropriate times and/or places for behaviors that are prohibited, as outlined above in "1. Form rules about desired behavior". See Table 8.8 for examples of the chanelling strategy.

Table 8.8 Examples of strategies for chanelling behavior

Example	Visual reminder
zones – used to help the child know where he can use certain behaviors. He needs to know when it is acceptable to exhibit the behavior. Signs can be posted in the selected location(s) and then practiced with the child.	 **My whining zone**
private places – wherever you want them to be but, usually, is the child's bedroom. This is the only place where certain things can be done, such as burping, releasing intestinal gas or masturbating. Help the child understand where his private place is by showing him and posting a picture like that shown. If he is about to burp, escort him to his private place and remind him of the rule.	 **My private place**
delaying – involves the child's putting off a certain behavior until a more appropriate time. This can involve using a Brain Box©, as described in Chapter 6 **Program Content**. The child's behavior is respectfully 'removed' from his consciousness and put away for later.	
Take 5 bag – gives the child something to do if he is expected to wait, such as when not interrupting. Children with autism often have a difficult time occupying themselves in positive ways. The Take 5 bag can contain gum, juice, a chew toy, a book or other object that the child enjoys.	

5. Interference

Interference is sometimes an effective way of preventing potentially difficult situations. A simple way is to engage the child in actions that are incompatible with the potential distress reaction. See Table 8.9 for examples of the behavior interference strategy.

Table 8.9 Examples of the behavior interference strategy

Examples Interference Strategy	Visual illustration
filling the child's hands – if the child tends to push others or pull hair engage him in incompatible behaviour. This can involve occupying his hands with carrying relatively heavy objects from one location to another.	
high 5s – this can help avoid other not-so-desirable options. Occupying the child's hands with high 5s or handshakes is physically incompatible with actions like hitting or pushing.	
keeping the child's mouth busy – if the child tends to screech or bite, it can help to engage his mouth. He can chew gum or a crunchy food just prior to the times when he is most likely to become distressed.	
keeping his mind on something else – being the leader in a line can become a 'blood sport' with children who physically vie to be at the front. Make up number tags like that shown. Assign numbers each day and tell the children that everyone 'gets a chance' to wear different numbers. This strategy gives the children visual support and advance warning. It also helps them learn to read numerals and understand their order.	

6. Control proximity

This involves moving people or objects to avoid an undesirable event. See Table 8.10 for examples of this strategy.

7. Problem solving

To make balanced decisions, the child must learn how to gather information about the problem and how to make choices. He also must look at details in a situation as well as in the total context. Decision-making has to be analytical and logical but the impact of the decisions on others needs to considered. Because of the need for this balance in decision-making, the person with an Introversion-Sensing-Thinking-Judging learning preference experiences many challenges, particularly with the Intuiting and Feeling that are necessary.

A Problem Solving Format which incorporates these features is presented in Table 8.11 with an example in table 8.12. A blank form is included in Appendix III.

Table 8.10 Examples of the proximity control strategy

Example	Visual illustration
gratitude – involves removing an object from a child in a positive manner. For example, if the child is dashing past you with a pair of scissors which are destined for a not very positive place, you would quickly remove them from his hands, saying: "Thank you so much – that is exactly what I needed."	
distance – involves placing physical distance between the child and anything that could cause a problem for him. The child can be moved out of the range of other children or of a 'target' child. Sometimes, a child with autism will choose one other child as the 'target' of his stress so, by increasing the distance between the children, probability of problem behavior is decreased.	
barriers – entail some degree of isolation of the child. The child can be moved to a work station or another location which has a physical barrier like a wall or carrel. This will allow the child to focus more on the task at hand and less on potential problem behaviors.	

Table 8.11 Problem solving format

Questions to be answered	Strategies and suggestions	
What's the problem?	Help the child define the problem. It is critical that the issues are clearly spelled out so that everyone understands them. Very often, children with autism will focus on non-central and/or non-critical information so it will be important to help him understand the most important features of the problem.	
What could I do?	Plan	What might happen?
	Together with the child, determine three possible actions that can help to solve the problem. At this stage, accept the child's suggestions, even if one or two seem 'absurd'.	Figure out, with the child, what might happen if you used each one of these plans. Look at both logical and emotional consequences, such as how he might feel and how other people might feel. Provide feedback to the child on his suggestions and decide if they are possible or not.

Which one will I try?	Help the child decide which one of the three suggested plans he should try out, emphasizing the impact on positive interactions and relationships with others.	
What will I say and do?	Say: Help the child decide exactly what he will say when using the plan. It is important to print out the exact words the child will use and to rehearse them with him.	Do: Help the child determine what he will do when using his plan. Spell out each step and rehearse with the child.
How did it work? Should I try something else?	After the child has tried his plan, help him evaluate how it worked. Include both logical consequences, such as did he get what he wanted, and emotional consequences, such as what was the impact on other people. If the plan did not work well, help the child start the process again by re-examining the definition of the problem, plans and actions for other possibilities.	

Table 8.12 An example of the problem solving format completed with a child with autism

What's the problem?	Sometimes I touch my friends a little too hard.	
What could I do?	Plan 1. I touch them more softly. 2. I stop touching other people. 3. I give high-5s.	What might happen? 1. Some people might not want to be touched. 2. I feel weird and don't know what to do. 3. Some people might not want to.
Which one will I try?	Give high-5s because I see my friends give high 5s.	

Table 8.12 continued

What will I say and do?	Say: give me five	Do:
		1. Put up my hand in the high-5 position.
		2. Wait for the person to put out his hands.
		3. Touch his hands gently with my hands.
How did it work? Should I try something else?		

Give the child as much leeway in this problem-solving process as you feel appropriate. Sometimes, letting the child experience a mildly negative response can be effective learning. For example, if the child decides that covering his mouth when he burps is a better plan than suppressing burps or going to the bathroom to burp, let him try it out to see what happens.

We need to start as early as possible to help the child learn active problem solving. Start within controlled settings and, once the child learns the process, it can be introduced into daily situations.

Expect the child to start using the Problem Solving Format on his own only after repeated practice. He will initially need support in using it but, over time, he will be able to do some problem solving on his own.

Another format that can be used is the *Social Rule*. It is more specifically focused and less usable by the child on his own. It is similar to the Problem Solving Format in that the issue is defined and steps are outlined for addressing the problem. The Social Rule Format is more specific about when, where and with whom the problem arises. It also defines the rationale for the rule and, perhaps most importantly, how the child can help himself remember to use the rule. An example of the Social Rule Format completed with a child with autism is shown below. A blank form is included in Appendix III.

Social skill: what to do when someone is bugging me

Definition: bugging means that something the person is doing or saying is making it hard for me to think and feel okay

When: when I feel distracted and it is hard to think and to feel comfortable

Where: at home, on the playground, in class

With whom: my friends, my brother, my sister

What to say and do:

1. stop, stay calm, and think about what I can do to help myself

2. ignore the other person

3. if it doesn't stop, say: "I don't like it when you do that."

4. if the person still doesn't stop, I leave and go to another place

5. if the person is still bugging me, I tell an adult

Reasoning: I do this because I can think better when I am calm and I can help other people understand when something is bugging me

How I can help myself remember: I can make a picture of a shield in my head that will help me ignore the other person and protect my brain

Social Stories™ are a highly effective format for presenting problem solving. Children with autism respond particularly well to Social Stories™ because they engage important *Learning Preferences and Strengths*. Social Stories™ allow the child time to review the information before entering a situation, they point out the most important cues in a setting, outline the appropriate steps to take and the reasoning for using the strategy and they are visual. By incorporating the rhythm of favorite books, such as Dr. Seuss or Robert Munsch, the child's Musical-Rhythmic strengths can also be engaged to focus his attention. Consider including topics or characters of high interest to the child, such as dinosaurs or a television character, in the story so long as it does not distract or divert attention. An example of a Social Story™ in book format is shown in Figure 8.2. It was written for a child who did not like to be singled out in group settings. The term 'leader' was used because it is more positive and understand-

How to be a good leader by Bobbi Smith	 I have many good ideas. I have lots of things I know in my brain.
 Sometimes, adults ask me to be a leader. They want me to help other kids do or say things.	 They might ask me to stand up. Then I have to do or say something. The other kids will stay sitting down.
 They might ask me to be in the center of a circle. They might ask me to be the only person who does something.	 Sometimes, I feel nervous and I say "no thanks".
 Next time an adult asks me to be a leader, I will stay calm. I will tell my brain that being a leader helps my friends learn.	 My friends can watch me and learn some of the things in my brain.
 The other kids will like to hear my ideas. They can learn the things I know.	 My teacher will be happy because I helped her teach the other kids.

Figure 8.2 Example of a Social Story™ in book format

able. The child liked to tell others what to do so that was highlighted, under the guise of being a 'leader', so that the child's concerns about being singled out might be outweighed by this.

Helping the child learn how to *self-prompt* to use his problem-solving skills and strategies is a major issue. It is usually best to ask the child about what he thinks would help him remember. Below is an example of a reminder for a child who loves cars and really wants to become a driver. The 'driver's license' was mocked up for him and his picture was placed on the front with identifying information. On the other side were the reminders of what to do when someone is bothering him. The license was laminated and the child kept it in his wallet. It was carefully explained to the child that this license *did not* mean that he could now drive a car!

Figure 8.3 Example of a visual reminder to cue self-prompting

Another form of problem-solving prompts is *Social Tickets* presented earlier as a means of supporting the child's selective attention. They are ticket-shaped cards used to help the child remember and recall what he can say in certain situations (see p.217). First, introduce each card one at a time, play-act an appropriate scenario and then practice the sentence or phrase on the 'ticket'. The ticket is then made available to the child, such as in his pocket or posted in a central location, to remind him about the words he can use. When you see an opportunity for the child to use a Social Ticket, you can give it to him or prompt him to get it for himself. After a short while, the child will begin to get and use the tickets on his own. Over time, he will no longer need to use the tickets to remind himself but they should still be readily available for him as back-up.

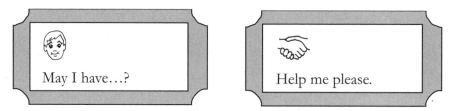

Figure 8.4 Example Social Tickets

Prompt Dice can be used to help children with autism use more variety in their approach to problem solving. Make a cardboard cube that has, on each face, a different alternative for dealing with a situation. For example, if a child wants a particular toy, object or game another child is using, he could roll a Prompt Die and select the option shown. Options presented on the die could be alternatives like "Can I play with that in five minutes?", "Can we play together?" or "I can play with that another day." Practice using the die in a one-to-one situation with the child so he understands the alternatives and their consequences. After the child seems to comprehend and use the alternatives, practice with a group of children before letting the child use it on his own.

    Shortcuts to the full problem-solving process can be used in some situations. I had spent a lot of time observing children and trying to figure out how to give them a sense of control when things seemed to be falling apart for them. I saw that some children became overwrought if an adult read the 'wrong' book, another child tried to take his toy or if someone did something that was not in his mental plan. I tried a number of different strategies but finally decided simply to teach the starter phrase "How about...?" When the child encountered a situation where he wanted to do something differently than the other person, he used the words "How about...?" and provided a suggestion, like: "How about we read the other book?" I found that, just by providing an appropriate starter phrase, the children were able to negotiate on their own. Another interesting and unexpected outcome was the more positive reception from other people. If a child says "how about" rather than screaming and melting down, he is more likely to have people respond positively toward him and, often, he got his way.

Promoting generalization of rules and strategies

The ultimate goal is to have the child use rules appropriately in everyday situations without prompting and to solve problems flexibly and independently.

Adults and other mediators in the child's life have an important role in promoting generalization of rules and strategies. By actively engaging the child in rule and strategy formation, his ability to extend them to other settings is enhanced. Independent use of rules and strategies is, however, an ongoing process that requires continuing support in day-to-day life.

The most effective way to promote use of rules and strategies is to activate problem solving in the child. By prompting him to recall rules and strategies on his own, we are helping him analyze a situation and select possible solutions. Table 8.13 gives some examples of adult responses in different situations that activate problem solving and those that leave the child as a passive recipient of directions. Notice the way the adult asks questions of the child to help activate his thinking and problem solving.

Table 8.13 Examples of ways to stop and activate problem solving

Situation	Child is passive recipient	Active problem solving by the child
you are working with a group of children and other children are being too noisy	"Be quiet. You're making too much noise."	"We are having a hard time hearing. What could you do to help us?"
it's cleanup time	"put the materials in the box, push in the chairs…"	"It's time to clean up. What do you need to do to make it the way it was before we started?"
one child is distracting another	"move away from Kim"	"It looks like you are having a hard time listening. What could you do to help yourself?"
one child is making disruptive noises while another is trying to talk	"be quiet"	"I think it is Mary's turn to talk. What could we do to help her?"
a child volunteers to help you	"get two jars of paint, ten pieces of paper. Pass one piece of paper to each child…"	"Let's look at what we have planned. What kind of things will be needed? Can you make sure everyone gets what they need?"
a child is whining	"stop whining"	"I can understand you better when you use your normal voice"

Table 8.13 continued

| a child interrupts while you are talking to someone else | "don't interrupt" | "I'm talking to Barb, what could you do if you need to talk to me?" |
| a child pushes another child. | "don't push" | "How are we supposed to use our hands?", "Are hands for pushing our friends?", "How do we treat our friends?" |

Checkpoint for avoiding distress reactions: What Learning Preferences and Strengths did we incorporate?

	Introversion	Sensing	Thinking	Judging	Visual-Spatial	Musical-Rhythmic
	✓	✓	✓	✓	✓	✓

| **Challenge:** | Intuiting Feeling | | | | Interpersonal | |

Notes: Problem solving, the main strategy that challenges *Learning Preferences and Strengths*, does so in the following ways:

- *Intuiting* – people with Intuiting preferences are able to see the larger scope of an issue and the over-riding concepts. The problem-solving process stretches the child to look beyond the details of a situation and begin to understand the wider implications and principles.

- *Feeling* – people with Feeling preferences value others' needs and try to meet them. Problem solving presses them to consider others' feelings and interactions.

- *Interpersonal* – the person with Interpersonal strengths has the ability to understand the feelings and thoughts of others. By pressing the child to project how others may respond to his plan for problem solving, he is being prompted to try to understand the other person's thinking, intentions and feelings.

Chapter 9

Putting the Pieces Together: An Overview of the *Learning Preferences and Strengths* Model

THE *LEARNING PREFERENCES AND STRENGTHS* MODEL

Advantages of the *LPS* model

In the *Learning Preferences and Strengths* (*LPS*) model, each child with autism is seen as a unique individual. There are, however, commonalities in their learning preferences and strengths, in particular for Introversion-Sensing-Thinking-Judging preferences and Visual-Spatial and Musical-Rhythmic strengths. Once we understand and appreciate those preferences and strengths, pieces of the puzzle fit together harmoniously and tension and misunderstanding are reduced. Tieger and Barron-Tieger (1997) use the analogy of gardening in relation to honoring learning preferences: The gardener accepts the growing requirements of each plant and provides conditions for it to flourish. If we are willing to do this for plants, why would we be reluctant to provide conditions for children to grow and flourish?

> In a world that understands autism, we will be able to embrace the virtues and vicissitudes of autistic perception and behavior and adjust our reactions accordingly... Given that we have some understanding, then we are in a position patiently and compassionately to address the needs of such people in a supportive way. (*How to Understand Autism*, Alex Durig 2005, p.127)

Learning Preferences and Strengths are areas in which the child can learn with greater ease and pleasure. They also allow us to view learning from the child's point of view – what things are important and meaningful to him, how he prefers to deal with objects, events and people and what his natural interests are. Blossoming of the child's *Learning Preferences and Strengths* will contribute to his self-esteem and feelings of self-acceptance and self-worth.

An important core of the *LPS* model is that each child is viewed as a learner. It does not focus on the deficits and pathology usually at the center of intervention programs. Deficit-oriented thinking often precludes recognition of the child's strengths and the ability to make meaningful changes in the child. Learning in the *LPS* program starts with what the child brings in terms of preferences, strengths, knowledge, skills, attitudes and beliefs. His developmental needs are opportunities for learning.

The *LPS* model takes a long-term view of the child. Children are more likely to become competent adults if they learn to develop their preferences and strengths and compensate for their weaknesses. The foundation skills for complete and accurate intake, integration and expression of information will help the child become a more effective learner throughout his life. Also, by promoting independent decision-making from an early stage, we are helping the child assume greater responsibility for himself and his choices. The focus of the *LPS* model is on helping the child to trust his own mind, know there is more than one right way to do things, evaluate his own work and behavior and to acknowledge his mistakes and rectify them. It develops a more responsible and autonomous learner who can feel a sense of power through his accomplishments and be more adaptable and flexible.

Using the *LPS* model, we found that principled predictions could be made in relation to the child with autism's:

- motivators
- energizers
- stressors
- preferred pace
- distress reactions
- trust needs
- calming strategies
- do's and don'ts of teaching
- areas needing continued growth.

A summary of these features is presented in Table 9.1.

Table 9.1 *Summary of major learning features of children with autism*

Motivators	Energizers
• tasks that can be analyzed • practical and functional activities • engaging all senses • concrete experiences and tasks with tangible results he can see • pursuing his interests deeply • situations when social and/or emotional factors are not primary • a plan to follow • clear indicators of progress • incorporating his affinities and areas of high interest • tasks and activities that he initiated	• logically organized materials • clear and stable step-by-step explanations and directions • valuing his ability to gather and organize detailed information • coming to closure, finishing a task before moving on to another task • breaks for exercise or quiet time • music and rhythm • visually-apparent rules and expectations • minimum conflict • clear goals and deadlines • quiet work environment where he can concentrate on the task at hand • being in control of his own schedule • enough time to work to his own standards

Stressed by	Preferred pace
• unknown activities or situation • being asked to change once he has made up his mind • things that do not fit logically into his mental frameworks • trial and error • lack of predictability, surprises • not following the agreed-upon plan • being singled out • last minute changes and uncertainty • highly complex tasks or situations • being prompted to move on to new tasks when he does not feel he perfected the previous • interruptions • decisions based solely on feelings • being pressed to compromise • being late or behind schedule • being pressured to meet a deadline • clutter or chaotic environments • poorly defined standards and goals • incomplete or sloppy work by others	• time to warm up to new situations, people and tasks • slower pace, especially for new tasks or events • methodical and steady • chances for reflection • time to practice and rehearse a strategy **Calming strategies** • time alone • getting away to a sensing environment • validation of competence and value • help organizing and accomplishing small tasks • help sorting priorities

Table 9.1 continued

Distress reaction	Raise trust by
• internalize his feelings of being out of control yet appear outwardly calm • become immoveable, resisting even minor changes • over-focus on details and possible cause of present problem • experience confusion, panic • become very negative, unwilling to tolerate anything unfamiliar and imagine disasters ('catastrophizing')	• abiding by the rules, being fair • being reliable • working systematically • being careful about facts • using familiar and practiced ways of approaching tasks or events • congruence between what you say and do

Do

- help him see the most important and relevant information in a task or situation
- celebrate his persistence
- praise his use of self-regulation
- emphasize practical application and results of tasks and activities
- provide reasoning for doing things in a certain way
- explain the logic in problem solving and social situations
- use a clear system of accountability known in advance
- guide his thinking in new directions ("Tell me how you see the problem…have you thought about it this way?")
- use known structure or organization for new things; he can be comfortable with variety and can be spontaneous so long as some features are kept the same
- use progress charts and tangible records but remember that successful completion of a task is often its own reward
- prompt him to ask for feedback about his interpersonal behavior
- model language and behavior for him that will support his development of social skills
- incorporate music and/or rhythm
- let him vent his feelings when stressed without passing judgement or giving advice
- help him deal with things causing him stress
- keep your sense of humor

Don't

- let him become bogged down in details
- allow him to stay away from social experiences ('use it or lose it')
- allow him to lock into a course of action without looking at enough relevant information
- permit him to become over-focused on completing a task; emphasize importance of taking time and ensuring all information was considered first
- allow him to over-control or suppress emotions; help him learn to identify and express them appropriately
- talk about the child within his ear-shot; he is private and may resent such violation of his privacy
- appear to use favoritism with others

Areas needing continued growth

- coping with and reducing internal build up of stress
- becoming mired down in details
- determining the 'big picture'
- thinking on his feet, brainstorming
- extending and refining his understanding, awareness, expression and validation of emotions and affect
- understanding that there are few strict rules and no guarantees in social situations
- using intuition and 'hunches'
- learning how his behavior and responses affect others
- extending his creativity beyond the here and now, such as by helping him learn to ask open-ended process questions
- coping and dealing with inconsistency
- showing personal interest in others
- providing criticism that is constructive and more focused on maintaining interpersonal relationships
- flowing with change and new experiences
- extending his range of emotional and affective awareness
- adhering too rigidly to routines and procedure
- failing to notice or ignoring others' emotional reactions
- relating to things he has not experienced directly
- standing back and determining what is important to him when stressed

Identifying the main *LPS* features, as shown above, helps us understand the child more quickly because we have a set of expectations. It is important to view the child with an open mind but the *LPS* model permits us to focus on what the child can do rather than on old notions of impairments and deficiencies. Autism is a condition that will not go away but, when his *Learning Preferences and Strengths* are used in clear and appropriate ways, the child can more fully realize his potential. With continued support, change will occur over the child's lifespan.

> Understanding the way children with autism spectrum disorder think is a large part of the 'art' of teaching them. (*A Mind Apart*, Peter Szatmari 2004, p.171)

Features of the *LPS* model

The main focus of this book was on developing program structure, content and processes that honor the child with autism's typical *Learning Preferences and Strengths*. Examples were also provided for ways to challenge the child's non-dominant preferences and strengths. This is because exclusive focus on areas of preference and strength can impede development in other areas which are needed for well-rounded learning and growth.

The major goal of the program is to provide the child with a safe environment where he is given reason to pay attention, understand and remember by making the learning personal, purposeful, meaningful and relevant. These were addressed in the three key program components: structure, process and content.

Program Structure emphasized developing a learning setting that is understandable and visually obvious to the child. This creates a 'safe haven' for him in that it is consistent and predictable. Scheduling in breaks, or quiet time, for each child helps ensure that he has regular opportunities to de-stress. Willis (2007) suggested that breaks provide a chance for the amygdala, an area of the brain associated with feelings and visual learning and memory, to cool down.

Program Process stressed engaging the child in a reciprocal partnership where he can make mistakes as well as experience successes. The Seven Pillars of Mediated Learning underline the importance of making objectives clear, promoting active participation, encouraging independence, increasing awareness of his thinking and learning strengths and needs and processing information more effectively.

Adult mediators of the child's learning are encouraged to use gently intrusive teaching methods. The teacher/mediator is a trusted coach and guide to the child. The child is an apprentice who learns from and collaborates with the adult to construct knowledge. Consistent effort is made to transfer learning to new

> (Learning) depends massively upon participation in a dialogue carefully stabilized by the adult partner...so much of learning depends upon the need to achieve joint attention, to conduct enterprises jointly, to honor the social relationship that exists between the learner and (adult). (*The Process of Education*, Jerome Bruner 1977, p.xiv)

contexts and tasks by helping the child understand when, where and why the knowledge is useful.

Learning is made explicit and visible to the child so he comes to understand what it means to learn and who he is as a learner. This metacognitive emphasis helps the child move from learning basic factual information and procedures to understanding concepts and principles and how he learns best. Through metacognition, the child finds value in what he does well and begins to understand that people cannot do everything in life equally.

The emphasis on understanding why we are learning something plus making the learning personally interesting and motivating provide an ideal emotional climate. The child is increasingly held accountable for his learning while the adult is providing him with support by listening and being attentive, showing positive emotion, being fair, being honest, being trustworthy and granting some autonomy and opportunities for decision-making. By its nature, there is a high rate of successful performance using the program process.

Program Content focused on learning, cognitive, social and communication skills, using an information-processing model. Self-regulation skills were an important part of that chapter as well. The manner in which these skill areas were presented emphasizes the child's becoming more responsible for his own learning and learning to ascribe achievement and failure to himself and factors he can control, like effort, ability or motivation. He is helped to analyze, reflect on and understand his own behavior and learning, become aware of his cognitive strengths and weaknesses and control his attitude and efforts.

Assessment is a critical part of each child's program. *Pre-assessment* provides information on the child's learning preferences and strengths, the learning processes he uses and those that require attention, his interests and his entry skills and understanding.

From this information, the child's Individual Program/Education Program (IPP or IEP) is developed. Using country, state or provincial standards and 'big ideas' of what we want the child to be able to do and understand over the longer term, we develop goals. We plan strategies with 'hooks' to draw the child in and set up opportunities for the child to experience and explore key principles and concepts. Activities are designed to promote understanding as well as automaticity of skills. Then we define what is acceptable evidence of the child's having achieved the goal.

Formative assessments are a critical part of progress monitoring. On an ongoing basis, we review the child's progress toward IPP/IEP goals, revising the goals and/or strategies as needed. In the assessment, we ensure the child is learning and engaged and we clear up any misconceptions. We also can encourage the child to assess his own learning.

Summative assessments are done at the end of the period specified in the child's IPP/IEP. We evaluate the child's progress toward achieving the goals, looking for evidence of his learning, knowledge and understanding and what he is able to do and in what situations or settings.

When assessing children with autism, there are a number of factors that need to be kept in mind. Their development is usually uneven, with advanced development in some areas and plateaus, cycles and spurts of growth in others. Sometimes what may appear to be a regression is a response to the child's development being challenged in another area. Also, learning changes the physical structure of the brain so that it organizes and reorganizes information but different parts of the brain may be ready to learn at different times.

The final chapter focused on redefining and examining *behavior* in children with autism in relation to their learning preferences. The issue of defining, understanding and expanding the child's optimal stress level was addressed along with identifying stressors, distress reactions and calming strategies. Strategies for regaining equilibrium and avoiding distress reactions were described and examples were provided.

EFFECTIVENESS OF THE *LPS* MODEL

We reviewed trends in the data collected in relation to *Learning Preferences and Strengths* in children with autism and saw a clear profile emerge. The behaviors and perceptions of people with Introversion-Sensing-Thinking-Judging preferences and Visual-Spatial and Musical-Rhythmic strengths converged strongly with those observed in children with autism.

The *LPS* model is a compilation of theories and practices. The principles and strategies used within it are rooted in educational and developmental theory and research. For example, ensuring that complexity of skills taught should be slightly in advance of the child's current level of mastery is grounded in the work of Lev Vygotsky (1978) and his zone of proximal development. Neuro-imaging studies support the emphasis on optimizing stress. Willis (2007) indicated that, with reduced stress, children's ability to process and store information in memory and develop high levels of cognition are enhanced.

Intervention and teaching practices are well supported by trends found in diagnostic and outcome assessments but, to date, there is no further empirical validation of the LPS program as a package. Therapists and parents who have consistently implemented the *LPS* model have reported substantial improvements in learning and development of their children with autism.

BECOMING AN EXPERT IN THE *LPS* PROGRAM

Becoming an expert in any approach takes time and feedback through self-reflection and input from others. Bransford *et al.* (2000) found that experts in any field have the following characteristics:

- notice meaningful patterns

- organize knowledge around key concepts, principles or 'big ideas'

- take time to understand and reflect on a task or event before proceeding

- approach new situations flexibly and adaptively

- monitor their current understanding and decide when it is adequate and when it is not.

To become an expert in effectively planning and implementing the *LPS* model will take time and consistent effort. You will learn the basic concepts, principles and strategies. It is important then to reflect on the patterns and larger concepts and take time to understand them thoroughly. Adapt your practices slowly, starting with program structure. Then introduce one content area at a time. Full concentration on program process should occur once you have structured your program well and have developed good facility with at least some areas of program content. Try out the concepts and strategies you have learned, remaining flexible and ready to adapt approaches as needed. Improvement in planning and implementing the *LPS* model may be in small incremental steps. Consulting with colleagues and friends about your journey will help you develop ideas and options.

Commit yourself to the longer term and rejoice in the improvements you see in yourself as the teacher/mediator and in the child. You need to reflect on your own thinking, strategies and motivation, accept the responsibility of learning the *LPS* approach and value children with autism. The techniques and strategies presented in this book will engage your ingenuity and creativity. Collaborate with others to develop ideas and options so that you can all share the creative load. To help you plan well-organized programs, a Lesson Planning Form and Lesson Planning and Implementation Checklists are included in Appendix III.

WHERE MIGHT THE FUTURE LIE FOR A CHILD WITH AUTISM?

Predicting the future for children with autism is just as uncertain as with any child. *Learning Preferences and Strengths* are assets that will help the child find meaning in life and make contributions. We cannot predict the final outcome but a great deal of research has been completed at the Center for Applications of Psychological Type (Macdaid *et al.* 1995) in relation to different learning preferences.

The career areas in which people with Introversion-Sensing-Thinking-Judging preferences have strong representation include:

- librarians, library attendants and assistances
- accountants, auditors, bank employees
- computer professionals
- engineers, especially electrical and mechanical
- electrical and electronic technicians
- electricians
- police officers
- dentists.

These may or may not be career possibilities for all children with autism but the children should never be underestimated. Also, if they do not reach these professional areas, related careers should be explored. Books, such as *Career Training and Personal Planning for Students with Autism Spectrum Disorder* by Vicki Lundine (2006), should be consulted for further information on career planning.

FINAL WORDS

I will now give the final word to a young man with autism whom I have known for 12 years. I mentioned him in the anecdote in Chapter 6 at the end of the Learning/Cognition section 1a. I asked MacKenzie to write about things that he learned with me that worked to help him through school, things that he learned with me that did not work, things he wished he had learned earlier and advice he would give to children with autism about learning and school. Below is his response.

> I would like to start off by saying that I am very fortunate to have had Dr. Heather MacKenzie as my speech therapist. It was the simple things, such as encouraging me to succeed despite my disability, which allowed me to overcome the obstacle known as autism. Through her, I learned the important aspects of communication: eye contact, body language, and vocal clarity, making sure that I wasn't slurring my words. I had also developed logic, and the enhanced ability to think differently in many situations, through challenging mind games such as puzzles and 'Whodunits'. This was extremely helpful in my school life, that if I did need help from a teacher, I was confident in communicating the problem.
>
> However, one of the things I wished I learned earlier was the importance of friendship, the foundation of a social life. When I was younger, I found myself more comfortable around adult groups, rather than with children my age. This reluctance to interact with those around me led me into a state of recluse, which then led to loneliness. When my classroom helpers discovered this problem and encouraged me to play with others on the playground, I had made a small group of acquaintances. It wasn't exactly the biggest group compared to others, but I knew those that remained beside me were my true friends.
>
> For those with autism like me, I leave you with this following message. Know that autism should never stop you in the pursuit of your dreams. With hard work and dedication, you can become more of a social being, an important part of society. Doubt of one's self can prove to be the biggest obstacle in your school and social life. Like any other disability, know that it can be overcome with your will. If however, you have any trouble at all, do not hesitate to ask for help; whether it be from your parents, teachers, or friends. Everybody needs help sometimes.
>
> *MacKenzie Whitney*
> *18 years of age*

References

Baron-Cohen, S. (1999) "The extreme-male-brain theory of autism." In H. Tager-Flusberg (ed.) *Neurodevelopmental Disorders.* Cambridge, MA: MIT Press.

Baron-Cohen, S. (2000) "Is Asperger syndrome/high-functioning autism necessarily a disability?" *Development and Psychopathology 12*, 489–500.

Baron-Cohen, S. (2002) "The extreme male brain theory of autism." *Trends in Cognitive Sciences 6*, 6, 248–254.

Baron-Cohen, S., Bolton, P., Wheelwright, S., Scahill, V., Short, L., Mead, G. and Smith, A. (1998) "Autism occurs more often in families of physicists, engineers, and mathematicians." *Autism 2*, 296–301.

Baron-Cohen, S. and Hammer, J. (1997) "Is autism an extreme form of the 'male brain'?" *Advances in Infancy Research 11*, 193–217.

Baron-Cohen, S. and Wheelwright, S. (1999) "Obsessions in children with autism or Asperger Syndrome: a content analysis in terms of care domains of cognition." *British Journal of Psychiatry 175*, 484–490.

Baron-Cohen, S., Richler, J., Bisarya, D., Gurunathan, N. and Wheelwright, S. (2003) "The systematizing quotient: an investigation of adults with Asperger syndrome or high-functioning autism, and normal sex differences." *Philosophical Transactions of the Royal Society: Biological Sciences 358*, 1430, 361–374.

Baron-Cohen, S., Wheelwright, S., Lawson, J., Griffin, R., Ashwin, C., Billington, J. and Chakrabarti, B. (2005) "Empathizing and systematizing in autism spectrum conditions." In F. Volkmar, A. Klin, R. Paul and D.J. Cohen (eds) *Handbook of Autism and Pervasive Developmental Disorders.* Hoboken, NJ: John Wiley and Sons.

Baron-Cohen, S., Wheelwright, S., Skinner, R., Martin, J. and Clubley, E. (2001) "The Autism-Spectrum Quotient: evidence from Asperger syndrome/High-functioning autism, males and females, scientists and mathematicians." *Journal of Autism and Developmental Disorders 31*, 5–17.

Baron-Cohen, S., Wheelwright, S, Stone, V. and Rutherford, M. (1999) "A mathematician, a physicist, and a computer scientist with Asperger Syndrome: performance on folk psychology and folk physics test." *Neurocase 5*, 475–483.

Baron-Cohen, S., Wheelwright, S., Stott, C., Bolton, P. and Goodyer, I. (1997) "Is there a link between engineering and autism?" *Autism 1*, 153–163.

Bransford, J. D., Brown, A.L. and Cocking, R.R. (eds) (2000) *How People Learn: Brain, Mind, Experience, and School.* Washington, DC: National Academy Press.

Bruner, J. (1977) *The Process of Education.* Cambridge, MA: Harvard University Press.

Cuomo, N. (2007) *Integrated Yoga.* London: Jessica Kingsley Publishers.

Durig, A. (2005) *How to Understand Autism – The Easy Way.* London: Jessica Kingsley Publishers.

Frith, U. (1989, 2003) *Autism: Explaining the Enigma.* Malden, MA: Blackwell Publishing.

Frith, U. (ed.) (1991) *Autism and Asperger Syndrome.* Cambridge: Cambridge University Press.

Gardner, H. (1983) *Frames of Mind: The Theory of Multiple Intelligences.* New York, NY: BasicBooks.

Grandin, T. (1995) *Thinking in Pictures.* New York, NY: Doubleday.

Grandin, T. and Scariano, M. (1986) *Emergence: Labelled Autistic.* Novato, CA: Arena Press.

Gray, C. (2000) *The New Social Story Book.* Arlington, TX: Future Horizons.

Half, R. (undated) Unsourced quote. Accessed on 6 February 2008 at www.worldofquotes.com/author/Robert-Half/1/index.html.

Happé, F. (1997) "Autism: understanding the mind, fitting together the pieces." Accessed on 10 February 2007 at www.mindship.com/happe.htm

Happé, F. (1999) "Autism: cognitive deficit or cognitive style?" *Trends in Cognitive Sciences 3*, 6, 216–222.

Haywood, H.C. (1990) *A Total Cognitive Approach in Education.* Presidential address, Second International Conference on Cognitive Education of the International Association for Cognitive Education, Mons, Belgium.

Lundine, V. (2006) *Career Training and Personal Planning for Students with Autism Spectrum Disorder.* London: Jessica Kingsley Publishers.

Macdaid, G.P., McCalley, M.H. and Kainz, R.L. (1995) *Atlas of Type Tables.* Gainesville, FL: Center for Applications of Psych. Type Inc.

Myers, I.B. (1998) *Introduction to Type.* Gainsville, FL: Center for Application of Psychological Type.

Perrin, N. (2007) Personal communication.

Quenk, N.L. (1993) *Beside Ourselves.* Palo Alto, CA: Consulting Psychologists Press Inc.

Quenk, N.L. (2000) *In the Grip*. Palo Alto, CA: Consulting Psychologist Press.

Sacks, O. (1995) *An Anthropologist on Mars*. Toronto: Alfred A. Knopf Canada.

Szatmari, P. (2004) *A Mind Apart*. New York, NY: The Guilford Press.

Tieger, P.D. and Barron-Tieger, B. (1997) *Nurture by Nature*. New York, NY: Little Brown and Company.

Vygotsky, L. (1978) *Mind in Society: The Development of Higher Psychological Processes*. Cambridge, MA: Harvard University Press.

Welton, J. (2004) *What Did You Say? What Do You Mean?* London: Jessica Kingsley Publishers.

Willis, J. (2007) "The Neuroscience of Joyful Education." *Educational Leadership 64*, accessed on 12 February 2008 at www.thehawnfoundation.org/wordpress/wp-content/uploads/2008/01/joyful_education_by_ds_willis-2.doc.

Wing, L. (1997) "The autistic spectrum." *The Lancet 350*, 9093, 1761–1766.

Appendix I

Some Free Internet Resources

LEARNING ACTIVITIES AND MATERIALS

http://abcteach.com – reading, math, science, social studies activities for kindergarten through grade nine

http://atozteacherstuff.com – lesson plans, thematic units, downloadable teaching materials and eBooks, printable worksheets, emergent reader books

www.bbc.co.uk/cbeebies – stories, rhymes, activities and games with favorite television characters

www.coloring.ws – printable coloring pages, jigsaws and games

www.dltk-kids.com – rich resource printable activities for preschool through elementary and some materials can be personalized

www.ed.gov/pubs/CompactforReading/kitcover.html – U.S. Department of Education reading activities for kindergarten through grade three

www.edhelper.com – many printable activities in both English and Spanish across the curriculum kindergarten through grade six

www.edhelpernet.com/Monthly/Themes.htm – preschool to elementary games, themes, social studies, science, math and reading activities

www.first-school.ws – preschool and kindergarten lesson plans, activities, printable crafts, worksheets

www.gamequarium.com – online games for preschool through grade six in the areas of keyboarding, math, reading, science, social studies

www.hardin.k12.ky.us/res_techn/countyjeopardygames.htm – jeopardy games in math, reading, social studies and science for 5 through 18 years

www.homeeducationresources.com/FREE1.htm – math, science, social studies, reading worksheets

www.kidsrcrafty.com – activity sheets, coloring pages, dot-to-dots, mazes, vocabulary and worksheets in both English and French

www.kidssoup.com/index.html – crafts, activities and games in English and German

www.kidzone.ws – activities for preschool to grade five across the curriculum

www.kizclub.com – activities in language arts for preschool and elementary age children

www.lessonplanspage.com – over 3000 lesson plans from preschool through high school

www.makingfriends.com/f_Friends.htm – variety of paper dolls with separate clothing (pants, hats, shoes, dresses, coats, etc.) and hair

www.makinglearningfun.com – alphabetically listed preschool activities

www.mes-english.com – vocabulary flashcards for four- to seven-year-olds

www.myteachertools.com – worksheets, themes, lesson plans, frameworks

http://newton.uor.edu/facultyfolder/rider/adjectives.htm – activities for correct use of adjectives in English and Spanish

www.nickjr.com/parenting/activity_finder/printables/index.jhtml – searchable activities for preschoolers featuring favorite television characters

www.pbs.org/teachers – lesson plans, classroom activities, interactive resources organized by subject, grade level, and curriculum topic

www.pitt.edu/~poole/eled.html – links to math, science, social studies, reading resources for early childhood through elementary school

www.preschoolrainbow.org – preschool and early childhood education lesson plans and activities

www.primarygames.com – online games and printable activities

http://printables.familyeducation.com – worksheets across the curriculum for preschool through elementary

www.readinga-z.com/newfiles/preview.html – free sample of downloadable levelled reading books in English, Spanish and French

www.sesameworkshop.org/sesamestreet – online stories, games, music and printable coloring pages

www.starfall.com – reading and writing activities for first grade, pre-kindergarten, kindergarten and second grade

www.teach-nology.com/printables – worksheets and other printables

www.teacherview.com – activity pages, themes and written expression

www.teachercreated.com/free – searchable database of over 400 lessons

www.theeducatorsnetwork.com/main/worksheetfeature.htm – reading, printing and math worksheets

www.theteacherscorner.net/printable-worksheets – math and reading worksheets

www.underfives.co.uk – preschool lesson plans, themes and activities

FILE FOLDER ACTIVITIES

www.angelfire.com/pa5/as/myprintables.html

www.enchantedlearning.com/filefoldergames

www.preschoolprintables.com/filefolder/filefolder.shtml

VISUAL ORGANIZERS

www.busyteacherscafe.com/wspages/graphicorganizers.htm

www.edhelper.com/teachers/graphic_organizers.htm?gclid=CIWHk7rbwIwCF
QurhgodjG58Wg

www.eduplace.com/graphicorganizer/index.html

www.enchantedlearning.com/graphicorganizers

www.freeology.com/graphicorgs

http://gotoscience.com/Graphic_Organizers.html

www.teachervision.fen.com/graphic-organizers/printable/6293.html

READER'S THEATRE

www.aaronshep.com/rt/RTE.html – elementary level

www.fictionteachers.com/classroomtheater/theater.html – elementary level

www.lisablau.com/archives.html – elementary level

http://pbskids.org/zoom/activities/playhouse/index.html – elementary level

SONGS AND RHYMES

www.bbc.co.uk/music/parents/yourchild/18mnths_3years/action_songs.shtml

www.childcarelounge.com/Caregivers/songstt.htm

www.edhelper.com/?gclid=CL-l_ayy9IoCFSLPhgodUFcBlA

www.gutenberg.org/files/10607/10607–h/10607–h.htm

www.kididdles.com/lyrics/busy.html

www.preschooleducation.com/stransition.shtml

www.preschoolrainbow.org/preschool-rhymes.htm

www.preschoolrainbow.org/transition-rhymes.htm

www.songs4teachers.com – free songs are in the left hand column

http://songsforteaching.com

http://songsforteaching.com/transitions.htm

www.teach-nology.com/printables/songs

www.theteachersguide.com/ChildrensSongs.htm

www.underfives.co.uk

CHILDREN'S BOOK DATABASE

www.lib.muohio.edu/pictbks – wonderful searchable database of over 5000 children's picture (non-chapter type) books for designing literature-based activities

Appendix II

Learning Preferences and Strengths Profile

Learning Preferences and Strengths Profile

Directions

This profile is designed to provide information on a child's typical preferences and strengths in learning.

Complete each checklist with your child in mind, thinking about how he responds most of the time.

Remember, we are looking for trends; that is, what the child is most likely to do when he is just being himself.

Once you have completed all of the learning preference and strength checklists, you can summarize them. The information you provide will help us understand your child better and to develop intervention/teaching strategies for him.

Child's Name: _____   Date: _____

School: _____   Grade: _____

Birth Date: _____   Age: _____

Gender: _____

How long have you known the child?_____

Person completing profile: _____

Relationship to child: _____

LEARNING PREFERENCES

Read each item on the left side of the checklist and then the corresponding item on the right side. Choose which item best describes the child *most of the time*. Try to check either the left or right item. Try not to skip any items.

Energy source			
The child usually:	Check if yes	The child usually:	Check if yes
1. prefers working or playing with others		1. prefers working or playing alone or with a few friends	
2. enjoys new situations and activities and meeting new people		2. is slow to warm up to new places, people and activities until he can experience it for a while and take it all in; likely considered 'shy' or 'withdrawn' by strangers	
3. is interested in other people and what they are doing; is viewed as friendly or sociable		3. focuses in depth on specific objects or topics of interest (e.g. trains, cars, dinosaurs)	
4. enjoys sharing personal experiences but may talk more than listen		4. holds back from sharing feelings and thoughts, sharing them selectively; more likely to listen than talk	
5. prefers to think out loud, feeling stifled if he cannot talk about his observations and ideas		5. needs time to think about things or watch others before doing them or answering questions	
6. prefers to pay attention to what others are doing and saying even if they are interrupting him		6. dislikes interruptions, shows frustration if interrupted during an activity	
Total checks Extraversion		Total checks Introversion	

Information gathering			
The child usually:	Check if yes	The child usually:	Check if yes
1. is more interested in hands-on tasks that he can see, touch, smell, etc.		1. is more interested in ideas and imagination than hands-on activities	
2. wants to try something out and explore it before learning more about it		2. wants to learn about something before trying it out	

The child usually:	Check if yes	The child usually:	Check if yes
3. is interested in objects and concrete information more than people and possibilities		3. is interested in possibilities, patterns and people more than facts and details	
4. notices and remembers details others may not		4. becomes impatient with detail and may miss some of it	
5. prefers established routines and familiar methods and schedules		5. becomes restless with routines, preferring new approaches	
6. enjoys details and facts but may miss the main idea		6. forgets facts and details but gets the main idea	
Total checks Sensing		Total checks iNtuiting	

Decision making

The child usually:	Check if yes	The child usually:	Check if yes
1. wants to know the reasons for actions and events; may ask 'why?' frequently		1. is interested in pleasing another person rather than questioning reasoning or rationale for actions and events	
2. identifies what is wrong or different in a person or situation		2. avoids telling others things that may be unpleasant or uncomfortable to them or to himself	
3. is unaware of how others feel; may seem detached		3. is sensitive to the feelings of others	
4. values fairness and consistency and is 'black and white' in making decisions		4. values harmony among people and seeks to maintain it; viewed as 'warm' and 'sympathetic' by others	
5. seems to lack knowledge of how his actions and words affect others; may seem aloof		5. is unaware of how rules and regulations can over-ride feelings and values	
6. holds firmly to a conviction or belief, regardless of what others think		6. agrees with others in a group regardless of what he thinks; prefers to avoid confrontation	
Total checks Thinking		Total checks Feeling	

Relating to the world				
The child usually:	Check if yes	The child usually:		Check if yes
1. wants events and activities decided and settled and expectations clear		1. wants to leave options open to new possibilities		
2. makes definite choices from among possibilities and options		2. samples many experiences, sometimes more than can be used or taken in		
3. is uneasy about unplanned events or actions, even if he usually likes the activity		3. changes what he is doing if other possibilities arise		
4. persists in seeking what he wants until it is achieved; may be viewed as 'competitive'		4. is flexible, adaptable, and tolerant; viewed as 'easy-going'		
5. prefers being orderly, organized, and systematic		5. prefers to leave things open to whatever might happen		
6. prefers finishing one project before starting something else		6. enjoys starting new projects and activities but has difficulty finishing them		
Total checks Judging		Total checks Perceiving		

LEARNING STRENGTHS

Read each item on each checklist and check all items that best describe the child *most of the time*. Do not be concerned about items you skip.

The child usually:	Check if yes	The child usually:	Check if yes
1. enjoys conversations and telling about experiences		1. asks questions about or investigates how things work	
2. imitates speech and expressions of others		2. has a good understanding of numbers and quantity for his age	
3. enjoys and learns easily from books and listening to stories		3. enjoys working on logic puzzles, brainteasers, or computer/video games	

4. enjoys rhymes and playing with words and speech sounds		4. has a good sense of cause-effect relationships for his age (i.e. if I do this, that will happen)	
5. has a good vocabulary for his age		5. enjoys organizing and putting information and objects into categories or in their place	
6. is highly verbal and enjoys discussing ideas		6. enjoys games that require strategies	
Total checks Verbal-Linguistic		Total checks Logical-Mathematical	

The child usually:	Check if yes	The child usually:	Check if yes
1. remembers routes to places		1. remembers music and musical patterns readily	
2. uses colors and shapes in a purposeful and visually pleasing way		2. keeps time to music, has a good sense of rhythm	
3. enjoys puzzles, mazes, 'I Spy' games or books		3. listens and responds with interest to music, song, rhythm	
4. enjoys three-dimensional construction like Lego™, Duplo™, Meccano™		4. enjoys listening to music and musical instruments and is sensitive to off-key music	
5. recognizes and remembers faces, objects and details he has seen previously		5. responds to music with movement (e.g. dancing, clapping, beating the rhythm)	
6. prefers watching videos and other visual media		6. enjoys playing musical instruments or singing	
Total checks Visual-Spatial		Total checks Musical-Rhythmic	

The child usually:	Check if yes	The child usually:	Check if yes
1. prefers to touch and handle available objects		1. forms and keeps friendships easily	
2. fidgets if required to remain still for a long time		2. adapts easily to different social settings	
3. is skilful at imitating others' mannerisms and gestures		3. works cooperatively with others	

4. likes working with his hands		4. enjoys working or playing with others	
5. enjoys dancing		5. seeks out the company of others	
6. enjoys running, jumping, climbing		6. is sought out by others to socialize	
Total checks Bodily-Kinesthetic		Total checks Interpersonal	

The child usually:	Check if yes
1. shows a strong sense of himself, his likes and dislikes	
2. tries to actively understand his own feelings and experiences	
3. is able to learn from his experiences in life, failures and successes	
4. enjoys playing or working independently	
5. is motivated to identify and pursue his goals	
6. is curious about 'big questions' about the meaning and purpose of life	
Total checks Intrapersonal	

Learning Preferences and Strengths Profile Summary of Scores

When you have completed all parts of the profile, go back and add up the number of check marks you placed in each column.

For the Learning Preferences, find the column for each section that has more checkmarks. For example, for Energy source, which column has more checks? If it is Extraversion, circle the E below. If it was Introversion, circle the I below. If there are an equal number of checkmarks in both columns, follow the standard MBTI® rules:

- if equal E and I, circle the E
- if equal S and N (Intuiting), circle the N
- if equal T and F, circle the F
- if equal J and P, circle P

For the Learning Strengths, find the two strengths that have the most checks. Circle only those two below. If there are equal numbers of checkmarks for more than two, circle all of them.

	Learning Preferences	
Greater number of checks (circle only one of each pair)	Extraverting	Introverting
	Sensing	iNtuiting
	Thinking	Feeling
	Judging	Perceiving
	Learning Strengths	
Two learning strengths with greatest number of checks (circle only two)	Verbal-Linguistic	Logical-Mathematical
	Visual-Spatial	Musical-Rhythmic
	Bodily-Kinesthetic	Interpersonal
	Intrapersonal	

Appendix III

Frameworks and Forms
for Observation and Planning

OBSERVING LEARNING PREFERENCES AND STRENGTHS – CHILD ALONE

Child's name:

Observer:

Dates/times in minutes:
(should be 10 to 15 minutes per observation period)

Settings:

Activities:

The child	Date:				Date:				Observations/comments
	Not at all or no opportunity	Rarely	Sometimes	Frequently	Not at all or no opportunity	Rarely	Sometimes	Frequently	
approaches me as soon as I enter his space									
responds when I speak to him									
tries to share an object or event with me									
lets me re-arrange a toy he is playing with									
lets me do something in a different order or way									
responds to my laughter with pleasure or to crying with look of concern									
puts away a toy or object he is playing with when requested									
lets me crash or disassemble a toy he was playing with									
responds to singing, music or rhythm									
Other observations/comments:									

OBSERVING LEARNING PREFERENCES AND STRENGTHS – CHILD IN A PEER GROUP

Child: _____

Observer: _____

Dates/times in minutes: _____
(should be 10 to 15 minutes per observation period)

Settings: _____

Activities _____

Participants: _____

The child	Date: Not at all or no opportunity	Rarely	Sometimes	Frequently	Date: Not at all or no opportunity	Rarely	Sometimes	Frequently	Observations/comments
approaches others as soon as he enters space									
responds when spoken to									
tries to share an object or event with others									
lets others re-arrange a toy he is playing with									
lets others do something he is doing in a different order or way									
responds to laughter with pleasure or to crying with look of concern									
puts away a toy or object he is playing with when requested									
lets others crash or disassemble a toy he was playing with									
responds to singing, music or rhythm									
Other observations/comments:									

INVENTORY OF CHILD LIKES AND DISLIKES

Child's name: _____ Date: _____

Informant: _____ Relationship to child: _____

Questions	Responses
What are the child's *favorite*:	
videos	
games	
TV shows	
computer programs	
books	
toys	
characters from videos, TV, games, and/or books	
What things does the child *dislike* in relation to:	
videos	
games	
TV shows	
computer programs	
books	
toys	
characters from videos, TV, games, and/or books	

OBSERVING LEARNING PROCESSES

Child's name:					Observer:

Date:

The child	Not at all	Rarely	Sometimes	Frequently	Observations/comments
works systematically left to right or right to left					
works systematically top to bottom or bottom to top					
labels objects, actions and events observed					
looks at person or task while listening					
responds to nonverbal cues					
attends and responds to key words					
determines most important and relevant information					
ignores non-central and/or irrelevant information					
notes and uses clues and signs to help himself determine what is expected					
notes and uses models to help himself determine what is expected					
says information over to himself to help retain it					
retains descriptions of objects or simple events					
retains simple stories					

The child	Not at all	Rarely	Sometimes	Frequently	Observations/comments
uses visualization to help himself retain verbal information					
connects information by grouping and/or categorizing					
looks for and uses patterns to connect information					
notes connection between present task/event with past task/event					
looks for similarities and differences in present information					
requests repetition if he does not hear or understand information					
requests clarification if he does not understand information					
exhibits understanding that another person may have a different visual perspective					
engages in reciprocal teaching where he is 'teacher'					
uses a plan to organize his responses					
revises communication based on listener feedback					
revises response based on ongoing evaluation of progress toward the goal					
tells coherent stories which include time, main characters, location, at least one main event and a conclusion					
exhibits the ability to identify main characteristics of at least three basic emotions					
Comments and additional observations:					

LESSON PLANNING FORM

Child:	Date:
Area of learning:	Teacher/mediator:

Pre-assessment of knowledge and skills in this area:

Goals (specific, observable, measurable):	Timeline:
1.	1.
2.	2.
3.	3.

Strategies/methods, activities/tasks and format (1:1, small group, larger group, with age peers):	Preferences, strengths and interests included:
1.	Learning processes included:
2.	Environmental modifications:
3.	

Materials/resources needed:
1.
2.
3.

Formative assessments (indicate date and change or lack of change noted, any changes to goal, strategies or materials):
1.
2.
3.

Assessment at end of time-line:
1.
2.
3.

LESSON PLANNING AND IMPLEMENTATION CHECKLISTS

Program structure	
Learning environment	
Have I ensured that:	Check if 'yes'
noise levels are reduced?	
visual stimuli are controlled?	
odors and scents are reduced?	
lighting is optimized?	
all needed materials are close at hand but out of sight?	
the child has a clearly marked place for his belongings?	
each work/activity area is visually obvious?	
the language level used is in keeping with the child's abilities?	
seating arrangements are appropriate to the task?	
Schedules, plans and routines	
Have I ensured that:	Check if 'yes'
the master schedule includes the number of items the child can tolerate and understand?	
schedules, plans and routines have an interactive component so the child can experience completion?	
schedules follow a consistent cycle?	
schedules are rhythmic, providing him with chances for less structured activities between tasks	
one-to-one tasks or activities are included?	
independent tasks or activities are included?	
group tasks and activities are included?	
schedules, plans and routines are depicted visually in ways that are meaningful to the child?	

Tasks and activities	
Have I ensured that:	Check if 'yes'
time expectations are clear to the child as appropriate?	
quantity expectations are clear to the child as appropriate?	
quality expectations are clear to the child as appropriate?	
tasks and activities are organized left to right or right to left?	
Learning preferences, strengths and interests	
Have I ensured that the child:	Check if 'yes'
is given extended time to process information and think things through?	
is given time to warm up to a situation, idea, activity, people and time to digest information before the actual event or activity?	
has opportunities for reflection and time to practice and rehearse in a comfortable environment?	
does not feel 'singled out'?	
is helped to determine which information is most relevant and important to the task, activity or principle?	
is helped to relate the present task, activity or principle to past experiences or overcome past negative experiences?	
has opportunities to see models and/or observe a task being done before being expected to do it on his own?	
has hands-on experiences to accompany tasks and activities?	
is given an objective and logical explanation of the task and approaches to it?	
understands the rationale behind expectations?	
is allowed to finish one task before moving on?	
is encouraged to work systematically and according to the plan?	
has visual support in order to understand task expectations?	
is spoken to using musical intonation and/or rhythm of words and phrases?	
is provided songs or chants to help him mediate his behaviour and thinking?	
has his areas of interest incorporated into tasks and activities?	

Seven Pillars of Mediated Learning	
Have I made sure:	Check if 'yes'
I use the word "we" when interacting with the child?	
the child is actively engaged in the task or activity?	
I respond to important and relevant behaviors from the child?	
the child begins to anticipate or wait for my responses?	
I relate the task or activity to other things the child knows and cares about?	
I provide a rationale for tasks, activities and strategies?	
I provide specific feedback to the child about his performance?	
I rejoice with the child about his successes?	
the child is allowed to choose some aspect of tasks or activities?	
I provide the child with specific feedback about the amount of effort he needs to expend or expended to achieve mastery?	
I model metacognitive strategies for the child?	
I try to ask the child more process questions, like "why" and "how", than questions which prompt him to simply identify or label?	
I help the child determine other tasks and settings where the strategy or principle can be applied?	
I help the child understand what he needs to do to improve his intake of information ?	
I help the child understand what he needs to do to improve his integration and elaboration of information?	
I help the child understand what he needs to do to improve his expression of information?	

COMMUNICATION SKILLS CHECKLIST

Child:
Completed by: Date:

Children will communicate many different things with actions and gestures, sounds, single words and sentences. Please look at each category below and determine how frequently the child uses each type of communication. Feel free to add any types of communication you did not feel were covered in the inventory. Please give examples of how your child presently expresses or responds to each communication type and put them in the column shown.

To help us decide on the types of communication we should work on with your child put a star (*) on the left-hand side beside items you feel are most important.

Communication type	How often used			Examples
	Never	Sometimes	Always	
Social				
1. Greets others spontaneously.				
Responds to other's greeting.				
2. Says farewell to others spontaneously.				
Responds to others' farewell.				
3. Calls others to get attention.				
Gets others' attention with gestures or actions.				
Responds to other's call for attention.				
4. Introduces self to others (gives name).				
Responds to others' introductions.				

Communication type	Never	Sometimes	Always	Examples
Repeats what he said when asked to clarify.				
Informative				
1. Asks others for information about: A. a thing ("what's that?")				
B. a person ("who's that?")				
C. an action ("what's he doing?")				
D. location ("where's Mom?")				
E. feature of an object – color, shape, size, etc.				
F. reason ("why?").				
G. process ("how?").				
2. Responds to others' request for information about: A. a thing				
B. a person				
C. an action				
D. location				
E. feature of an object				
F. reason				
G. process				
Requesting				
1. Asks for things he wants or prefers.				
Responds to others' questions about his wants or preferences.				
Offers help to others.				

Communication type	Never	Sometimes	Always	Examples
2. Gives warnings ("stop", "don't")				
Responds to other's warning.				
3. Asks permission to do things.				
Responds to others' request for permission by accepting/rejecting ("yes"/"no").				
4. Asks others about what they plan to do.				
Tells others about what he intends to do before doing it.				
Affection				
1. Expresses affection ("I love you").				
Responds to others' expression of affection ("I love you too").				
2. Expresses appreciation ("thank you").				
Responds to others' expression of appreciation ("you're welcome").				
3. Tells others about positive or negative feelings ("I like/don't like...") or things that are bothering him.				
Agree/disagrees with others' feelings ("me too/not me").				
Turn-taking				
1. Interrupts others.				
2. Takes long speaker turns, not giving others a chance to talk.				
3. Perseverates on certain topics.				
4. Responds with one- or two- word answers or comments.				
5. Continues a topic started by another person.				

Communication type	Never	Sometimes	Always	Examples
Nonverbal				
1. Keeps appropriate social distance when talking with others.				
2. Uses head nods or shakes head to acknowledge others.				
3. Looks at the listener when he speaks.				
4. Understands and adjusts to other's feelings.				

Please describe situations that are most challenging to your child socially (e.g. meal times, eating out at restaurants, when you are talking on the phone, when he is teased by others, when he wants to join other children in play or wants to enter a group).

STRESSORS, DISTRESS REACTIONS AND CALMING STRATEGIES CHECKLIST

Child's name:	Date:
Completed by:	

Please look at each category below and determine how frequently the child responds with anxiety or other behaviors to each type of stressor. Each item is in two parts, one for school settings and the other for home. Stressors may be different in different settings so please complete both where applicable. Feel free to add any types of stressors not covered in the inventory. Please give examples of specific things that tend to cause anxiety or stress in the child.

Stressor type	How often observed at **school**			How often observed at **home**			Examples:
	Never	Sometimes	Always	Never	Sometimes	Always	
1. Organization of tasks, materials and activities not visually obvious.							
2. Too many options or unclear expectations.							
3. Others do not do a task as the child expected.							
4. Change in plans without forewarning.							
5. Child's concerns are ignored or negated.							
6. New possibilities presented after child has started an activity.							
7. Too much information is presented to the child at once.							
8. Child is tired from working too long or too hard.							
9. Child is pressed to complete a task faster or within a limited time.							

Now, look at each category below and determine how frequently the child exhibits each type of distress reaction. Each item is in two parts, one for school settings and the other for home. Distress reactions may be different in different settings so please complete both where applicable. Feel free to add any types of distress reactions not covered in the inventory. Please give examples of specific behaviors the child tends to exhibit.

Distress reaction types	How often observed at **school**			How often observed at **home**			Examples:
	Never	Sometimes	Always	Never	Sometimes	Always	
1. Focuses on sensory acts involving touch, taste, smell, movement, sound or sight.							
2. Engages in organizing or other detail-oriented activity.							
3. Acts out without thinking.							
4. Shows subtle signs of anxiety such as tensed body, dilated pupils.							
5. Rejects even familiar, enjoyable activities.							
6. Erupts into a melt down.							
7. Exhibits or expresses usual fears or dangers.							
8. Increased rigidity even to minor changes.							
9. Loses things and seems to have difficulty dealing with details.							
10. Becomes over-focused on fears and worries.							
11. Denies obvious fears or worries.							
12. Refuses to do task or go into situation which is causing stress.							
13. Expresses suspicions about other people or uses them to make excuses.							

The final step is to look at strategies that tend to calm the child. Determine how frequently the child is calmed by each of the strategies below. Each item is in two parts, one for school settings and the other for home. Calming strategies may be different in different settings so please complete both where applicable. Feel free to add any calming strategies not covered in the inventory. Please give examples of specific strategies used.

Calming strategies	How often observed at **school**			How often observed at **home**			Examples:
	Never	Sometimes	Always	Never	Sometimes	Always	
1. Breaking task or activity into smaller parts.							
2. Connecting present activity or event with past experiences.							
3. Time away from the stressful situation.							
4. Time to engage in sensory activity.							
5. Concrete validation of his competence and worth.							
6. Reminding of previous positive outcomes with task or event.							

Other observations/comments:

PROBLEM SOLVING FORMAT

What's the problem?		
What could I do?	Plan 1. 2. 3.	What might happen? 1. 2. 3.
Which one will I try?		
What will I say and do?	Say:	Do:
How did it work? Should I try something else?		

SAMPLE PRESCHOOL LITERATURE-BASED CURRICULUM PLAN

September		
KEY:	☆ Primary book or concept • additional or adjunct book or concept	
Literature	☆ *Brown Bear Brown Bear What Do You See?* (Eric Carle) • *Goldilocks and the Three Bears* (Jan Brett and others)	
Adjunct themes	• Summer • Family	
Concepts	Cognitive	☆ look at one object or feature at a time ☆ flexibility (e.g. cats can be purple) • others look back at us • left to right systematic search and progression • clues (e.g. in the page margins) can help us guess or predict
	Academic	☆ color names ☆ comparison, same/different • rhyming • categorizing (e.g. animals, children, two-legged and four-legged animals, animals found in the sea, air, on land) • size labels, synonyms for size words (e.g. small and tiny)
	Social-Behavioral	☆ reciprocity in asking and answering questions • turn-taking • afraid, feelings, facial expressions • different voices for different characters
	Sensory-Motor	☆ looking with our eyes to find things • games (e.g. hide and seek) • textures of different animals • movements of different animals • sounds of different animals • smells, textures and temperatures of different foods in *Three Bears*
	Self-help	☆ I can look with my eyes to find things • meal-time routine, spoon feeding with *Three Bears* • bedtime routine with dressing and undressing for *Three Bears*
	Social-Communication	☆ answering "yes" or "no" to questions ☆ reciprocity ☆ narrative ('once upon a time') structure • use "I" and "me" when referring to self • use sentence frame ("I see a (color) (object)") • use of "what do…?" questions

STORY FORMAT (SIMPLE)

When – setting (time)
Who – main characters
Where – setting (place)
What happens – three main events
1. Beginning
2. Middle
3. End
How does it end?
How do the main characters feel? Why?

STORY FORMAT (MORE COMPLEX)

Setting (time)
Main characters
Protagonist ('good guy')
Appearance
Traits
Strengths
Weaknesses
Antagonist ('bad guy')
Appearance
Traits
Strengths
Weaknesses
Setting (place)
Three main events
1. Beginning
2. Middle
3. End
How does it end?
How do the main characters feel? Why?

SOCIAL RULE FORMAT

Social skill: _____

Definition: _____

_____

When: _____

Where: _____

With whom: _____

What to say and do:

1. _____

2. _____

3. _____

Index